MBA
FUNDAMENTALS

INTERNATIONAL
BUSINESS

Kaplan MBA Fundamentals Series

MBA Fundamentals Accounting and Finance

MBA Fundamentals Business Law

MBA Fundamentals Business Writing

MBA Fundamentals Project Management

MBA Fundamentals Statistics

MBA Fundamentals Strategy

From the #1 graduate test prep provider, Kaplan MBA Fundamentals helps you to master core business basics in a few easy steps. Each book in the series is based on an actual MBA course, providing direct and measurable skills you can use today.

For the latest titles in the series, as well as downloadable resources, visit:
www.kaplanmbafundamentals.com

MBA
FUNDAMENTALS

INTERNATIONAL BUSINESS

Rajesh Iyer, PhD

PUBLISHING

New York

This book is dedicated to my family:
To my parents, my greatest teachers.
To my three daughters, Rajeshwari, Diya, and Siya.
Most important, to my wife, my constant support and companion.

* * *

© 2009 Kaplan Publishing

Published by Kaplan Publishing, a division of Kaplan, Inc.
1 Liberty Plaza, 24th Floor
New York, NY 10006

Printed in the United States of America

Library of Congress Cataloging–in–Publication Data

Iyer, Rajesh.
    MBA fundamentals: international business/Rajesh Iyer.
       p. cm.—(MBA fundamentals series)
    Includes index.
    ISBN 978-1-4277-9844-2
  1. International business enterprises.   2. Intercultural communication—Economic aspects.   3. International trade.   4. Investments, Foreign.   5. Personnel management.   I. Title.   II. Title: International business.
    HD2755.5.I97 2009
    658'. 049—dc22
                                               2008040369
10 9 8 7 6 5 4 3 2 1
ISBN-13: 978-1-4277-9844-2

Kaplan Publishing books are available at special quantity discounts to use for sales promotions, employee premiums, or educational purposes. Please email our Special Sales Department to order or for more information at kaplanpublishing@kaplan.com, or write to Kaplan Publishing, 1 Liberty Plaza, 24th Floor, New York, NY 10006.

Contents

Introduction vii

PART I: International Business in a Multicultural World 1

   1. Introduction to International Business and the
      Importance of Globalization 3

   2. Culture and International Business 11

PART II: International Financing and Foreign Direct Investment 33

   3. Understanding International Trade and
      Foreign Direct Investment 35

   4. The International Monetary System and the
      Foreign Exchange Market 59

PART III: Global Strategies and Planning 81

   5. Choosing a Strategy 83

   6. Modes of Entry in International Business 107

PART IV: Transactions, Supply Chains, Human Resources, and Profits 131

   7. Communications and Paperwork. 133

   8. Global Production, Supply Chains, and Logistics 153

   9. International Human Resource Management 175

   10. Evaluating Profits and Building for Future Growth. 197

Appendix A: Where to Get More Information 221

Appendix B: Trading Partners and What's Traded 233

Glossary 243

Index...257

About the Author 279

Introduction

Trading is as old as mankind. Early in human history, one person traded with another to obtain goods and services. The first things traded may have been services, food, animal skins, attractive stones, ornamental animal teeth, or weapons. A person who was unusually good at knapping arrow points might exchange some arrowheads for good-quality flint or animal skins, or for other products made by similarly skilled specialists. As humans scattered across Earth and increased in skill, resources, and levels of production, trade across greater distances—even across political borders—became not only profitable but essential. Trading routes were established over common roads or routes. The legendary Silk Road (including both land and sea routes), named for the silk laboriously carried along it from China to the Middle East and beyond, was merely one of the best-known routes. More trading routes were developed to ship salt, spices, amber, tea, incense, and other such high-value products. Each exerted great effect on transportation and city-building and influenced the development of various cultures and philosophies, all while increasing the power, wealth, and social standing of those who traded—or even controlled whole routes of trade.

To us, the famous castles along Germany's Rhine River may seem romantic survivors of a medieval past. In reality, they were strong points used by local rulers to defend territory, to expand land holdings, and to extract tariffs from traders moving goods along the river. In particular, the Pfalzgrafenstein castle, situated in the Rhine itself, was originally built, manned, and equipped to prevent boats—if necessary, by force—from passing without paying tolls or tariffs on the goods they carried. Modern import duties are a contemporary equivalent of rulers' ancient habit of charging fees to allow goods the privilege of entering or passing through their territories. Today's international trading relationships, treaties, practices, and procedures owe a great deal to this heritage of ancient trading practices.

The goal of this book is to provide you with the information you need to begin participating in the global marketplace. Here, you'll find practical information about the basics of international business, as well as fundamental guidance about the procedures, opportunities, and considerations vital to individuals operating an international business. Two appendixes are included: one providing sources for additional help and information and another listing U.S. trading partners and the most important goods and services exchanged. The glossary provides definitions of words commonly used in international business, and the index gives you quick access to the text's content.

"Going global" brings with it new challenges, but it also offers new rewards and markets. Applying what you learn here can help you make such a venture profitable.

PART

INTERNATIONAL BUSINESS IN A MULTICULTURAL WORLD

Introduction to International Business and the Importance of Globalization

WHAT IS INTERNATIONAL BUSINESS?

International business is business across national borders. That's a very basic definition—one that glosses over the many potentials for profits and the many pitfalls and problems that can be encountered. The exchange of goods, services, and capital across countries can be extremely challenging. The goal of this book is to give some knowledge of the opportunities, as well as some background about the challenges and an introduction to strategies for success in international business.

This chapter will explain the types of international business, describing the most critical factors affecting international business and explaining some reasons to engage in international business.

WHAT ARE THE TYPES OF INTERNATIONAL BUSINESS?

You'll need to know some important terms and concepts to learn about international business. The buzzwords used to describe international business are largely interchangeable: world, global, international, multinational, transnational, micro-multinational, borderless, and many more.

For the purposes of this book, however, we'll use a few simple terms and definitions.

National Business

A **national business**, or domestic business, is any business that has offices and employees in only one country. A national business differs from a multinational or transnational business (described below) on the basis of its ownership. If a company owns or controls resources in only one country and is not owned by a foreign business, it is a national business. Although it might not sound "international," a company employing three employees in Akron, Ohio, might be an international business, depending on its business transactions. For example, a domestic business participates in international business when it engages in any transaction with a foreign company. Thus, contracting with a call center in India, buying sugar from Brazil, and selling shares to a Saudi Arabian investment bank are all examples of international business.

Many national businesses participate in international business by contracting with foreign companies but do so without purchasing holdings in other countries. Often, competitive advantage can be gained by contracting internationally for cheaper components or manpower, or for an international client base. Advances in information and communication technologies have made it easier for smaller domestic companies to connect with international buyers and suppliers. This shift is commonly called globalization. **Globalization** is the unification of global markets and production. As trade barriers decrease and information, communication, and transportation technologies improve, businesses are increasingly viewing the world as a single market.

Buying and selling aren't the only ways for a domestic business to engage in international business. Another method is pursuing a joint venture with a business abroad. This is one of the potential methods of international business entry that we'll discuss in greater detail later on. The important thing to remember now is that a joint venture can be an excellent way for your business to limit risk while developing international business competencies—by working with a partner instead of with a supplier or a client.

Outsourcing is another way to take your national business into the global environment. **Outsourcing** uses another company to perform some business function. Outsourcing doesn't always mean sending the work to another country, but in today's global market, it often does. In addition to potential cost savings for your company, outsourcing an activity can help direct your employees' energy toward what they do best while maximizing the efficiency of your company's resources.

Multinational Business

A **multinational business** is a company with holdings in multiple countries. Although there are many ways to become multinational, the most straight-forward is through the acquisition of a foreign firm. A multinational firm typically has a headquarters in one country and uses foreign subsidiaries either to support its business with products or services or to gain access to a foreign market. Note that the management of subsidiary branches of a multinational business is distinguished from outsourcing; instead of *using* an independent subcontractor abroad, a multinational business claims at least some degree of ownership in its foreign subsidiaries.

If your business is thinking about acquiring production capabilities abroad, doing so probably looks good for the bottom line. In many cases, using labor abroad can provide huge cost savings for your company, but the decision to do so should factor in the potential difficulties that arise in crossing cultural borders. Initially, buying an existing factory in Mexico might look extremely profitable—in a pure production cost analysis. But an in-depth look is required. Your analysis and final decision ought to include the complexities of managing employees in another culture. Will your company's existing hiring policies work in Mexico? Will you use a "local" manager, or will you send one from your home office? What steps will you take to ensure that you overcome communication barriers?

The following chapters will address these and other related questions, but for now, remember that a multinational business has many challenges. Decreasing barriers to trade have increased companies' potential for making profit across borders, but making that potential profit a reality is difficult without a working knowledge of the foreign culture and business environment. For this reason, multinational businesses often allow their subsidiary companies a great deal of independence.

Transnational Business

A **transnational business**, or global business, is a type of multinational business that operates as one entity rather than as a collection of units in different countries. In addition to having holdings in multiple countries, a transnational business uses the competencies of the host nation and the subsidiary nations together so that the company as a whole can respond to the global environment with greater efficiency and effectiveness. Simply put, a transnational business is a more cohesive multinational, one in which redundancies in all departments are eliminated as operations in different countries function together, rather than autonomously. Most multinational businesses run their foreign subsidiaries as colonies of their company. Although the thinking that "Americans know best" is widely prevalent among young multinationals based in the United States, multinationals that allow for more open communication between their foreign and domestic managers are often the ones that are the most successful and stable. To be a transnational business, a multinational business needs to do what business is always supposed to be doing: maximize efficiency, effectiveness, and profit.

Transnational collaboration is difficult to achieve. Sometimes it is an elusive goal for an international enterprise. It requires effective communication and extensive knowledge of the cultures of all the participants, brought together in a corporate culture that supports cooperation. This challenge can only be met through careful planning and partnership cooperation between all the participants.

WHAT FACTORS SHAPE INTERNATIONAL BUSINESS?

Market Growth

The expansion of businesses across international borders is driven by the same motive as all business is: profit. For example, as production capacity increases in China even as Chinese labor costs remain lower than costs in the United States, it becomes more and more profitable for U.S. companies to produce a variety of goods in China. Similarly, as China develops a stronger, wealthier middle class, selling goods in China becomes more attractive. As you can see, the market rules remain the same for international business. Companies must find the most efficient methods of production and sell to those markets that offer the highest potential profit. As international trade becomes easier, the path to maximizing business profit doesn't necessarily lie in a company's home country or in the same country where you've been working. As new markets emerge, you must be able to analyze the size, profit potential, and possibilities of changing markets.

Legal Environment

One of the most important changes driving global business and international trade is the legal environment of business. Trade agreements between countries and among regions are strengthening in their levels of enforcement and expanding in their scope. International trade is being encouraged and facilitated by reduced tariffs and increasingly free movements of products, manpower, and information.

Most economies used to be largely self-sustaining and protectionist. People were restricted from crossing borders or from working abroad, and nations taxed goods that crossed their borders, whether coming or going. But as such restrictions and costs are reduced or removed, international business grows. Globalization is causing significant shifts in production, a situation that some nations find threatening. Although the challenges globalization poses to individual national economies are cause for certain concerns, the overall increases in global production that also result are very impressive. In the same way, your company's potential for international profit can be impressive as well.

Another aspect of the legal environment that must be taken into account is the laws of each nation in which you are operating. Every country brings with it its own laws and a legal system to go with them. You must take each nation's legal system into consideration when you make business decisions. For example, Budweiser might view Saudi Arabia as a huge market completely devoid of competition. But a look at the Saudi legal environment makes the picture clearer. In Saudi Arabia, among certain other Middle Eastern countries, alcohol is illegal to produce, consume, or import. This same sort of consideration applies to the labor, health, and safety standards of foreign nations that your company may be considering as potential targets of international business.

Financials

International business adds a complication to the way capital normally operates. Although the international market for capital works much the same as the national market for capital, the picture is clouded by currency exchange. The required return on an investment is the cost of capital, but if the cost of capital is figured in euros, that can change the equation dramatically—and in ways that can change daily.

INTERNATIONAL MONETARY SYSTEM

Different countries use different currencies. The method by which currencies are valued against each other is through the international monetary system. The price of money within an economy is subject to the inflation or deflation of the currency, a situation that can itself be difficult for your business. And when multiple currencies are involved, the picture becomes much muddier. Later chapters will discuss in more detail the issues that surround fluctuations in currency exchanges and the ways that a strong or weak dollar affects your business and its capability to operate and compete in an international environment.

MARKET FOR CAPITAL

Another force driving the growth of international business is the world economy. Easier movement between national economies allows for a greater pool of investment dollars and opportunities. This can translate into a competitive advantage for your business, whether by accepting investment from a country with a lower typical required rate of return, or investing in a country with a higher one. For example, investing in a country that has a weak financial market can bring high rates of return, because where capital is the hardest to obtain is usually where you can "charge" the most for it.

FOREIGN DIRECT INVESTMENT

Foreign direct investment (FDI) is direct investment in a business in another country. It is important for your business to examine your potential investments and investors—this isn't a one-way street, after all. International businesses are increasingly investing in American companies, making this is just another aspect of the international business environment that managers should understand.

Cultural

The most basic rule of understanding cultures from country to country is this: assume difference. Language barriers certainly spring to mind as examples of cultural differences that are essential overcome, but even two countries sharing a common language can have wide gaps in standard business practices on both formal and informal levels. One of the hardest things for a firm entering international business is adapting to cultural differences and then working within them. Ignorance of cultural differences can have devastating effects on international ventures. The next chapter will discuss how you can learn to overcome cultural gaps and how you can identify and avoid the most common pitfalls of American managers abroad.

WHY BOTHER?

If this book is starting to seem like a collection of complications, you're on to something. International business, like all business, is filled with uncertainty. This book will alert you to the difficulties of doing business with different countries that have different cultures, laws, and currencies; those who ignore these very real challenges are unlikely to succeed internationally. Some of the challenges of international business are enough to deter many businesses from going global. But with the appropriate background knowledge, and commitment to learning on the part of you and your company, engaging in international business can bring tremendous growth and equally rewarding profits. Take, for example, Advanced Fibre Communication (AFC), a small telecommunications startup in Petaluma, California. Founded in 1992 by Donald Green, the company now has annual sales of more than $130 million, and some five hundred employees. AFC's success began in 1995, when Brazil's telecommunication industry started its deregulation. AFC began participating in international trade shows through the help of their local Commercial Services. AFC sold its first major contract—$8 million—in Latin America to the Brazilian telecommunications operating company Telerj for digital loop carrier systems. Such equipment was nothing new in the United States, and AFC grew because it beat its competitors into the Latin American market. Now, sales in Brazil account for approximately half of AFC's annual sales. All it took was knowledge of international opportunities and a tolerance for the uncertainty that comes with entering a new environment.

KEY POINTS TO REMEMBER

- There are three types of international businesses: national (having offices and employees in only one country), multinational (having offices or employees in more than one country), and transnational (a type of multinational business that functions as a unified whole).

- The methods by which a domestic business can engage in international business include joint ventures with, outsourcing through, buying from, and supplying to foreign companies.

- The ways of engaging in international business as a multinational company include through mergers, acquisitions, and investments, whether as investor or subject of investment.

- Many factors affect the international business environment, including international market growth, various countries' legal environments, the international monetary system, international financing, and cultural differences between nations. Each of these brings with it practical implications for every international business.

Culture and International Business

WHAT IS CULTURE?

Ask any American undergraduate sociology student what culture is, and he or she will probably respond "culture is an adaptive mechanism." He or she might even give you the textbook elements of culture: language, technology, governance, religion, economics, education, and structure (among others). Understanding culture is a discipline unto itself, but the practical goal for you is learning the differences between your culture and another, and how to modify your behavior to do business with or in another culture. Sometimes these differences are easily noticeable, such as India's legacy of a caste system or China's Communist party. But even subtle differences can make for a serious day-to-day difficulty. The sales representative from India speaks English, but that doesn't mean she speaks American English. In America, smokers often ask, "Do you mind if I smoke?" before lighting a cigarette. In China, it would be considered rude to ask someone to put their cigarette out. It's the details of a culture that can easily trip you up. Obviously, this chapter won't teach you everything you need to know about any one culture, but you will learn how to approach a new culture.

In addition to general aspects of culture, there are also aspects specific to business culture in different countries. Chinese buyers will spend a good deal of time looking at your company's reputation before they consider signing a service contract, and you need to plan around this delay, remembering that they'll pass on a great deal if it's offered by someone they don't trust. Japanese firms use far more debt financing than

American firms typically use in their financial structure, and you should know about this business norm when trying to discern the value of a Japanese company.

This chapter will give you a framework with which to compare cultures across a number of dimensions. We'll discuss some easy steps you can take to be more successful in international operations. Some of this information may seem intuitive, but intuition often breaks down in a new environment. Remembering these general principles and doing the necessary research on whatever culture you are transacting with will help your business succeed.

HOFSTEDE'S MODEL OF CULTURAL DIMENSIONS

One of the simplest and most popular models for comparing cultures is Geert Hofstede's cultural dimensions. Initially, Hofstede proposed four dimensions of culture: power distance, individualism vs. collectivism, masculinity vs. femininity, and uncertainty avoidance. After additional research, Hofstede added a fifth cultural dimension: long-term orientation. We'll explain this model in some detail to give you the vocabulary and framework with which to further research and interpret another culture.

Dimension	High	Low
Power Distance	Comfort with unequal concentration of power	Discomfort with unequal concentration of power
Individualism	Focused on individual goals	Focused on group goals
Uncertainty Avoidance	Comfort with ambiguity	Discomfort with ambiguity
Masculinity	Aggressive and separated by gender	Passive and more equal between genders
Long-Term Orientation	Attempt to change norms	Comfortable with norms

Power Distance

Power distance measures how comfortable a culture is with control. A society that accepts an unequal distribution of power, like a totalitarian regime, is said to have high power distance. Note that this doesn't quite mean that a country with low power distance has equally distributed power; it means it has a society that supports the equality of power and perceives itself as having a fairly equal distribution of power. Typically, a country with representational democracy has a low power distance, but if the system seems corrupt to the people and they are unhappy with the system, the country actually has high power distance. An interesting exception to this rule is India, which rates as having a high power distance, although it is the world's largest democracy. Power distance is not to be confused with subordination, although it may sound that way. Many cultures with high power distance are nationalistic and may shun the thought of a joining or working with an American enterprise. On the other hand, a foreign subsidiary in a country with high power distance might be more willing to accept decision making being kept in a home office elsewhere.

Individualism

Individualism measures where a particular culture falls on the spectrum from collectivist to individualist. An individualistic society, such as the United States, will likely have strong safeguards on personal freedoms and property rights. A collectivist society, such as China, stresses the supremacy of the needs of the group over the rights of the individual and is less likely to protect individual freedoms. A collectivist society might also be quicker to accept a new human resources policy if they understand how it helps the company as a whole. An individualistic society is likely to have relatively more entrepreneurial activity and to lend itself to tougher employment contract negotiations.

Power distance and individualism have a great deal of interplay in a culture. A collectivist society, such as most Communist or formerly Communist states, is likely to have both low individualism and high power distance. This relationship doesn't always hold, but there is a strong correlation between them.

Uncertainty Avoidance

Uncertainty avoidance is simply the overall tendency within a culture to tolerate ambiguity. Uncertainty avoidance is not as institutionalized as some of the other cultural dimensions of Hofstede's model, but it is still fundamental. A country with a popular, small government and heavily regulated industry can be identified readily as having low individualism and high power distance, but empirical evidence of uncertainty avoidance is harder to find. Perhaps the only way to measure it is entrepreneurial activity, something we'll revisit later. Uncertainty avoidance should not be confused with risk-averse behavior; uncertainty avoidance is more about not knowing the odds than about placing a bet. One of the ways that uncertainty avoidance can be measured is in terms of professional longevity. In a country with high uncertainty avoidance, workers likely stay with a company or job for longer periods of time.

Masculinity

Masculinity measures two things simultaneously: how close the attitudes of the genders are in a culture, and how assertive that culture is relative to others. In a "feminine" culture, the attitudes of women and men are fairly similar and are more modest and caring. Note that although often related, the "masculinity" of a culture isn't necessarily an indication of equality or inequality in legal or social terms between men and women in a given society. Other sources have renamed this dimension of Hofstede's model as quantity of life vs. quality of life, for the masculine vs. feminine names apply specifically to the traditional Western views of masculine and feminine ideals. Such differences are important as businesses attempt not only to work with foreign nationals but also to market their products in other nations. For example, one major American company attempting to market laundry products in India ran ads showing men doing their own laundry. The ad campaign failed miserably; consumers could not relate to men who did their own laundry.

The differences between genders in different cultures are important on many levels. For our purposes, probably the simplest use for the dimension of masculinity is that a relatively masculine culture is likely to be more aggressive and to place a greater emphasis on personal goals, as opposed to a feminine culture, which is likely to focus on understanding and mutual goals. In Hofstede's original study on cultural dimensions, Japan rated the most masculine, and the United States was in the middle of the pack.

Long-Term Orientation

Long-term orientation and short-term orientation refers to the tendency for different decisions horizons in different cultures. A culture with long-term orientation is likely to take longer to accept your bid but is also likely to work harder to get you to accept theirs. Cultures with short-term orientation have less belief in the efficacy of the individual and are more likely to work "within the system," holding "traditional" values. They are also typically more concerned with reputation than with results. The simplest way to describe the difference is this: Short-term orientation countries say, "This is the way it is." Long-term orientation countries ask, "How can we do it better?" Many East Asian countries rate high on long-term orientation. One of the ways that it's expressed is in their focus on reciprocity. In short-term oriented cultures, the focus is on "making a deal." Long-term oriented cultures view favors and gifts as a sort of investment that will eventually be paid back. In fact, in this type of cultural setting one of the ways to succeed is to have a reputation for returning a favor. Later in this chapter we'll discuss the concept of saving and losing face as a manifestation of long-term orientation cultures.

Hofstede's model allows us to compare various cultures and their elements through a clearer, systematic approach. For example, instead of saying that the United States is a predominantly Christian nation and Iran an Islamic nation, we can compare how the religious backgrounds of the two countries relate to a difference in power distance. Iran has a higher power distance than the United States, something that can be at least partially explained by the correlation of religious differences to general ideology in those cultures. We'll continue to use this vocabulary to explain the elements of culture.

How Countries Compare in Hofstede's Model (Measured on a Scale of 1–100)

	Power Distance	Individualism	Uncertainty Avoidance	Masculinity	Long-Term Orientation
High	China, 80	**USA, 91**	Russia, 95	Japan, 95	China, 118
	Brazil, 69	Germany, 67	Columbia, 80	Hungary, 88	Brazil, 65
	Spain, 57	India, 48	**USA, 46**	**USA, 62**	India, 61
	USA, 40	Russia, 39	India, 40	Argentina, 56	**USA, 29**
Low	New Zealand, 22	China, 20	China, 30	Sweden, 5	Australia, 31

Note that numbers for long-term orientation do not correspond to the 1–100 scale; the measurement was developed in a subsequent study rather than at the same time as the four original dimensions.

ASPECTS OF CULTURE

- **Language**
- **Technology**
- **Legal Environment**
- **Economics**
- **Religion**
- **Education**
- **Social Structure**

There is no complete model for culture, and not a whole lot of agreement on what is and isn't a part of it. But we'll discuss some of the generic aspects of culture where there are most likely to be gaps between you and your foreign buyer, supplier, or partner. These gaps can sometimes be turned to your competitive advantage, as in the case of technology. It's a general principle of business that a problem is an opportunity for profit, and technology deficiencies in foreign countries can be just such an opportunity for your company. The important things for your business are to realize that the gaps are there, to know how to get around them, and to understand their subtleties.

The term "culture shock," which applies to strong anxiety in a new environment, gets used all the time in the context of international business. In the face of a new and different environment, it's easy to feel overwhelmed. By examining the differences between your own culture and another in terms of the elements explained in this chapter, the big world of China, India, and anywhere else becomes a whole lot smaller— and a lot less intimidating.

Language

Language differs from country to country. When the difference is obvious, it's easier to deal with and manage. But many language gaps appear small. If you don't notice these gaps, however, you'll run into trouble. When dealing with a foreign agent for whom English is a second language, you should make an effort to avoid idiomatic expressions, and to be cautious about literal translations of foreign idiomatic expressions. Idioms and slang are the last and perhaps most difficult part to learn of any language, partly because they are subject to frequent change. However, fluent speakers use idioms routinely. For example, *J'ai une faim de loup* is the French equivalent of the American idiom "I'm so hungry I could eat a horse." But it literally translates as "I have hunger of/for a wolf." A Frenchman saying "*J'ai une faim de loup*" does not mean that he's about to offer you wolf tartare; he's simply very hungry. Similarly, a "speed bump" to an American is a sleeping police officer in Mexico. Remember that even the simplest idioms are hard to interpret for someone in another culture. So if you tell your partner in Argentina that a spike in retail sales between October and December is "par for the course," there's a good chance the agent will have no idea what you're talking about. Idioms are difficult also because they are subject to change through generations. If you refer to your product as being "the cat's meow," your foreign partner will have no idea what you're talking about—and neither will most of your employees under the age of forty.

It's also important to remember that translations aren't perfect. If you're speaking to someone through a translator, or simply speaking to someone for whom English is a second language (no matter how fluent they may appear), take the time to clarify and make sure that you each understand each other. This is especially important in written communication. It's easy to forget how much information is carried in tone of voice or body language. It might seem simpler to e-mail back and forth with international partners, but you must take care that your communication is understandable to someone else, and make sure you get it right the first time. Many times, misunderstandings occur because people are embarrassed to ask for clarification if it may make them look incompetent. Ask the questions you need to ask in order to ensure that you understand. It's not a mistake to ask a follow-up question, but it is a mistake to ship steel beams to Shanghai that are six feet long, instead of six meters.

Technology

Technology gaps between nations and competencies with technology are an important consideration for your business, but what are perhaps more important for your business are the potential gains your company may make by exploiting the gaps of technology. Bringing a premium technology to an emerging market and the technology's early adopters can be very profitable. The trend in global technology has been somewhat toward unification, but there's still a lot of money to be made by being the first to a new market. Voice-over-Internet Protocol (VoIP) is the perfect example both of changing communication technology—because it reduces the cost of international communication—and of a technology gap being an opportunity. American companies are selling VoIP in Mexico. The technology is not terribly advanced, but by the time it was offered in Mexico, it was nothing new in the United States. The profit potential for the first companies to offer in Mexico was incredible, because the technology was effective, efficient, easy to adopt, with few direct competitors in the market (the technology being new to the marketplace in Mexico). This can also be analyzed in the context of long-term orientation vs. short-term orientation. Cultures with a long-term orientation are more likely to consider future trends when making an investment and are thus more likely to adopt a new technology when they see a potential for growth and predict its increased future use.

Changes in technology globally are making the world smaller every day, and technology gaps are narrowing. Commercial jets and larger freight ships have drastically reduced the cost of moving goods from one country to another. The Internet and improved cellular networks have allowed for increasingly cheaper and more effective communication between buyers, suppliers, and offices abroad. Obviously, technologies aren't on a completely even playing field worldwide, but portable devices are spreading around the globe. We'll address some of these technical advances in later chapters.

Legal Environment

Governance includes both the legal and the political structures of a country. In terms of political structure, different countries have very different political bodies, but in general the differences are in how distributed decision making is in a country. The more bureaucratic a nation is, the more work it is for your business to break in through permits and permissions and competitions of government contracts. On the other hand, a nation with fewer political decision makers can be subject to capricious decisions. This part of the legal environment of international business is easy to think of in the framework of low or high power distance. Countries with high power distance typically have more restrictive, totalitarian governments. Countries with low power distance tend to have more democratic forms of government. This is an area where you may need to hire an expert. If you're bidding on a foreign government contract, an encyclopedia entry on how the Russian parliament operates is not going to be enough; you'll need someone well versed in the legal structuring.

The legal structure of foreign nations is very important for your business to consider, especially when it's different from your own. There are two types of legal systems: civil law and common law. Common law is determined by previous legal decisions and customs and allows for varying degrees of interpretation on the part of judges. Civil law systems rely on detailed codes that spell out the law with much less room for interpretation. Common law countries include the United States, parts of Western Europe, and many former British colonies, such as India. Civil law countries include Russia, China, and Japan. A civil code can be harder to learn but easier to understand, because when there's a part of the code that applies specifically to your industry, it tends to be straightforward.

Furthermore, separate from the unique legal environment of a foreign nation or that nation's government, it is important for you to consider the global legal environment and the political context of both countries. For example, it will be awhile before you can set up a factory in Cuba.

One of the most important legal principles in international business is comity, or legal reciprocity. Comity means two things:

1. Specific legal rights in your home country apply in the foreign nation where you are transacting business—and vice versa for foreign businesses in your country.

2. Professional distinctions, certification, and licenses in your home country apply abroad. This can be a very significant consideration in some countries where bureaucracy (or corruption) may slow or stop the process of getting the legal right to perform a specific task or to do business.

Comity agreements and treaties exist between many nations and vary in their details, so you'll need to research them, considering how to handle comity clauses in your contracts. Sometimes comity treaties between nations settle this issue for you, but this is an area where your business— especially if it's a small firm—needs additional research and counsel. We'll discuss this further in later chapters. But in terms of legal environment as an aspect of culture, it's important to remember that in some situations, you leave at least some of your rights behind when you get on a plane.

Finally, one of the important considerations for your business, in terms of the legal difficulties in international business, is that not all courts are created equal. The judicial systems of many countries are, at best, biased towards nationals and, at worst, corrupted by nationals. It might be in your best interest to establish a court in a third country—many contracts establish the British courts for the settlement of disputes.

Economics

Economic structure is closely tied to political and legal structure. Different countries have very different amounts of government involvement in industry and widely variant attitudes towards foreign investment. Some countries actively seek out investment dollars from abroad and take aggressive steps to create tax incentives, readily available work permits, and smaller tariffs on goods. Other governments take a strong part in industry and may be involved in the production of certain goods or services. Often these nationalized industries are monopolies. Even where that isn't the case, a delicate balance exists for American businesses. The national government might deregulate an industry such as energy but still place significant handicaps on privately owned companies that enter the marketplace.

When it comes to economics in the global market, it's almost impossible to cover the topic briefly. Ask an economist how the price of gold in South Africa affects the interest rate in Russia, and you'll need to sit down before the answer ends. Understanding economics on a global scale is very difficult—so much so that its complexity makes some businesses shy away. On the other hand, companies that expanded in China over the last decade profited greatly by the average annual growth rate— over 10% each year. The international economic environment is complicated, but it warrants your attention, for a growing market abroad can be the best way for your business to compete. New markets open up in the face of changing legal environments and increased buying power, so pay attention. Your business will appreciate you landing a deal in the next China, wherever it is.

Religion

Religion is a surprisingly easy issue for your business to deal with once you have the appropriate information. Whatever the religious requirements of a nation are, do everything in your power to comply with them—and don't expect anyone to have a sense of humor about their religious beliefs. If you're dealing with a Muslim country, don't offer the sales rep an alcoholic drink: it's that simple. Although the issue of religion can seem highly contentious and complicated, all you need to do in order to practically handle religious issues in other nations is to find out what their religion prescribes and forbids, acting accordingly in every way possible.

Granted, talking politics and religion are generally ill advised in a business setting, so it should seem fairly intuitive that you should be as respectful as possible of religious differences. In the context of international business and cultural differences, it's important to know at least something of the religious environment of the nation you are working in, especially regarding any ongoing religious conflict. There are many countries where religious tension can get in the way of your business. Asking a Serb in Bosnia to hire a Croat manager can become a prickly business because of a long and ongoing political struggle. That's the kind of information you should know before going into that country's business environment.

Education

Education is an important factor for your business to consider when you're looking at any production or service abroad. A country with a large pool of highly educated workers may be necessary for some industries and may be an indication that manual labor is cheaper elsewhere. Education systems play an important part in the socialization of any person, but insofar as it applies to the context of international business, two things are important. First, the attitude a given culture has toward education is a reflection of its power distance and social structure. Countries such as France, where collegiate education requires certain scores on a nationalized test with a definite cut-off point, have a strong social stratification based on college degrees. Similarly, the education system of Japan, which stresses education almost to the point of reverence, teaches children to respect the authority of their teachers from an early age; the nation's high power distance is affected by that principle.

Another aspect that you need to consider, and one that we'll address more in depth later in this chapter, is to ask yourself what people have been taught about you. In many countries, English is taught in the classroom even if it is not the official language of that country. That might make communication easier (although many former British colonies learn a sort of variation of English somewhere between Commonwealth English and American English), but you should still try to find out what individuals in a foreign country are taught about America itself—not merely popular cultural perceptions about what America and Americans are like, but what the education system actually teaches about America. Japanese students, for example, learn about the atomic bomb differently than American students do. Arabs have a very different portrayal of the Gulf War than we might. And whatever parts of American culture get exported also have an effect on the preconceptions of Americans abroad.

Increasingly, foreign nationals come to the United States to study and then return to their home country to work. These individuals are often hired as liaisons to deal with American businesses, and you may run into a few in your international travels. They are probably the most educated regarding America, and consequently your best possible interpreters of language or cultural gaps.

Social Structure

Social structure is an important consideration even in cultures that don't have the legacy of a caste system, as India has. Depending upon how rigid class distinctions are in a given culture, your business can have a hard time getting certain tasks done. In some cultures, some tasks are seen as being "beneath" individuals of a certain social standing, and you'll have to hire additional employees of lower social class to perform them. It's an important consideration when trying to make production decisions, especially when beginning a new venture or product. Tension between classes can also lead to antagonism between workers and managers, as it did in England up until the last twenty years or so. Class consciousness can lead to a higher number of labor disputes, which increases production costs—even in countries where there isn't a framework for labor disputes, or where strikes are illegal. Discontent with management will cost you.

Furthermore, classes are largely economically based, and understanding the economic power of a social class is another part of knowing your market when selling to a foreign nation or populace. And, just as with potential religious tensions, you should have some background knowledge of class struggles in a country. In many places in Africa, class delimitations are made by tribal identity, another complication that you ought to be aware of when entering a new culture.

CULTURE COUNTS

Remember that this list of cultural aspects is incomplete. However, it is a good start for you to research and consider. You should never expect that the way things are in your culture and business (standards, etiquette, practices, or beliefs) are universal. Assume that things are always done differently somewhere else, and if you're wrong, you'll just be pleasantly surprised. The general rule for dealing with the differences in these aspects between cultures is this:

Assume there to be a gap between your culture and theirs.

Learn what the difference is and what it means for you.

Tweak your behavior to accommodate.

Expect exceptions to generalizations about a culture.

Reassess your business in its new environment.

Remember to **ALTER** your business. International business has no hard-and-fast rules, which is why some businesses seem to think of entering international markets as a separate beast. However, instead of viewing it as something totally new and foreign to you, think of it as regular business with a few minor changes.

There might not always be a big difference between the legal system of the United States and the United Kingdom, for instance. But start with the assumption that they are different, and learn how your rights to representation change in a British court. Then plan to structure your contracts with a clause stating in what country's courts your disputes will be heard. Don't fear the difference if you do go to a British court; find a way to use the differences to your advantage. This five-step process is a simple way of preparing yourself for cross-cultural interaction.

CROSS-CULTURAL LITERACY

The ability to understand and learn about another culture in a functional relationship is called cross-cultural literacy. This is what international businesses need to cultivate in their employees in order to successfully operate in an international environment. When hiring, look for a background in a foreign language; look for bilingual candidates, individuals who are expatriates of another country or who spent some time living, studying, or working abroad. Those tend to be the candidates with cross-cultural literacy. Even if your prospect lived in Spain for a year and you're trying to find a liaison for a German client, a person who has learned to adapt to one culture successfully already—no matter which—has the skill set and thought patterns necessary to adapt to another one.

And it is important (as we'll remind you throughout this book) to remember this is a two-way street. It's just as important for managers to know they have to alter their expectations of foreign nationals as it is for you to remember that expectations for you might need a similar adjustment.

AMERICA, AS SEEN BY EVERYONE ELSE

The perception of Americans as overbearing, loud, and rude can be a serious obstacle for you when seeking out a partner or client abroad. The general dislike for Americans is so strong in some countries that it will be difficult for you to get in the door; even if you do, it will be harder still to shed the "defects" commonly attributed to Americans around the world. "The Ugly American" is born out of actual experiences that foreign nations have had with Americans. Even if the generalization is unfair (it isn't always), you ought to consider how your business will work to escape the perception abroad.

Dealing with these preconceived notions of what Americans are like is another area where a little research can go along way and is something that is especially important before a first meeting with a foreign company unfamiliar with your country. The inexperienced foreign national will pre-suppose that you will behave just as the generalized "Americans" do, and every action smacking of arrogance and aggression will solidify this view of you. If you take the time to find out before your meeting some general idea of how Americans appear to the culture you are trying to work with, then you can take action to break those stereotypes and dissociate yourself with any negative ideas that people around the world have of Americans. Unfortunately, when interaction between two cultures or organizations is limited, each characterizes the other by the few times they do cross paths, and in this respect every American shapes the perception of American business internationally. Your colleagues will appreciate you taking this responsibility seriously.

Part of the reason that businesses need to go global is that "everybody else is doing it." As your business finds increasing numbers of international competitors or competitors going international, you'll have to compete. And when it comes to foreign competition, they sometimes have an edge over you. American culture is exported, whether it's pop culture or American products. So your Chinese competitor has at least had some exposure to America culturally, especially if he speaks English fluently, something that is increasingly the case. Can you name a famous Indian novel? A Chilean rock star? A French supermarket chain? America imports some culture from abroad, but typically by accident or through someone else's design. Elsewhere, foreign nationals are actively seeking to import American culture and products.

CULTURE WITHIN A CULTURE

Finally—and perhaps the most difficult complication—don't assume a culture to be homogenous. In any given country, there are many different groups: economic, social, religious, and so on. Social psychologists use the term "outgroup homogeneity effect" to describe the natural tendencies of individuals to overestimate the similarity of members of unfamiliar groups and to appreciate the range of familiar ones. You have some idea at least of how diverse America is, because you have a wide range of experience with Americans. But if you have limited experience with Japan, your natural tendency—simply because you have limited information—is to assume on a conscious or unconscious level that all Japanese people are more or less the same. This is obviously not the case. Even though you know this abstractly, be careful of how assumed similarity affects you in the real world. Appreciating the variations will prove beneficial to you and will help you expect the many exceptions to national generalizations that you will encounter. For example, you might think of New Zealand, as a former British colony, as having a culture much like that of the United Kingdom, but that view isn't just simplistic, it's wrong. The indigenous Maori population is a significant portion of the populace and controls a large amount of land, given to it as reparation. Furthermore, the Maori are divided into subtribes, or Iwi, some of which struggle with cultural tensions spawned out of land wars almost two centuries prior. To think that marketing that targets members of one Iwi will target New Zealanders of British or Dutch descent is just plain wrong—and it will cost you money if you don't appreciate the differences between the groups.

HOW TO DO IT

Now that we've covered some of the concepts of the cultural environment of international business, it's time to talk about how to learn what you need to know. In order for you to engage in international operations successfully, there are a few general tips that apply to doing business in any different culture. Most of these should seem intuitive to an experienced manager, but their applications in the international context may be new to you.

The model is simple and involves constantly correcting and refining how you do business abroad in order to improve and build a better working relationship:

1. Get it right the first time. Research as much as you can to adapt before you start working abroad. But, if you don't . . .

2. . . . Get it right the second time. A slip made in ignorance can be forgivable, but once you've already been corrected, be careful not to repeat your mistake, because if you don't . . .

3. . . . There might not be a third time.

Do Your Homework

Before doing business with or in another country, try to find out as much as you can about that particular culture. Speak with someone who knows from experience, and do your best to modify your behavior. Even if your company hires a liaison, that doesn't mean you don't still need to bow in Japan.

This applies to the discussion in Chapter One regarding the forms of international business. To be multinational, you'll need to learn a great deal about the new culture with which you'll be interacting. Hiring someone who speaks both languages isn't enough. You'll need to research the laws relating to your industry and the government's position and policies toward welcoming foreign investment—and the communication barrier doesn't stop with an interpreter. The more you know before the first meeting, the better off you'll be.

Pay Attention

When doing business across cultures, you should expect to have a few misunderstandings. Rather than trying to know everything about another culture, try to learn from your mistakes. Reasonable people going into cultural gaps will know that there will be a certain amount of misunderstandings of various degrees of seriousness and will plan around them. But when you make a cultural faux pas, be sure to correct it in the future; continuing the same mistake will hurt your image and the image of your business. Displaying conciliatory behavior after a misunderstanding and remembering not to repeat it is the best way you can hope to overcome gaps in culture.

Some cultural differences can be worked around, such as language difficulties, but some can't. The Spanish siesta is a cultural practice so deeply ingrained that there isn't much working around it. It seems strange to Americans to leave work, go home, and nap for an hour or more in the middle of the workday, but some cultural differences you'll just have to learn how to live with—and get a little shuteye yourself, even.

Be Patient

Although you can't expect unlimited forgiveness for your mistakes, you should remember to be patient with foreign nationals when it's them and not you committing the social faux pas because of their ignorance of your culture. One of the most difficult things to adjust to in any working relationship involving international businesses and employees from other cultures is reminding yourself that there are many things that are common to your culture but not others. There is a big difference between a mistake, an insult, and a misunderstanding when it comes to conflict across cultures. It's important that your business be able to deal with the errors of your foreign partners in a constructive way.

Don't Be Afraid of Sounding Stupid

If you or your company are unsure of what a foreign counterpart is expecting of you, take the time to clarify it. It will help you both develop better communication across cultures; that way, you'll get it right the first time. Besides, asking a simple question is painless and can lead to discussions that add to your working relationship.

Avoid Thinking Someone Else Is Stupid

If work comes back wrong from a foreign subsidiary, it's easy to think that a mistake was made on their part. But before you get on the phone to say how wrong they are, consider that standards of quality can be different in different cultures, and remember that learning curves can be painful. You need to discern the difference between actual incapability and a communication breakdown. And it's important—of paramount importance in certain cultures—to be polite when correcting, so choose your words carefully. American procedures and methods are not the only way of doing business. You must allow for different practices and standards in other nations. Be clear in your communication, but avoid being condescending.

Saving and Losing Face

Face is often discussed in the context of understanding East Asian culture (particularly China), but your business should follow a general rule in any international dealings: Be careful how you criticize. The problems of communicating across cultures, managing global operations, and working in an increasingly unified world market are hard enough without having to deal with personality conflicts on top of everything else. When difficulties arise, work hard to understand why something went wrong rather than merely attempting to place blame. If you can work with your foreign colleagues instead of against them, it will be much better for your business in the long run. This might sound like nothing more than a management truism, but it needs emphasis in an international business book. In China, saving face is so important that causing someone to lose face, even if accidentally, can have serious consequences. Sending the wrong level of employee to greet a Chinese businessman—something that might seem innocuous to you—might be perceived as a loss of face.

These problems are easy to avoid. What you need is some planning, the right attitude, and a little spin. You're not sending managers to your factory in Chile because they produce an inferior product; you just want to match production standards there with your other facilities. Instead of saying, "we need to fix what you're doing wrong," present it as "we need to integrate you in what we're doing right." It's just that simple most of the time. And yet, when you examine the issues that expatriate managers have when they start telling their foreign employees how to "fix" what they're doing, you can see that many managers aren't taking the time to handle the delicate situation of reputations in an international context—or simply haven't been trained how to do so.

HOW TO LEARN IT

One of the appendices of this book is a section on other resources you can turn to for more information, but this chapter stresses the need to research cultural differences and details some of their complexity. So how do you learn?

The first resource to turn to is the U.S. State Department. At www. state.gov, in the country profiles background notes, you can find a demographic breakdown for every country that includes some economic statistics and a brief history of the country. The entries are short, but they can provide you with quick facts about any country's cultural environment. The State Department Web site also includes articles and links to articles about contemporary issues in the country. This information is kept current and updated relatively frequently, so it's a good resource to turn to as a first pass at learning about a new culture.

One resource that you might not readily think of is travel books about the country. Tourism titles will include a good deal of the smaller cultural practices of a country, even if they aren't geared toward business. They won't typically give a lot of information about the culture or its current ideology, but they will teach you about proper etiquette in conversation, something that can be hard to learn any way other than by experience. Travel books will also teach you some of the basic and common vocabulary of the language of that country, something that can be very helpful indeed. Using an interpreter is necessary in some situations, but you should take the time to learn basic greetings and courtesy language in the relevant language. Here are some words and phrases you should know, in the forms appropriate to various classes and genders:

Hello.

How are you?

Please . . .

Thank you.

I don't speak [language].

Goodbye.

The single best resource you can turn to when preparing to deal with an unfamiliar culture is someone who's done it before. A colleague who has done business in the country you're going to will have a relevant perspective on doing business in that culture, and you can learn from his or her experience.

KEY POINTS TO REMEMBER

- Cultures can be compared across five dimensions: power distance (comfort with inequality), individualism (focus on the individual), uncertainty avoidance (tolerance for ambiguity), masculinity (aggression and gap between genders within the culture), and long-term orientation (commitment to the established order).

- Cultures have many characteristics that can create gaps in beliefs and behavior. These include language, technology, legal environment, economics, religion, education, and social structure, among many others.

PART

INTERNATIONAL FINANCING AND FOREIGN DIRECT INVESTMENT

Understanding International Trade and Foreign Direct Investment

The possibilities of investor individuals and countries offering capital for venture and growth is at least as old as maritime trade. From the first Phoenician merchants to the era of discovery and the Columbus voyages through the exports and imports that accompanied the Industrial Revolution, Church, state, companies, and individuals have been assessing risk and potential return. These partnerships grew the world. Commercial development relied on creating financial vehicles bearing equanimity in return for investment. With the diversification from maritime commerce to manufacturing, banks rose to prominence in financing, managing, and creating the financial tools needed to spur growth. Even Marxism had the opportunity to weigh in on international trade, supplying theory for labor and raw materials. Eventually, the difficulty of travel and schisms of nationalism in places such as Europe made borders porous in economic trade.

Today, with economies around the world becoming global, countries and companies are attentive to the possibilities of greater returns using the opportunities opening up beyond national borders. Much of this multinational diversification comes from the homogeneity of communications and knowledge brought about by the inventions of the past 100 years—such as telephones, airplanes, and computers—in fact, by all of modern technology. This same technology allows the world to devise better means of financing and to think about commerce more in terms of transportation and other logistics than in terms of physical borders.

Never before in human history have there been so many opportunities for businesses to look beyond their home communities, beyond their native countries. For example, anyone with the inclination to do so can become part of international trade through investment. One result of this change is that a growing amount of capital is invested from the worldwide markets as foreign direct investment (FDI). But what is foreign direct investment, and how does it work in the global economy? Let's begin by defining FDI.

FOREIGN DIRECT INVESTMENT DEFINED

Foreign direct investment (FDI) is the investment outside an investing entity's country of origin or residence. Usually, this entity is a company, or the country itself, wanting to increase revenue through investment returns. To qualify as foreign direct investment, the capital must contribute to building, owning, or maintaining a long-term production facility, raw material production site, or a power plant manufacturing business that directly contributes to the creation of goods in another country. An FDI is most frequently an investment in a factory or similar facility or facilities. The facility serves as a means of production (MoP). The concept of means of production is a relatively new concept in economics. The term was introduced during the Industrial Revolution, when factories and mass production of goods began to significantly affect the economies of nations. It is a concept that describes the necessity of having the tools and materials needed to create products (goods and services). In simple terms, this necessity generates a market for foreign direct investment.

Briefly, here's how this works. Let's say a company (let's call it XYZ, Inc.) wants to sell comparatively inexpensive knit cotton fabric in the U.S. market. Rather than simply buying and importing the fabric, XYZ, Inc., decides to buy an existing small and inefficient cotton fabric knitting mill in Tirupur, Tamil Nadu, India. XYZ, Inc. plans to upgrade the knitting mill with more efficient and modern equipment, and to expand both the mill and its production. The financial investment XYZ makes to buy the mill and upgrade it is foreign direct investment.

Both the U.S. Department of Commerce and the United Nations have established standards that define and control foreign direct investment. The standards are important, for, according to the International Trade Administration, the United States receives more foreign direct investment than any other country. The direct investment does not include just the capital; the investment must also include control over the foreign entity. By U.S. Department of Commerce and United Nations standards, to qualify as a foreign direct investment, the purchase must provide the investing company with control over the purchased entity. The UN's standards define control as owning 10 percent or more of the ordinary shares or voting power of an incorporated firm, or the equivalent in an unincorporated firm. If the investing company does not control 10 percent or more of the foreign company, the investment is known as a foreign portfolio investment. These standards form the basis for the technical definition of a multinational company, and such details are important. Once a company qualifies as a foreign direct investment investor, it automatically becomes a multinational company for tax purposes. Thus, these technicalities have significant implications for taxes and the bottom line.

If you are considering foreign direct investment as a means of entering the international market, you need to consider the various types of investment available and the trade environments that exist in the areas where you are considering investment. This knowledge will help clarify how foreign direct investments are tracked, how they are affected by economic conditions within countries, and how investing companies gain the information needed to make intelligent foreign direct investments. Let's begin by looking at the issues of balance of trade and balance of payments.

THE BALANCE OF TRADE AND THE BALANCE OF PAYMENTS

As you begin to shop for a potential foreign direct investment, one of the things you need to investigate is the economic health of the nation in which you are considering investing. One of the major indicators of national economic health is balance of trade (BOT). The value of exported goods and services is compared with the value of imported goods and services within the borders of the country where investment might be made. The resulting figure has different implications depending on whether it is positive or negative. A negative balance of trade indicates that a country is importing more value in goods and services than it is exporting. This is a trade deficit. A trade deficit is important because of how it affects investment decisions in different economic climates. It quantifies how much of what a country produces in goods and services is moving beyond that country's borders. A negative balance of trade is a transfer of wealth from the inside of a nation to its outside.

The second concept is balance of payments (BOP). This concept acknowledges that there are a great many other factors contributing to a country's wealth besides the products and services created inside its borders. The balance of payments extends its consideration beyond goods produced and services bought and sold to include the positive or negative values of, for example, tourism, foreign aid, military expenditures, and foreign investment for a given country.

Now that the components contributing to the balance of payments are defined, a clear understanding of the process to determine value is required. Determining the balance of trade and the balance of payments is an accounting procedure, much like any other determination of fair market value. The two types of accounts within the balance of payments are current accounts and capital accounts. (There is a subset of the capital account, the financial account, that we do not need to detail for our purposes.) Both of these accounts can be simplified to determining ingoing and outgoing values.

Here, we should pause to clarify a very important point. The current account for a balance of payment should not be confused with the similarly named account in banking.

In theory, the current account for balance of payment determinations should be equal to the capital account; these two accounts are the balances of each side of an equation. Each account is comprised of economic categories that contribute to the balance of payments. Current accounts are comprised of merchandise (goods), services, and investments. These items are what we think of as the goods and services created by means of production. Capital accounts add the value of the means of production into the equation through the sale of land and the market value of cash and currency, designators of agreed value for exchange. For the purposes of foreign direct investment strategies, the stronger the current account surplus, the greater the indication of thriving export sales. For the purposes of foreign direct investment, consider current accounts as how much of a country is being bought and sold; the capital accounts can be defined as how much of a country is owned by other countries and how much of other countries a country owns.

As you evaluate the implications of a nation's balance of trade and balance of payments, you can evaluate the economic health of a potential investment nation. Is the business climate strong? If you will be producing goods in this nation, does this economy have the potential to allow you to sell not only to your home country, but also to other trading partners of the nation? What marketing and sales options will you have? What are the opportunities and problems you are likely to face if you make that foreign direct investment? And what do the economic conditions in the nation you are considering tell you about the types of foreign direct investment you should consider in that nation? Basically, it comes down to, how many eggs do I put in my foreign direct investment baskets, and how do I decide where to place each egg?

There are two basic types of foreign direct investment: horizontal and vertical. Each has advantages and disadvantages that influence your choices.

HORIZONTAL VERSUS VERTICAL FOREIGN DIRECT INVESTMENT

When a multinational company decides to invest, it must make decisions about the best use of its investment capital. In selecting an investment strategy, the company can choose either horizontal or vertical investment strategies.

Horizontal investment refers to capitalizing in such a manner that the same product is produced and/or marketed in multiple countries. This means duplicating production and/or marketing facilities and staff and their associated warehousing facilities. This type of investment makes sense when local preferences are critical to product sales and when delivery costs are high in comparison with the cost of production.

Vertical investment is chosen when a company places different sections of production and/or marketing in different countries. The strategy is investing in such a manner that the costs for each phase of production are the lowest possible. This strategy is most beneficial when the product(s) being produced do not need to be customized by market and when the costs associated with transportation are only a minor part of the cost of production.

Multinationals choose the investment strategy that works best for their individual situations. Horizontal investment is used to expand the market for existing widely accepted products or services by introducing those into a new foreign market. Vertical investments can be used to cut costs and increase profits, or in a distribution channel for marketing a product abroad.

Factors that weigh in on a company's choice between horizontal and vertical investment include geographic, social, and economic costs. Transportation cost is a good example of how these factors can come into play. One of the reasons for engaging in horizontal foreign direct investment is reducing transportation costs. It's obvious that producing goods close to the end market keeps transportation costs low. However, you must also consider that transportation is only one cost of many in the production and delivery of a product to market. The costs of transportation need to be weighed against the value-to-weight ratio. In situations in which the product has a low value-to-weight ratio, as is the case with textiles and perishables, lowering transportation costs can improve the bottom line. However, for other products, such as electronics, this might not be as beneficial, for transportation cost is a smaller portion of the overall cost of the product.

Once you decide on a vertical or horizontal investment strategy, the next decision is the method used to implement that strategy. Will you simply buy into an existing firm, or will you develop a totally new business operation? Or will you adopt some hybrid strategy using both investment procedures?

GREEN-FIELDS VERSUS MERGERS AND ACQUISITIONS

A company going multinational needs to decide whether to take the green-field operations route or to focus investment on mergers and acquisitions. Green-fields are investments in new facilities and involve creating entirely new manufacturing and power operations. Alternatively, a company making foreign direct investments may decide to use mergers and acquisitions to invest in existing companies. Acquiring a company means that it has been bought and is solely owned by its new purchaser; the original company no longer exists. In some cases of foreign direct investment, a new owner may not buy all of a foreign company, only an amount sufficient to exercise control over its operation. A merger implies that the target company and the purchasing company go forward as a completely new company, although an equal status rarely occurs. Generally, a merger is actually just a friendly acquisition with CEOs in gentlemanly agreement to call it a merger.

Acquisition is the most common form of foreign direct investment, mostly because it takes the least amount of time to complete the deal and begin the business of business. However, you should heed a word of caution regarding acquisitions and foreign direct investment. One of the pitfalls for choosing acquisition as a method of investment is that American managers have a tendency to overestimate the amount of value a foreign acquisition will bring to a company. That usually translates to overpayment for the acquisition. Choosing a green-field enterprise path presents its own list of caveats. These are characteristically more time-consuming to bring into operation, and the potential for unforeseen complications caused by regulations administered by an unfamiliar government can be daunting. However, both types of investments have been made successfully, and you need to carefully consider whether the green-field or acquisition route is best for your company.

Of course, if you are making multiple investments under your overall FDI strategy, you have the option of combining investment types. You might use the acquisition approach in one country or one aspect of your investment while employing the green-field approach in another. For example, if you are acquiring a textile factory in a nation, you might also create from scratch a textile distribution center to distribute the products of the factory.

Once you decide on the type of foreign direct investment(s) you will use, you then need to locate the capital necessary to implement your plan. Unless you are fortunate enough to have sufficient capital available for the investment, you must now secure the capital to make that investment. Turning to your local banker is often not a good (or even viable) answer to this need. You need access to the foreign investment market.

HOW TO FIND INVESTORS AND INVESTMENTS FOR DIRECT INVESTMENTS

The most reliable and reputable source for researching the foreign direct investment market is through the U.S. Department of Commerce's Foreign Commercial Service Agency, which falls under the International Trade Administration. The Foreign Commercial Service was created exclusively to support the development of U.S. exports, and it publishes materials that are created for the investor who seeks direction and information. This agency also provides opportunities to interact with and learn from specialists in areas of foreign trade through seminars and conferences on international trade. They specifically provide free prospectus information and can even provide advice about exports. This agency also offers for-fee product surveys in foreign countries for potential investors, but these surveys are limited to countries that are major trade partners. However, as a one-stop source for resources and networking on foreign direct investment, it is better than immediately engaging the services of an international trade broker. For more information on the International Trade Administration's Foreign Commercial Service, go to its Web site, http://trade.gov/cs/index.asp.

FOREIGN PORTFOLIO INVESTMENTS: THE EXAMPLE OF CHINA'S INTEREST IN THE UNITED STATES

Just as there is an onshore market for financial products, there is a foreign investment market that responds to the drive for capital to grow foreign securities and financial products. These are foreign portfolio investments (FPI).

With FPI, rather than investing in factors of production, a company invests in financials, such as government bonds issued by a foreign country. Thus, instead of a company owning a portion of a factory in a foreign country, that same company could own shares of the foreign company that owns the factory. This is foreign portfolio investment. Another difference is that foreign portfolio investment in financial instruments does not require active management, unlike FDI, which requires active oversight. Other examples of foreign portfolio investments are bonds, stocks, and other securities issued by a foreign company or country.

Just as there is hedging within the onshore financial markets, futures contracts are issued to guarantee payment as a foreign investment. It is important to assure that investments are made in a stable portfolio. In London, the International Commodities Clearing House keeps a registered members list and provides to those members such services as maintaining and organizing the clearing of futures contracts; it also assures the fulfillment of transactions. The ICCH services mostly Great Britain and Europe. With foreign direct investment for United States entities, the company looking to invest in foreign portfolios can seek out seasoned assistance with financial products through the U.S. Department of Commerce's Foreign Commercial Service Agency.

As with any investment in financial products, there are some general factors that affect whether there is a good climate for portfolio investments. One is whether the country where the investment will occur has a lower comparable tax rate than the rest of the market. Another consideration is whether the interest rate for the investment will occur at a higher comparable rate than the rest of the market. The exchange rate where the currency is at its strongest is also a major consideration for investors. For all foreign portfolio investments, these matters fall in the capital account within the balance of payment calculations.

One good example of response to these conditions is China's investment in the United States, especially in its securities market. China not only holds more foreign exchange reserves (FER) than any other country in the world, but also is acquiring FERs at a faster rate than any other country. China's high savings rate and the structured restraint of the yuan's appreciation put China in an ideal position to purchase foreign exchange reserves from countries with relatively low savings growth. One of those low-savings-growth nations is the United States, which relies on foreign capital from China and other countries having high savings rates. As of June 2007, China accounted for almost 20 percent of the foreign-held U.S. securities covering the national debt. It is second only to Japan for the amount of U.S. foreign exchange reserves it holds. The big picture debates around this issue are

- How sustainable this level is, and for how long
- The risks inherent in this extent of reliance
- Methods of evaluating costs of borrowing compared with benefits over time

Financial experts propose that this situation could put the U.S. economy at risk, for China might

- Attempt to influence U.S. policies
- Pull out of its U.S. holdings for better interest rates

The general consensus is that any actual large activity to divest of foreign exchange reserves would be deficits for China, and the reciprocating damage to the U.S. economy would ripple into China's domestic economy. Essentially, divesting into foreign markets solidifies commitments between countries' economies.

Although some Americans may regard foreign investment in this nation as a potential problem, U.S. companies have been heavily investing in other nations.

UNITED STATES FOREIGN DIRECT INVESTMENT ABROAD

The United States is the biggest investor in foreign direct and portfolio investment in the world. The trends of America's investments abroad have been the most prolific of any other country. The second and third largest investors, Britain and Germany, do not total as much foreign direct investment business as the United States does alone. For the most part, the ebb and flow of foreign investments' direction and size is governed by the relative rate of

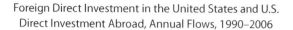

Foreign Direct Investment in the United States and U.S.
Direct Investment Abroad, Annual Flows, 1990–2006

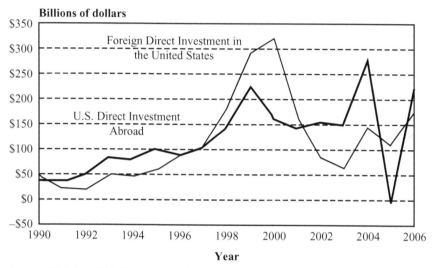

Source: CRS from U.S. Department of Commerce data

growth between the United States and foreign countries. The outlook for foreign direct investment, with over $235 billion invested in foreign countries in 2006, up from $8 billion the previous year, shows a strong upswing because of these conditions. Almost three-quarters of these investments abroad are in developed countries—mostly in Western European nations.

With the United States' long-term and continuing foreign investment in Western European development, it has become a trend for countries to create as inviting an investment climate as possible. Ireland is just such a success story. In part, perhaps, because of the commitment of the United States to the 1990s peace agreement, Ireland has shared America's love of technological development. To that end, Ireland has provided an accommodating structure for foreign investment in its technology sector. Examples of this welcoming effort are a workforce prepared for this sort of work, goals for exports in a friendly and technology-hungry European market, and the economic climate as a whole. Today, software investment in Ireland accounts for almost 25 percent of Ireland's total foreign investment.

Foreign direct investment is not a one-way street. Just as Americans invest abroad, other nations invest in the United States.

FOREIGN DIRECT INVESTMENT IN THE UNITED STATES

Many of the factors that make the United States a good foreign investor globally also make it a good foreign investment. By 2000, it was the largest single recipient of foreign direct investment, although it has trended downward since then. Although the Western European states receive more direct investment than the United States when taken together, no single country receives more individually. As mentioned, Japan and China heavily invest in the United States, having diligently nurtured reciprocating conditions to match factors such as low interest rates that the United States promotes as attractive for investors. Some of these investors are institutional investors, who are hedging in international markets. The United States has an economic environment welcoming to businesses seeking to expand existing products or markets. A good example of such exploitation of an intentional niche is the Mexico-based Cemex's expansion into foreign markets. Cemex is Mexico's largest multinational business, and the world's largest manufacturer of cement. It became so by way expanding into foreign markets, mostly through acquisition. The United States is home to 25 percent of its plants.

WHY INVEST ABROAD?

There are as many reasons that businesses invest in international markets as there are combinations of business motives and market incentives. Usually, when one thinks of investment on an international scale, it is assumed that the motive is an immediate profit potential. This is not always the case. Sometimes the learning curve that a business encounters entering the international investment world, or that even a seasoned multinational encounters when broaching a new market, is an investment choice approached as a goal for future profit potential. Some businesses may even choose to limit exposure to the volatility of foreign markets by investing only minor sums as a way to gain exposure and experience with a tolerable minimum of risk. This way, they can learn more about the market while developing the competency to compete. This tactic plays out well for both investment in an existing business or in a green-field enterprise.

When it comes to investing in the U.S. markets, foreign investment still favors (by historic cost) the established markets of manufacturing, banking, and wholesale and retail trade. The newest rising star is professional and scientific services. The most lackluster performance is information. However, as with any social science over time, economics are an expression of climate. Although these last two categories were both poorer performers through the first five years of the 2000s, they started to pick up in 2005. Considering that the decade started with the bursting of the technology bubble, with outsourcing, and with 9/11, the market adjustments around these three industries are unsurprising. They could be interpreted as reflecting the success of tried-and-true incentives over situational issues that cause fluctuation. Part of this recovery in shaken markets demonstrates the strength of foreign market responses to incentives. In particular, there are now more entrepreneurial foreigners prepared to avail themselves of the full benefit of incentives.

Innovation is the hallmark of entrepreneurism. Often, innovation within a small business is a factor in survival. Entrepreneurs and small businesses are capable of attracting foreign investment because of their innovation. Frequently, small businesses build on the foundation of simple but high-demand products that have the characteristics needed to propel their manufacturers into a globalized world.

When the Small Business Innovation Development Act was passed, it spawned the Small Business Innovation Research (SBIR) Program to help small businesses make the leap to a global market. Seminars and workshops have been organized by knowledgeable experts in foreign direct investment to help small business owners learn how to access and leverage international investments. Small businesses receive this support from the federal government as an acknowledgment of the history of small businesses advancing change and building "capacity to create wealth." Studies such as those done by a Duke University Pratt School of Engineering research group established that 25 percent of the technology and engineering companies started in the United States in the decade between 1995 and 2005 could boast a founder who was not a United States citizen at birth. In fact, many of those responsible for the success of nascent technology and engineering success in the United States are foreign-born. They have become generators and drivers of intellectual property in our country. The majority of these innovators were from China or India. This phenomenon is so prevalent that Duke titled its study "New Immigrant Entrepreneurs."

No matter where a foreign direct investment is made, the political, cultural, and regulatory environments in the country of the investment will significantly affect businesses and their success. Thus, in addition to other considerations, the foreign direct investor should look carefully and thoroughly at the politics, culture, and regulatory environment in any nation where FDI is being considered.

POLITICAL ENVIRONMENTS AND FOREIGN DIRECT INVESTMENT

The political environment for the countries of both the investor and recipient companies of foreign direct or portfolio investments can have a significant effect on how attractive investments might be. Between 1990 and 2004, the global economy expanded by 50 percent. The five countries with the largest growth were in the double digits for trade expansion; all were developed nations (Ireland was one). Although nationalism and protectionism are now specters of the past for any developed nation, even with trade barriers thinning, there are sound reasons for countries to retain caveats around free trade agreements and the global market. The Doha Development Round is a series of talks begun in 2001 to lower trade barriers and facilitate trade among countries with disparities in prosperity. These talks provide good examples of the issues. Developed and developing countries are divided on agriculture imports, tariffs, remedies, and services as of mid-2008. For the United States and other developed countries, tax breaks (which act as an export subsidy) are a source of incentive for foreign direct investment. This, in turn, helps domestic firms to compete abroad or to entice foreign firms to invest in facilities to produce products outside their own countries. In both instances, tax breaks offset higher costs.

There is a type of insurance that assuages certain risks for different types of foreign direct investment. One type of investment insurable by the government is known as outward investment. This is the investment that goes out to another country for investment in resources, or in imports or exports that foreign commodities use. Losses covered by this insurance are those used for nationalization or for war. Exposure not covered includes tax incentives for companies investing on profits brought back into the country, local business subsidies, governments supporting industry nationalism, labor markets and agriculture groups, and security industries.

Inward investment is viewed by its recipient as outward investment; whether an investment is outward or inward depends on whether you are the investor or on the investment's receiving end. Comparable to outward investment's insurability is the restriction of inward investment ownership rights by some countries. Evaluating inward investment involves such incentives as tax breaks, low-interest loans, subsidies, grants, and the lifting of well-defined restrictions. What makes this attractive to investors is the long-term payoff, despite the possibility of short-term loss.

The overall effect of this policy is to decrease the risk of investing abroad. This is because the countries that receive investment mandate that nationals hold a certain percentage of each venture. Although this does add additional complications, the risk reduction that also accompanies it makes investment all the more attractive. One way this works is by a restriction on ownership, such as that a foreign company may only control up to a specific percentage of a domestic firm. India, for example, mandates that a foreign company may control no more than 26 percent of a domestic newspaper.

Working in multiple nations will mean that a business must deal not only with institutions in its home country and its host country, but also with a variety of international institutions and services. Understanding the role of these organizations can help make investment truly profitable.

INTERNATIONAL INSTITUTIONS AND INTERNATIONAL TRADE

International institutions serve a number of purposes within international trade. Some are involved with standards, some with facilitating transactions and promoting trade, and some with promoting economic freedom and social justice. Not all the promulgated ideas and directions these organizations advocate are accepted universally, but not all the activity of international financial organizations is esoteric or restrictive, either. Good examples of how large international institutions affect the day-to-day operations of product export and import business can be found in the form of customs house brokers.

Customs Broker Houses

Any product that enter or exits a country is governed by an enormous number of criteria and a great body of associated paperwork, which must conform specifically to national and international policies, laws, and standards. Customs broker houses are assurance centers that meet these needs for their clients. These clearinghouses cover many areas of specialty, according to the needs of their clients' businesses. They take the responsibility for everything involved in the transaction, including destinations, tariffs, routings, and other very specialized needs customary to imports and exports. Ultimately, products managed by customs broker houses clear customs.

With globalization, the role of customs broker houses is evolving. As they act as a centralized point of raw data and logistics for international trade coming and going in the United States, their access to critical business information makes them the de facto nerve center for strategic information. Thus, not only have they contributed to the expansion and development of markets as globalization takes hold, but they have also expanded and developed their own niche within the global market by being able to offer diverse and divergent management services in the international trade business. These services provide trades with opportunities to bring new products to market, to explore market potentials, to reduce costs of business, and to assess and evaluate existing and future markets.

There are many types and specialties of customs broker houses, but generally a trader can expect a good customs broker house to be able to handle

- Foreign suppliers
- Federal guidelines for imports, including contaminants
- Storage during customs clearance
- Bonds and insurance

In the process, the customs house broker will be required to assure that all regulations, requirements, and restrictions are met.

One source of the regulations that must be met in international trade is the body of standards and policies set by the World Trade Organization (WTO), an organization created to provide a framework for smooth international trade and to set standards governing its operation.

The World Trade Organization

The standards and policies of international trade are negotiated and overseen in concerted agreement by over 150 member nations of the World Trade Organization, an organization that has drawn up and ratified terms among producers of exported and imported goods, services, and intellectual property. The World Trade Organization is a multilateral trading system that provides stability and reliability for over 97 percent of international trade. Over two-thirds of its members are developed or developing countries; all rely heavily on the assurances of its high-level function in trade to keep peace when economic factors can incite conflict. Through agreements, trader nations know they are safe from threats that nationalism and protectionism might override the expanded availability of the raw materials, assembled products, and components upon which they have come to rely as the basis for their foreign direct and portfolio investments.

The decisions of the WTO are reached by consensus, with a three-level parliamentary structure. The hierarchy works as follows:

- Ministerial Conference: the highest level of decision makers, meeting at least every two years
- General Council: the second tier of decision makers, comprising ambassadors, Geneva delegates, and appointed representatives from member nations' capitals
- Committees, work groups, and parties: those responsible for production of individual agreements, environmental and developmental concerns, member applications, and regional trade agreements

A Secretariat position assures good communications between the organization and outside interests and provides technical and legal support to WTO members and hierarchy for all needs and capacities of governing structures and members.

Essentially, the World Trade Organization claims and holds its power on the world's international trade by providing

- Oversight of accord among members
- An arena for trade issue discussion
- Accepted arbitration of dispute
- Evaluation of trade policies
- Support of developing countries' trade, technical, and training issues
- Collaboration with other international trade agencies

The World Trade Organization is the only organization of its kind in the world. It is also the youngest international trade organization, founded in 1995. It has its roots in the General Agreement on Tariffs and Trade (GATT), a predecessor organization dating from the 1950s. The mission of the World Trade Organization is to facilitate the terms and agreements of trade and to facilitate and promote trade. Its role is "to ensure that trade flows as smoothly, predictably, and freely as possible." Not everyone agrees on what defines this process and what procedures in international trade achieve this mission; as mentioned previously in this chapter, the Doha social and economic inequities reveal a schism in application of economic theory that is the subject of ongoing discussions. The World Trade Organization has provisions for dispute, with a multi-layer review and arbitration procedure. Typically, WTO disputes are over broken agreements.

The WTO dispute resolution review process takes into account many of the similar considerations expected of an international review and assessment organization. The Dispute Settlement Understanding procedures are available to countries concerned about agreements and rights. The main focus of these procedures is to assure that the rules are enforced to maintain trade at a smooth pace. The process has procedural checkpoints all along the way. Failing resolution with consultation, the WTO has a well-wrought, stepped procedure with considerations for ruling panels of experts and appeals. Redress for policy review is also available through the Trade Policy Review Mechanism, which serves as feedback for policies. The Trade Policy Review Mechanism is also responsible for assessing and supporting new policies in countries, and for improving transparency throughout the organization.

Disagreements with policies and practices within the WTO are not lightly founded. There is a growing consensus that the economics and theory of trade of the World Trade Organization should be held account- able for destabilization of solid markets in developed countries, for irre- sponsible draining of resources and labor, and for inequitable shifts in intellectual property. The most memorable protest over such issues was the riot in Seattle, Washington, during the Ministerial Conference of 1999. Recent polls show that such sentiments may be the rule, not the exception.

One of the concerns expressed by the developing nations at Doha, by the United States economy, and by the protesters in Seattle a decade ago was the effect of multinational trade agreements on the local econo- mies. A key issue involved is free trade versus fair trade. The "free trade" position is that products should be available internationally without the interference of government regulations and tariffs. Those supporting free trade believe that government interventions only serve to increase costs to both consumers and producers. The "fair trade" position is that a market- based approach is the way to establish equanimity in developing countries' economies, to stabilize conflicts, and to end cycles of poverty. Advocates of both positions seek to build a world free of war, poverty, and depriva- tion. The differing viewpoints on how to go about reaching this goal are two sides of the same coin. For the foreign investor, it can come down to being open to either opportunity for expanding market niche. At the same time, the investor walks a razor's edge: the pitfalls of either could produce spiraling results.

The current economic climate in the United States mirrors the heavy foreign investment that the United States relies upon from countries such as China. Most economists concur that free trade is taking the brunt of the blame for what is really a business cycle fluctuation, "post-Reaganomics" adjustments in production within our borders, and a "zero-sum game" pos- ited as the both the devil and the savior, when in actuality it has nothing to do with the effects we see in the economy. Both free trade and fair trade recognize the issues:

- Environment: too lax a position, and governments willing to compromise their own environments to produce goods will compromise all environments; too stringent, and developing countries will be frozen out of competition
- Oppression: removing government restrictions opens opportunities for small businesses to compete on a global scale, allowing the rise of a middle-class economy in developing nations, but it also exposes developing nations to class servitude to wealthy economies
- Wages: both sides of the equation must balance; to what extent are richer countries their brothers' keepers? Must the United States sacrifice its own standards of living to be amicable with the superpower of China in 20 years, to protect its national security, or to have an economic equanimity with its own border countries that raises standards for all concerned?

Both free and fair trade agree on mutual objectives; it is merely their method that is at issue.

For business in the United States, the most crucial aspect in the opinion polls and for the economy is wages. Because we are now tied to our bordering neighbors by regional free trade agreements, international labor standards significantly affect us, and the continuation of our wealth is tied to the continuation of theirs.

NAFTA and CAFTA

The United States has two regional trade agreements with its bordering neighbors. The first is the North American Free Trade Agreement (NAFTA), which binds it to Canada and Mexico. In the early 1990s, Canada and the United States constructed NAFTA as a free-trade deal. By the time the agreement was signed in 1992, Mexico was on board as well. Although all three countries signed, approval by their national legislatures was another issue altogether. The agreement was unpopular in all three nations. In order to smooth passage, the North American Agreement on Labor Cooperation (NAALC) was added as a supplement to codify an agreement for solidarity in resolving labor issues, and to promote improved working conditions through cooperation between trade unions and social organizations.

Environmentalists had concerns as well. To ease fears that gains in environmental standards would not be lowered as a negotiating tool in agreements, the North American Agreement on Environmental Cooperation (NAAEC) was established. It obliges the three nations to meet their own environmental standards and laws, with a focus on addressing environmental issues involved with trade. Because of this treaty's focus on agricultural liberalization and environmental concerns, other nations show little interest in signing with the other three nations. But other countries in the Americas are joining other agreements or creating separate agreements. The issues addressed by NAFTA are similar to those common to global free trade: agriculture, wages, the environment, and oppression. Especially concerning features of NAFTA to other American countries are

Chapter 11, which stipulates that an entity can sue any member government if it takes actions adversely affecting his or her investments

Chapter 19, an antidumping, or predatory pricing, stipulation that allows for a bi-national panel, instead of (or as well as) a judicial review

Overall opinion in the three countries is widely divergent:

- The United States views Mexico as the winner.
- Canada sees itself as the NAFTA loser.
- Mexico enjoys the highest level of public support for NAFTA, but most Mexicans still see the United States as the winner.

The Dominican Republic Central America Free Trade Agreement (CAFTA) was signed in early 2004 by nations that included the United States, Costa Rica, El Salvador, Guatemala, Honduras, and Nicaragua. Because the Dominican Republic signed a little later in the year, the agreement is often referred to as DR-CAFTA.

The protests in Seattle and backlash by American consumers demonstrate how public opinion has changed regarding free-trade practices. Recent U.S. opinion polls show that almost three-quarters of those polled feel that U.S. trading partners benefit more from free trade than the United

States does. Other poll results indicate that over half of respondents feel that free trade has hurt U.S. business, and almost 80 percent stated that the U.S. workforce has been compromised. Overall, results show overt concern that jobs have been sent overseas even as wages are capped by trade policies. The major issue surrounding this dissatisfaction is whether or not the United States will enter an era of protectionism.

Markets reflect changing attitudes in economic climates. If the majority of Americans see the United States as being in a recession, then whether the nation is in a recession or not, individual Americans and individual business leaders will handle their capital and investments as if we were in a recession. Although no definitive statement can be made yet as to what long-term or unforeseen effects worldwide trade regulation might have on the economic climate, it is easy to see how the decisions of the World Trade Organization, NAFTA, and CAFTA affect business, even at the customs house brokers level. Other areas of business and international transactions respond to the policies and standards of international trade organizations as market factors. In the end, whether it is the free trade approach or the fair trade approach that ultimately does more to improve worldwide living conditions and to progress toward peace through economic investments and links, there is a clearly evident link between economic growth and democratization.

Within the environment overseen by the WTO and multiple trading agreements, foreign investors need to make choices about market segments for investment. As is the case with overall strategy, making market segment selections involves deciding which of the available strategies are best for you.

MULTIDOMESTIC VERSUS GLOBAL STRATEGY

For the foreign direct or portfolio investor, some strategic choices are required to determine what market segment is most appropriate for investment. If a company is thinking of investing with a multidomestic strategy, it will need to have autonomous units in multiple countries. Therefore, a method of decentralized decision making must be in place; horizontal foreign direct investment is called for. A global strategy needs additional coordination between units that cross international borders; to succeed, consideration should be given to the production process design and limitation of duplication of processes, making vertical foreign direct investment the ideal way to control necessary production factors.

The multidomestic strategy reflects a group of companies with similar products or services. Competition is compartmentalized and independent from one country to the other. A customized product has national competitors, and local companies are at an advantage over global competitors. General Motors provides a good model for this structure. Its European sites are not centralized, allowing its operating units to perform independently.

A global strategy base is similar in products and services but benefits by competing across borders. Its centralization makes it resemble a hive; the practices of the headquarters are replicated at all locations. This type of company is found in situations involving considerations for customers as global companies. For example, if the global company conducts costly research and development, it is more likely to require more than one market over which to spread its costs; information travels back to headquarters. Intel is a good example, keeping costs low to compete in the global market through low-cost production in India and China.

CHOICES AND MORE CHOICES

Any business seeking to "go global" has to plan carefully for success. With so many choices out there, there are both a multitude of chances for failure and myriad opportunities for business and growth and profits. Overall strategy must be selected based on solid research and careful consideration of the options available. As with many types of business decisions, the information you gain during the planning stages can pay off handsomely after investment. Today's global marketplace is, in many ways, smaller than it was for businesspeople only a century ago, and with the Internet, air transportation, and other globalizing factors, it's likely to get a lot smaller in the years to come. The astute businessperson will look for and plan to meet the challenges in international trade as our business world becomes more and more international.

KEY POINTS TO REMEMBER

- Foreign direct investment (FDI) brings money into a country for the purpose of using it to create profit for investors.

- Before investing in a country, consider its balance of trade (the value of its exports minus the value of its imports) and balance of payments (the value of its credits minus the value of its debits) to evaluate how likely an investment candidate it is.

- FDI can come in various forms accompanied by varying degrees of risk: as horizontal (consolidated in one country), as vertical (divided among many cooperating countries), as green-field (using newly built facilities and other infrastructure), or as mergers or acquisitions (using already existing facilities and infrastructure).

- The U.S. Department of Commerce's Foreign Commercial Services Agency can help you as you prepare to do business through exporting. You can also study the examples of many other companies that invest abroad, and even those of some that bring their investments to the United States.

- Your investments abroad can certainly capitalize on foreign markets' ready supply of inexpensive labor and materials, but choose your investment targets wisely—avoid political hot spots and be well informed about host-country regulations that may inhibit your efficiency or growth. Also, be sure to learn what trade agreements will affect your business affairs at home and abroad.

The International Monetary System and the Foreign Exchange Market

All organizations providing goods and services—from the tiniest microbusiness to the largest multinational corporation—fall into one of two categories: nonprofits and for-profits. Nonprofits have goals that are driven by concerns other than making a profit. For-profit organizations seek to sell a sufficient quantity of goods or services to generate income that exceeds the total cost (including raw materials, components, labor, administration or overhead, transportation to markets, taxes, etc.) of providing those goods and services. The difference between the costs of providing goods and services and the amount received is either profit or loss. Profits and losses are measured in money. A successful international business must deal with multiple types of money and have the capacity to understand, use, and account not only in its home country currency but also in the currencies used in its foreign areas of operation.

If you are new to the concepts of currency exchange and unfamiliar with how currencies are traded and exchanged in international business transactions, this will be a valuable chapter for you. There are many options available in international exchange that can help you reduce potential risks, determining in advance the income you will receive in a transaction and providing options for negotiating contracts. Understanding these options will be easier if you grasp some of the background behind today's international banking operations and currency exchange practices and markets. Let's begin by looking at the origins of money and banking services.

THE ORIGINS OF MONEY

The need for money, or an accepted symbol for value, was plain to even the earliest human communities. Barter, or the exchange of one type of good or service for another, has not totally vanished from the world even now, but the problems associated with a pure barter exchange system were apparent early on. For example, someone who raised sheep and needed grain to feed them soon found that the physical exchange of sacks of grain for sheep posed practical problems of transportation and storage. In the face of such practical problems, the adoption of widely accepted forms of symbolic value—money, in all its varied forms—became essential as soon as humans started forming villages, towns, and cities.

At its simplest, money is nothing more than a symbol. It can represent labor, goods, and/or perceived value. Money has been around for millennia and over this lengthy period has taken many forms. Strings of cowry shells were the basic monetary unit in China during the Shang Dynasty (c. 1500–1000 B.C.). The shekel has been traced back to about 3000 B.C. in Mesopotamia, where it was used to specify a standardized mass of barley. This unit of weight was also used to define other values such as units of silver, bronze, and copper. Thus, originally, the shekel was both a unit of weight and a unit of currency. Similar specifications have persisted almost until today. The British pound was originally a unit based on a quantity of silver weighing one pound.

In the Middle East, monetary systems were formalized about 1760 B.C. in the Code of Hammurabi. Even earlier collections of laws regulating commercial activity included the codex of Ur-Nammu (king of Ur, c. 2050 B.C.), the Codes of Eshnunna (c. 1930 B.C.), and the codex of Lipit-Ishtar of Isin (c. 1870 B.C.). Modern businesspeople would understand these ancient codes, which set the rate of interest on debt and prescribed fines punishing "white collar crimes" and other violations of the law.

Physical Forms of Money

Many of the objects used as money in early times were fragile and easily broken. Cowry shells, for example, are easily smashed, whether accidentally or deliberately. Clearly, more durable forms of money were needed.

Once humans gained the ability to use metals (bronze, gold, silver, etc.), governments rapidly turned to metals for coinage. Objects made using gold, silver, or bronze can be dropped and handled roughly without sustaining significant damage. Furthermore, these metals can be formed into objects with unique symbols on their surfaces identifying their source, value, weight, minting date, purity, and other details. Some of the early forms of metal money were rings of bronze or other metals that could be marked in distinctive ways and easily carried on larger, less valuable rings. During the Chou Dynasty in China (*c.* 700 B.C.), the coins were shaped like knives or axes. In the fourth millennium B.C., the Egyptians used gold bars of a set weight as a medium of exchange, just as the Sumerians had done, somewhat earlier, for silver.

Many scholars of monetary history identify the first true coin as one minted in Lydia (in western Turkey) about 650 B.C. These were small slugs of electrum (the natural alloy of gold and silver) stamped with a lion insignia (for King Gyges) on one side and bearing marks indicating weight and purity on the other. These coins were so successful that other nations soon adopted similar forms for their money.

Paper money was first used in China, where many called it "flying money," as it was easily blown away in the wind. The first attempt to use paper money came during the reign of Emperor Han Wu-ti (140–87 B.C.), but it was a failure. Because the paper was made using the hide of the white stag, a rare animal, the supply was too limited to sustain production in the quantities necessary for commerce. Just over 800 years later, a new and much more successful Chinese paper currency was issued. The Mongols adopted the idea of paper currency during their control of China and introduced Chinese-style paper money in Iran in 1292. The first European paper money was printed in Sweden in 1601.

EARLY BANKS AND THEIR GROWTH

Once money was available (whether as metal or paper), the need for financial services soon followed. It is likely that the earliest banks were developed by the sacred prostitutes of ancient Babylonian temples. The income from their trade brought in significant wealth, a situation that allowed them to lend money for business ventures and to build up yet additional wealth. Banking as a business grew rapidly and rulers such as Hammurabi included banking regulations in their law codes. Some of the most sophisticated early banks were organized by the Ptolemaic rulers of Egypt. With a central bank in Alexandria, the Egyptian banking system had local offices that provided financial services for businesses and wealthy individuals throughout Egypt. Meanwhile, banking services in much of the Roman Empire were largely under the control of private Greek owners and, in a continuation of tradition, often operated from temples. These financial organizations disappeared in Europe after the collapse of the Roman Empire.

In the Arab world, banks and banking continued to operate and grow, usually under the leadership of Jews and Christians. By the ninth century, Arab nations had a sophisticated banking system. The historic record includes mentions of head offices in Baghdad and branches in other cities. These financial offices helped traders and business leaders through the use of checks (the Arabic word is *sakk*). These checks were guaranteed by bonds and transferred by letters of credit. Thus, in the ninth century, it was possible to draw a check in Baghdad and cash it in Morocco, a significant convenience for those engaged in international trade.

Spurred by financial and business necessity, European banks started to reemerge around 808 A.D., when Jewish merchants in northern Italy worked together to create an unsophisticated type of bank for depositing cash. It would take another 400 years—and a special war tax on citizens in Venice—for a committee to evolve into a bank serving that maritime city state.

Although the presence of money and banking services has provided businesses with much-needed methods of exchange, the fact that forms of money are tied to political entities (nations) has meant that international businesses must deal with the multiple national currencies. This, of course, is not a new problem. International businesspeople have faced it since the first international trader accepted money in one kingdom to buy goods in a place ruled by another monarch. Whether along the Silk Road, the Salt Road, or the spice routes, the comparative value of different currencies has complicated international trade for millennia.

THE GOLD STANDARD AND INTERNATIONAL TRADE

One way that international trade was sustained over the centuries was by the use of gold for the payment of imported goods. This worked well until the level of international trade soared as the Industrial Revolution brought dramatic increases in the quantity of goods traded internationally. Physically shipping large amounts of gold for payment from country to country soon became impractical. Another answer was needed.

The policy adopted was pegging national currency to gold in what is known as the gold standard. Nation set relationships between their currencies and gold and agreed to convert their currency to gold upon demand at a fixed rate. By 1880, many nations had adopted this policy, including the United States, Japan, Great Britain, and Germany.

Some economists and political leaders claimed not only that the gold standard made international commerce easier, but also that it would be a powerful force in creating balance-of-trade equilibrium, a situation in which a nation's imports and exports are equal, or in balance. Although the mechanism for this is simple—even today, some modern economists recommend a return to the gold standard to achieve balance-of-trade equilibrium—the gold standard collapsed at the beginning of World War I, was briefly revived during the interwar years, and was eventually abandoned altogether during World War II.

THE BRETTON WOODS SYSTEM

In mid-1944, World War II was still raging, but Allied optimism was growing. Of major concern to the United States and her allies was the international economic environment that would prevail once Germany and Japan were defeated. Allied economic and political leaders placed much of the blame for the Second World War on the chaotic economic conditions of the interwar years, when foreign exchange controls distorted and weakened the foundations of international trade. These leaders wanted to avoid the economic debacles of the 1920s and 1930s.

With these goals in mind, 730 delegates from all 44 Allied nations met at the Mount Washington Hotel in Bretton Woods, New Hampshire, in the first three weeks of July 1944. Out of this meeting came agreements that set up a mechanism to regulate the international monetary system. International exchange rates were effectively pegged to the U.S. dollar, which, in turn, was based on a fixed relationship to gold ($35.00 per ounce of gold). In addition, the Bretton Woods delegates founded the International Bank for Reconstruction and Development (IBRD)—now one of the five institutions that comprise the World Bank Group—and the International Monetary Fund (IMF). The IBRD and the IMF became operational in 1945, although the IMF did not actually begin financial operations until March 1, 1947.

In the years immediately following World War II, the stable international monetary system created at Bretton Woods contributed to economic security and helped support the economic rebirth of many nations, notably Germany and Japan. However, by 1970, economic conditions had changed. The U.S. economy was being challenged. Involvement in the Vietnam War had tarnished the United States' international standing. And, most important, the United States was now experiencing inflation and running annual trade deficits. The United States was no longer the dominant economic power in the world. Furthermore, the emergence of international banking consortia and the rise in international monetary interdependence contributed to economic trends that weakened the role of the U.S. dollar in international trade.

By February 1973, the pegged exchange rate system set up at Bretton Woods in 1944 had to be abandoned. The currency exchange market closed in February 1973 and then reopened in March using a floating currency exchange system. With some modifications over the decades, this floating currency exchange system is the one now in place.

Although today's floating currency exchange system offers advantages for many nations, it also poses challenges. To preserve the value of their currency in a floating currency market, nations must work hard to protect their currency and its value both inside and outside their borders while concurrently facilitating the exchange of the currency with others. This is not an easy task. Money, as you will recall, is a symbol. In a floating currency market, the value of that symbol can change rapidly. Inflation is one of the factors that drive fluctuations in the currency market.

Inflation and Currencies

The value of any particular currency is heavily dependent on the quantity of that currency in circulation versus the value of the products and services produced by that county. In addition, there is a less quantifiable aspect to currency valuation. This is the perceived value of that currency, not only for today, but also for next week, next month, and the years ahead. When a currency is in excess supply and large numbers of people begin to lose confidence in its value, inflation soon follows. When inflation occurs, purchasing power declines. When purchasing power is lost, both domestic and foreign confidence in the value of the currency sink, and, spiraling, purchasing power drops again because of rising prices—causing confidence in the currency to sink even more. As this situation evolves, governments often print yet more money. But this only exacerbates the situation. In some cases, inflation becomes so rampant that use of the currency becomes very difficult or even impossible. When this happens rapidly, it is known as *hyperinflation*.

In the 20th century, there were several notable examples of hyperinflation. One of the best-studied examples was the inflation that overtook the German mark in 1922 and 1923. The impact of this monetary cyclone could easily be seen in the skyrocketing costs of mailing a letter in Germany. On July 1, 1922, the cost of mailing a domestic letter weighing 2 grams or less was 1 mark. On July 1, 1923, it was 120. Then things went completely out of control. By November 26, 1923, the cost of mailing a 2-gram letter had risen to 80,000,000,000 marks. The introduction of the Rentenmark currency on December 1, 1923, finally brought the inflation of the German mark under control.

Less well-known today—but even more disastrous—was the hyperinflation that destroyed the value of the Hungarian pengo in 1945 and 1946. Only nine months after V-E Day, the exchange rate for the pengo was so unfavorable that the currency was essentially worthless. In February of 1946, the exchange rate for a pengo was approximately 300,000,000,000,000 to a U.S. penny. More recently, nations such as Bolivia and Argentina have faced long periods of rampant inflation. The duration of these inflationary periods is often extended not only by political, monetary, and financial issues but also by thousands of individual and business decisions based on the assumption that inflation will continue. Stopping or slowing inflation is not merely a matter of reducing the supply of the currency in circulation and improving the business climate of a nation, it is also a matter of changing the hearts and minds of the individuals who use the nation's currency.

MONEY AND PSYCHOLOGY

For a nation, the ability to issue currency that is internationally recognized and accepted is more than fuel for business activity. It's also a matter of national pride, a sign of power and sovereignty, and a reflection of the political health and stability of a country. Many seemingly unrelated things can influence the condition of a national currency. Civil unrest, drought, storms, the rise and fall of political and military leaders, the sudden arrival of thousands of refugees, the outbreak of an epidemic, war, and even political changes in other nations can all influence the perception of a particular national currency. The astute international business leader understands and respects not only the technical influences on a currency but also the psychological and political aspects of currency conditions, taking all these issues into account while operating an international company.

One of the issues that an international business must consider when deciding whether to enter a particular nation's market is the issue of convertibility of the nation's currency. It would, for example, be quite expensive if you entered a national market and made a profit but then could not convert those profits into your own currency and take that money out of the country. This is the issue of convertibility.

Convertibility and Foreign Exchange

When a nation places no restrictions on the conversion of its currency into foreign currencies, the currency is *freely convertible*. Both residents and nonresidents are able to buy an unlimited amount of that nation's currency using foreign currencies. Some currencies are *externally convertible*: only nonresidents may convert unlimited amounts of the currency into foreign funds. When neither residents nor nonresidents may convert a currency into a foreign currency, it is *nonconvertible*.

The goal of a nonconvertibility policy is the protection of a nation's foreign exchange reserves and the preservation of its abilities to meet payment obligations on foreign debt and to buy imported goods. Nonconvertibility restrictions are also put into place to prevent citizens from exchanging large amounts of currency into a foreign currency during times of economic problems or severe inflation. Citizens' conversion of their currency on a large scale is *capital flight*, a move that usually causes a severe drop in the value of the nation's currency on the foreign exchange market.

Many nations place some restrictions on the conversion of their currencies into other currencies. The restrictions range from relatively minor (limiting the amount of money a person may take out of the country for things such as trips, or how much of a nation's currency a tourist may take home) to major (prohibiting a domestic business from taking currency out of the country).

A policy of nonconvertibility can cause severe economic problems for a nation and severely restrict its international trade. For example, the former Soviet Union had a standing nonconvertibility policy. This meant that even if foreign firms generated excellent profits in the Soviet Union, they could not convert the rubles they earned as profit into their home currencies and take them out of the country. Under such conditions, there was little foreign investment in the Soviet Union.

Although a policy of nonconvertibility places severe restrictions on dealings with a nation, it does not necessarily mean that trade is completely out of the question. Depending on the exact terms of the nonconvertibility regulations, it may be possible to be paid in something other than that nation's currency. Such exchanges are known as countertrade. You might exchange your products for products from that nation. In a sense, this is a return to the barter system. It does not work in every instance, but doing so has been a profitable option for the exchange of high-value items such as airplanes and road construction equipment.

There have been many examples of very successful countertrade contracts. For example, Saudi Arabia once bought ten 747 jet planes from Boeing, paying not in currency but in crude oil discounted 10 percent below then-current world oil prices. Similarly, in 1986, Caterpillar sold earth-moving equipment to Venezuela, accepting 350,000 tons of iron ore as payment. Caterpillar then traded the iron ore to Romania, which paid Caterpillar in farm products, which Caterpillar sold on the international market for dollars. Since 1985, when an estimated 20–30% of world trade involved some sort of countertrade agreement, the use of this type of arrangement has decreased, primarily because more world currencies are freely convertible. Nevertheless, countertrade agreements still constitute between 10 and 20% of world trade. Thus, countertrade contracts remain an important form of trade in international business.

In a freewheeling market such as the currency exchange market, there are always risks and the possibility that one participant or group of participants can behave in a manner that can injure or damage other participants in the market. There is a need for oversight of this market.

Overseeing Foreign Exchange

The need for stabilizing the foreign exchange market became apparent in the period between World War I and World War II. Not only did hyperinflation seriously devalue currencies in Germany, Austria, and other European nations, a multinational economic depression (known as the Great Depression in the United States) further stressed economies around the world. Some nations adopted a policy that became known as "beggar thy neighbor." What happened under this policy was that one nation would purposefully devalue its own currency with the goal of making its products less costly and more competitive in the world market. These nations were taking the risk that their businesses would be able to export more and that their national economies would greatly improve. Given the economic conditions of the time, these nations cared little that their hoped-for economic growth might come at the expense of their neighbors. It was a form of economic warfare that generated political conflict and enmity and helped set the stage for World War II.

INTERNATIONAL FINANCIAL INSTITUTIONS

One of the most important goals of the Bretton Woods meeting was developing international financial agencies that could oversee international financial activity and provide stability in the financial exchange market.

Although the fixed exchange rates that were set at Bretton Woods are gone, other legacies of the conference remain an important part of today's international exchange picture. These include several influential international financial institutions, which are supplemented by currency boards and central banks in individual nations.

The World Bank

Today, the World Bank is one of the members of the World Bank Group. The other members are the International Bank for Reconstruction and Development (IBRD), the International Development Association (IDA), the International Finance Corporation (IFC), the Multilateral Investment Guarantee Agency (MIGA), and the International Center for Settlement of Investment Disputes (ICSID). The activities of these organizations focus on providing assistance to developing nations. Their goals are supporting human development (education and health), encouraging the improvement of agriculture and rural life, protecting the environment, promoting the development of infrastructure (roads, power generation, water distribution, etc.), and supporting the development of stable regimes that are not corrupt, that use leadership to serve, and that emphasize the peaceful transfer of power.

Founded in 1944 by the 44 nations that established the Bretton Woods system, the primary purpose of the World Bank is to make low-interest loans to developing nations, usually for development projects. Such loans can help struggling nations build roads, water systems, hospitals and other health care facilities, railroads, airports, harbor facilities, and other parts of infrastructure that can improve the lives of ordinary citizens and enhance opportunities for economic growth and development. In this way, the World Bank helps nations improve their economic condition and maintain the value of their currency.

The International Monetary Fund (IMF)

Founded concurrently with the World Bank, the IMF is a safety net for national currencies. The most common forms of assistance to economically struggling nations are loans issued to help bolster the economy of the country.

Such loans usually come with covenants that require nations to implement specified economic reforms. For example, in response to multiple cases of currency devaluation in Turkey, the IMF has made 18 loans to Turkey. In each case, the IMF sought to get Turkey to agree to close insolvent banks, tighten monetary policy, abandon the fixed exchange system for the Turkish Lira, and privatize government-subsidized or government-owned industries.

SPECIAL DRAWING RIGHTS (SDRs)

Special Drawing Rights are an international reserve asset. They were created by the IMF in 1969 to supplement the official reserves of member nations. SDRs are allocated to member nations in proportion to their IMF quotas. The value of an SDR is based on a basket of key international currencies (currently U.S. dollars, the Euro, the Japanese yen, and the British pound sterling). The basket of key international currencies is reviewed every 5 years by the IMF Board. The next review will take place in late 2010.

For most private organizations, SDRs are not a direct factor in international exchange. Although SDRs are used as the basis for the international fees of the Universal Postal Union (the organization responsible for the worldwide postal system), the transfer of roaming charges for international mobile phone services, and carrier liability for international transportation (such as for international flights and damaged cargo and oil spills involving ships), private commercial firms will not deal directly with SDRs. However, the use of SDRs by individual nations can improve the economic health of a nation and improve the stability of its currency and its position in the international market.

Currency Boards

The primary job of a nation's currency board is to assure that its national currency will be converted upon request into another currency at a fixed exchange rate.

Central Banks

A nation's central bank maintains various controls on the overall national economy. Among these controls are the required reserve ratio (the proportion of total deposits that a bank must hold in reserve) and, in countries where it applies (such as the United States), a federal interest rate that functions as the basis for all of other loan interest rates in the country.

Central reserve assets are the assets held by a central bank to back a nation's currency. These assets may include gold, silver, their own currency, and other currencies (often U.S. dollars). These assets allow the nation to pay debts, providing stability to the nation's currency and backing the nation's banking system.

The Bank for International Settlements (BIS)

The BIS functions like a bank for central banks. It has a limited role in enforcing monetary policies, instead acting more like a collection of central bankers monitoring and researching the effects and trends of the macroeconomic environment.

INTERNATIONAL EXCHANGE RATES

The foreign exchange market can operate using a variety of types of exchange rates. These facilitate the transfer of money and help determine each nation's position in the global market.

Fixed Exchange Rate

Fixed rates value currencies against one another at agreed-upon rates that are stable over extended periods. At various times, many nations have used fixed exchange rates. The rates may be governed by international treaty or, if only a few nations are involved, by agreements between a small number of nations. Many developing nations use fixed-rate exchanges for trading currencies among themselves. The key attribute of a fixed-rate exchange system is that the rates of exchange are those that governments agree upon and undertake to maintain.

Pegged Exchange Rate

Pegged-rate exchanges, set the currency of one nation—usually a smaller or developing nation—at a specific rate against another nation's currency, usually a larger or more economically stable nation with a stronger currency. The value of the pegged currency fluctuates with that of the stronger currency.

Floating Exchange Rate

Floating exchange rates are determined on the international currency market in much the same way that corporate stock values are determined on Wall Street or corn or soybeans are valued on the Chicago Mercantile Exchange. You might say that floating exchange rates are decided by the forces of nature. Because significant fluctuations in this market are possible—even probable, over time—a nation using a floating exchange rate currency is vulnerable to sudden changes in exchange rates. However, using a floating exchange rate does allow a nation autonomy in the control of its own money supply, allowing it to avoid having to meet conditions set by fixed exchange rates. Many developed nations, including the United States, use a floating exchange rate for their currencies.

Spot Exchange Rate

Spot exchange rates are the rates at given points in time. These rates have stipulations that a transaction take place within a very short window of time—for example, two business days. Because spot exchange rates can fluctuate dramatically over time, and trends can be difficult to predict, a spot exchange rate is not the best measurement of a currency's valuation.

INTERNATIONAL OPERATIONS

There are a number of terms and concepts you should understand before venturing into foreign exchange transactions. Understanding the forces and activities that make up the world of foreign monetary commerce don't just give you a step up in the game—they're nothing less than necessary for those involved in international business.

Currency Market Investing

Currency market investing is investing in money—usually, in several different currencies. This may be done by investing in a currency fund or through direct purchase of currency.

Arbitrage

Arbitrage is the purchase and resale, at a known profit, of a currency or other asset over a very short period of time. Suppose you note that on one market you can purchase 50,000 of country X's lira for only $10,000 U.S. dollars. Then, moments later, you find another market where you can sell 50,000 of the same country's lira for $15,000. If you move quickly, you can buy 50,000 of lira and immediately resell them for a 50% profit. The principle behind arbitrage is using information about prices on various markets to make a quick, known (risk-free) profit. The lack of risk in making a quick known profit is the key point of arbitrage. Information from many sources is required, along with cash (or instant borrowing power) and a sharp attention to detail.

Vehicle Currency

A vehicle currency is a currency used to facilitate the exchange of other currencies. Both the U.S. dollar and the Japanese yen are widely used vehicle currencies. The British pound has also served as a vehicle currency. Vehicle currencies play an important role in the currency exchange market. Let's look at one possible example. Theoretically, a person or business wanting to change Venezuelan bolivars into Czech korunas could simply find somebody with korunas to sell who wanted bolivars, and then make the exchange. But, because of the comparatively small number of bolivar owners who are wanting korunas, it is much easier (and less expensive) to change the bolivars into U.S. dollars and then change the dollars into korunas. Because of the ubiquity of the U.S. dollar, changing bolivars into dollars finds many more possible buyers. Similarly, exchanging dollars into korunas is much more attractive. Because of the dollar's popularity, most buyers are paying dollars—and most sellers are wanting dollars. In such exchanges, the U.S. dollar is a vehicle allowing the prompt and easy exchange of money from one currency into another.

The concept of vehicle currency is also important in the exchange of a number of commodities, especially major grains (such as corn, wheat, and soybeans) and crude oil. Many markets for these products—no matter where they are located—use pricing in a vehicle currency (often the U.S. dollar). This makes prices and exchanges much easier for all concerned.

Forward Exchange

A forward exchange is an agreement between two parties to execute a contract for exchange at a specified date in the future. The forward exchange rate is the rate(s) agreed to in the forward exchange. The forward prices may be the same as spot prices, but that is not usually the case. In most instances, the forward price may be higher (at a premium) or lower (at a discount) than the spot price. Forward prices for most major currencies are quoted for a variety of maturities, including 1, 3, 6, 9, and 12 months. Maturities in excess of 1 year are becoming more common; for good customers, maturities of 5 or even 10 years are possible.

Trading at a Premium/Discount

Any asset can be traded at either a premium or a discount. The net asset value is the underlying value of the asset. When the market price of the asset is higher than the net asset value, it is said to be trading at a premium. When the market price of the asset is lower than the net asset value, it is said to be trading at a discount. Just as profits can be made by trading in stocks, bonds, funds, and so on at either a premium or a discount, so profits and benefits can be had whether trading currencies at a premium or a discount.

Bid/Ask Price

The bid price is the price a willing buyer offers for a product. The ask price (or offer) is the minimum price a seller will accept for the product. The difference between these two prices is the bid/ask spread.

Purchasing Power Parity (PPP)

Purchasing power parity is a concept developed by Gustav Cassel in 1920. Under PPP, the exchange rates for currencies are based on the compared purchasing power in each nation, calculated using a standard basket of identical goods. The base idea is the law of one price—the theory that in an ideal world market, each good sold should have only one price, no matter where it is sold. PPP takes into account such factors as costs of living and rates of inflation. There are differences—often quite large ones—between PPP rates and exchange rates. The most widely used PPP exchange rate is the Geary-Khamis dollar, sometimes called the "international dollar." But PPP exchange rates are controversial. One problem is that individuals in different nations consume different baskets of goods and services—whether by choice or by necessity—and their patterns of consumption often differ widely from each other. Furthermore, issues of quality are not fully considered under PPP. Nonetheless, PPP exchange rates do offer insights into currency exchange that can be helpful when studying lengthy periods of time.

Working with Multiple Currencies

As long as a business operates in only one country, the issues of the comparative values of different currencies do not arise. Suppose you buy products in U.S. dollars. You pay your bills in U.S. dollars. You sell your products and services in U.S. dollars. All this is fairly straightforward. But currencies are tied to political entities (nations, or unions of nations), and an international business must, therefore, deal with the complexities of multiple currencies. Things can get complicated when you are selling your products in two countries, and are being paid in two different currencies. And they can get even more complex if you're buying products using one currency, paying workers in another currency, selling products in multiple countries, receiving payment in multiple currencies, and having to figure profit or loss in your home country. With this much complexity involved in international trade, operating an international business would not be practical if nations and businesspeople had not developed methods of foreign exchange.

YOUR BUSINESS AND INTELLIGENT USE
OF THE CURRENCY EXCHANGE

At its simplest, foreign exchange is the trading of a set amount of one currency for an agreed-upon amount of another currency. These exchanges are handled in foreign exchange markets.

Unlike the New York Stock Exchange or the Chicago Board of Trade, there is no one physical location where currencies are traded in pits occupied by shouting and signaling traders in an atmosphere of confusion and noise. No bells open or close trading on the currency exchange floor. Instead, the exchange of currencies is handled by a network of offices located around the world that are connected via international computer links. Currencies can be exchanged around the clock. The principal center for foreign exchange transactions is London. Other major centers include New York and Tokyo. There are additional offices in places such as San Francisco and Sidney, Australia.

Despite differences in detail, in many ways the foreign exchange market is a lot like a commodity market, except that the commodity is not corn or soybeans or coffee; it's money. There are products and opportunities in the market that can help you improve the financial picture of your company and reduce the risks inherent in the currency exchange market.

Businesses have four major uses for the currency exchange market:

1. Payments received in foreign currencies must be converted for domestic use.

2. Payments made to foreign businesses must be converted to the currencies designated or required.

3. Businesses may make investments in foreign currencies when they have spare investment cash or wish to acquire financial assets in a foreign nation.

4. Businesses may speculate in foreign currencies, hoping for short-term profits in excess of what they might earn from other financial investments such as stocks, bonds, or U.S. dollar money market accounts.

The last two uses of the currency exchange market are similar to investments in commodities, stocks, or funds sold on the Chicago Board of Trade or the New York Stock Exchange.

One of the primary concerns in negotiating an international business contract involves the designation of the currency used to value or settle the contract. For example, if you are a U.S. publisher selling to a bookstore chain in Australia, how do you price the books? You have three choices. You can price them in U.S. dollars (in this case, the producer's currency pricing, or PCP), but you could also sell the books for Australian dollars (local currency pricing, or LCP). You and the buyer might want to price the books in a third currency (vehicle currency pricing, or VCP), or your contract may specify payment in any combination of PCP, LCP, and VCP. The choice of currency or currencies for payment in the contract is a matter of negotiation between the buyer and seller—and there may be any number of reasons why either a seller or a buyer might prefer any of the options. For example, the publisher might want to purchase rights for a major book by an Australian author and prefer to have Australian dollars available to make that payment. Or the buyer may have spare U.S. dollars available from a sale of Australian books to a U.S. buyer and prefer using those dollars to pay.

The key thing to remember about the currency or currencies specified in a contract is that this is a negotiable point. Before setting the currency of payment on an international contract, consider your own position and the currency needs you will have when payment will be received. By being flexible about the currency used for payment, you may be able to not only make a more favorable deal on the current contract, but you may also improve the position from which you approach future contracts for your business.

Once the currency for a contract is set, you must consider how to reduce the risk that you will lose money on the deal because of changes in the exchange value of the currency used in the contract. One way to reduce this risk is by using a futures contract.

Futures contracts are agreements to buy a specified quantity of something at a future date at an agreed-upon price. Futures contracts for currency can be very useful for international businesspeople. Suppose you sign a contract with a supplier in Japan for delivery of 50,000 parts 6 months down the road. Based on today's exchange rates, these parts will cost you $120,000. But you do not know whether the value of the yen will rise or fall against the dollar in the coming six months. To avoid the risk of having to pay substantially more than $120,000 for the parts in six months, you buy a futures contract for the yen you will need when you must pay the Japanese supplier. If the value of the yen goes down against the dollar in the next six months, you'll lose some potential profit. On the other hand, you eliminate the risk that the yen will go up in value against the dollar, increasing your cost. Working with a known cost for the yen allows you to obtain parts at a cost you know in advance.

Many businesses use future contracts to reduce the ambiguity and risk of the currency market. But the futures contract strategy is just one of many possible approaches to reducing your risks. Another way of managing this risk is to hedge your contract with securities in the currency in question. If you're selling $1 million of equipment to a company in Russia but you're not sure how the ruble will be valued against the dollar when delivery occurs, your company can hedge the risk by purchasing short-term Russian securities, such as government bonds. If the dollar depreciates, the profit from the securities will offset—or help offset—the loss.

When making sales to foreign companies or institutions, some companies negotiate payment terms that require prepayment in U.S. dollars. The payment is held in an escrow account at a corresponding international bank. The escrow account will pay you when you meet your delivery obligations under the contract. This can allow customers in countries with significant inflation to pay in higher-value currency than would likely be the case at delivery time. And, depending on the particulars of the account, the customer may also receive interest on the deposit. Meanwhile, you have a guarantee of payment in U.S. currency at delivery, which greatly reduces your risk and allows you to plan based on what you know you'll receive. This arrangement works well for many high-ticket items, such as custom-built research-grade instruments and medical diagnostic equipment.

Another possible strategy for dealing with fluctuating currency values is using indexed contracts. Under such contracts, payments are indexed to the value the currency will have on the market at the time of payment. Although there are advantages to the seller under these contracts, such contracts are less advantageous for the buyer and are specifically banned by some nations that impose currency controls. Indexed contracts are one of the less frequently used strategies in international trade.

Successful international businesses learn to respond to the foreign exchange market, not just to live with it. Whether the dollar is down or up against another currency, opportunity for profit exists in the international market.

KEY POINTS TO REMEMBER

- Today, currencies are exchanged using floating exchange rates, which are affected by inflation.

- Convertibility is determined by the nation issuing a currency—and whether or not you can bring home your foreign profits is an important consideration in international trade. However, countertrades are one option when working with nonconvertible currencies.

- The international institutions overseeing the currency exchange market include the World Bank, the International Monetary Fund, and the Bank for International Settlements.

- Businesses can invest in currency—just as they can in other assets—using a vehicle currency to facilitate the exchange of other currencies. The U.S. dollar and the Japanese yen are often used today as vehicle currencies.

- Purchasing power parity (PPP) is an exchange rate based on the compared purchasing power of each nation compared with the purchasing power of the others.

- Currency exchanges are handled in an international market that operates around the clock using international computer links.

- International businesses have four major uses for the currency exchange market:

  - Conversion of foreign currencies received in payment

  - Purchase of foreign currencies for payments

  - Investments of financial assets

  - Speculation hoping for short-term profits

- Contracts can be written using many currencies or even multiple currencies.
- Risks can be reduced using
  - Futures contracts
  - Prepayment deposited in an escrow account
  - Indexed contracts
- Remember—profits can be made whether your nation's currency is down or up against another.

PART

GLOBAL STRATEGIES
AND PLANNING

Choosing a Strategy

When it comes to international business, the saying "measure twice, cut once" comes readily to mind. The fates of many international expansions are determined by the strategies that are behind them at the outset. This chapter will discuss various strategies for expansion in the international marketplace and talk about why firms choose the strategies they do. A lot of risk comes with expanding internationally, and there are a few common pitfalls. The most common pitfalls come because of inexperience with the new cultural environment, inability to adapt a product or service to local needs, and the lack of an effective distribution system. The right strategy, however, can help your company avoid these pitfalls.

First, we'll discuss what businesses are trying to get out of their international operations. Later in this chapter, we'll explain how different global strategies achieve desired goals. The important thing for you to remember is that going international is supposed to make your business stronger and more competitive; that's why you're expanding internationally in the first place.

WHAT ARE THE ADVANTAGES?

Cost Savings

There are two main ways that international operations may provide cost savings for your firm. One common cost savings comes from reducing production costs by producing in a country with relatively lower wages, or more natural resources, or any number of other factors that can reduce the cost of goods sold. Sometimes foreign manufacturing operations are established by producers of bulk goods simply to eliminate transportation costs to a new market. When it comes to deciding where to produce, there may also be a cost savings found in a country that encourages foreign direct investment. All of these cost savings are derived from production decisions. Locating in the most cost-efficient location will increase your profits, but you'll need to be careful. We'll address production decisions in later chapters, but for now let's just say that by definition, where you produce is the criterion that decides the kind of international business you'll have.

International operations can also provide cost savings for your company by helping you achieve certain economies of scale by expanding your production scale. By expanding from domestic production levels to global production levels, your per-unit cost of goods will decrease, even as your sales volume increases. This aspect of the international business environment is often overlooked by novices, but it's important for you to consider. The world market allows an incredible amount of potential for growth. Some businesses only think of going abroad when their domestic market is saturated or highly competitive, but other companies have the foresight to expand when the market is favorable. As we'll discuss later in this chapter, going international is an important step in the life of your business, and not one that should be seen as an escape route from an increasingly competitive or saturated domestic market. The economies of scale gained by going global are bought at the price of uncertainty in new national environments and the costs of learning how to do business in a new environment abroad.

Differentiation

Necessity is the mother of invention. One of the potential benefits of international expansion, though it is hard to calculate, is that your company will have to improve in certain ways in order to compete internationally. Your international experience can aid all aspects of your business. In adapting your product to the needs of foreign local consumers, and in developing an organizational structure that can achieve the goal of product customization and a more responsive management team, you will learn a lot. Much of what you learn can be applied in your domestic business operations.

A trend in businesses today is to create "flatter" organizational structures. With these flatter structures, unnecessary hierarchy is removed to increase the flow of information from sales rep to CEO and back. Flatter organizations were one part of Jack Welch's overall strategy for GE when he became CEO of the company. By making the company less hierarchal, Welch was able to make the GE giant much more responsive—and thus much more suited to the fostering of innovation.

Because of the rapidly changing nature of international markets, international business organizations are virtually required to form a flatter structure. However, domestic businesses may also find that the lessons of international business can be applied within their home countries. Many people talk about leveraging competencies in international business, and your company's strengths are certainly an asset in your international expansion. But you'll have to develop new strengths to succeed abroad. In turn, you can bring these home with you to help your domestic operations. Businesses that are successful in adapting their products and services to the needs of customers in foreign markets may find that a good idea for operation in China may also be a good idea for operation in the United States. When responding to needs abroad, your company may develop a new product out of necessity and then sell it anywhere for profit. Of course, as we'll discuss later in this chapter, an organization's strategy can either aid or hinder that synergy.

Location

One reason to expand internationally is simply to get somewhere else—somewhere with favorable trade policies, with profit potential, with a new consumer base, with different competencies, with natural resources, with lower production costs. Simply put, America isn't the best place to make everything, and it isn't the best market in which to sell everything. As mentioned earlier, location choices can provide a great deal of cost savings. Depending on what your company sells, transportation costs may be a significant portion of your international business model and can be easily cut when you can reduce the distance across which you need to transport goods. Many multinationals now use a sort of regional manufacturing plan. Diebold, the ATM and bank vault manufacturing company, expanded operations in China, Brazil, France, and Germany. By manufacturing abroad, it drastically reduced the cost of manufacturing in the United States and of shipping its product abroad. Its manufacturing facilities serve as a sort of regional office, so that the ATMs sold in the U.K. are produced in France or Germany, and the electronic voting machines for use in Columbia are made in Brazil. These offshore facilities also help Diebold be more responsive to local needs. In China, people use ATMs to pay their bills; Diebold's Chinese division designed ATMs that could do that. These new ATMs might well find a new market in the United States.

Location can also provide other strategic advantages for your company, such as access to a technology or process found in only in a certain country, or natural resources found within certain national borders. Sometimes the advantage isn't entirely in the cost or in the market; sometimes simply working within a country that has a government on your company's side is reason enough to locate production facilities in that nation.

Talent Pool

Contrary to what sometimes seems to be popular belief, Americans aren't the best at everything. One reason to expand internationally is because there are talent pools abroad that can be accessed to your company's benefit. Dell has been doing just that by developing computer production facilities in India. Many countries have large numbers of educated and skilled workers who work for wages lower than those of their counterparts in education or skill in the United States. For a long time, Americans exported know-how in the international business environment. Proctor & Gamble's original expansion in the European market was fueled by competencies in marketing and developing brand-name products and in creating a consumer base with loyalty to those products. Today, these skills can be found in companies around the world, not just in American companies. That dilutes the strength of a competency such as Proctor & Gamble's.

The recent past has given rise to a particular form of corporation that capitalizes on the diverse international talent pool: the micro-multinational. Micro-multinationals tend to be either Web-based businesses or software design firms. They recruit talent from all over the world to work in a type of virtual office. Modern communication technologies make this not merely a viable but an attractive option for new ventures to pursue. Depending on the nature of the industry and the quality of the employees, the company may be able to function without a headquarters or other administrative overhead. Such savings can give a competitive advantage to the micro-multinational. These small international businesses are relatively new, making their performance not yet certain, but in the coming years the number of micro-multinationals is expected to increase dramatically.

ADAPTING YOUR STRATEGY TO THE LOCAL ENVIRONMENT

When considering a strategy, it is important to find what advantages the local economy offers, and what it doesn't. Expanding in Tokyo probably won't bring about a reduction in production costs (apart from economies of scale), because Tokyo is a wealthy city with relatively highly paid workers and some of the most expensive real estate on the planet. But Japan does offer a well-educated workforce and a lot of experience in international business. If you need an educated workforce with international business experience, Japan might be the place your company needs to go for at least some of your operations. Low-cost products produced elsewhere might complete the picture and close the gap in Japan's advantages. In addition to the specific advantages from above, the chief advantage of engaging in international operations is that there is nearly always a better way to do what you're doing, and the international marketplace nearly always has an answer.

Many managers think of going abroad in terms of access to a new market with increased profit potential, or of access to cheaper labor, or of any of the other reasons outlined above. But when you consider international expansion, think of it as a way to increase your company's overall competitive advantage and strategic position. International expansion should never feel like a side project; it must be an integral part of your business.

As we've stated before, the potential for profit is what brings companies to the international marketplace. The complication they find there is their stumbling block. The cost savings, value of new locations, talent pools available, and differentiation gained from international operation are all compelling reasons to start looking at overseas operations, but before we even get to the different strategies, let's first take a look at two of the largest pitfalls that your strategy will need to avoid.

AVOIDING DUPLICATION

International businesses can have a certain amount of redundancy, especially in the case of expanding with green-field operations and acquisitions, where new systems have to be developed or purchased without consideration for existing functions. Whether your company is departmentalized by industry, region, or product, setting up international operations for the first time will probably combine all three. You'll probably start with a limited product line, focusing only on the market you're entering. You will need to hire some support staff and company infrastructure positions from the local citizenry in order to manage foreign employees. This isn't the only way to manage, but you should know that expatriate managers, especially first-time expatriate managers, have a higher failure rate, many times because of issues not directly related to the business (e.g., a spouse unwilling to relocate). So a local manager is typically a better bet, but much as expatriate managers have a culture gap between your foreign employees and themselves, local managers have a cultural gap between themselves and you.

Once your international operations are established and your presence felt in the marketplace, some of these redundancies can be eliminated. How many marketing departments does your company need, after all? Hypothetically, one. Practically? More. When your company expands internationally, it may not yet know what it needs, simply because it hasn't done it yet. So your tendency will be toward over-management and duplication of resources. However, be mindful of this tendency, and try to keep it in check.

CREATING YOUR COMPETITION

One of the long-term strategic pitfalls in international expansion comes because you have many opportunities to sow the seeds of your own destruction. If your company finds initial success in international expansion, that only increases the attractiveness of your new market to your competitors. Of course, this is the case for domestic business as well, but in the international context, it means that your company not only needs to set up sustainable operations in a new market quickly but also needs to control and protect whatever market share you gain in that new market. Once you've established a beachhead of operations, your company will need to move quickly to secure the position indefinitely. And you should remember that direct competition isn't the only danger. McDonald's learned this the hard way when their first Chinese location was bought out from under them because they had failed to adapt to the local political environment.

The other—and probably more common—way to create your own competition is through your suppliers abroad. The more information and technology that you share with suppliers—particularly proprietary information about your product—the more potentially dangerous your supplier becomes. Although every contracted manufacturer professes commitment to the principle of not competing with its clients, the fact is that some suppliers do develop their own brands. The difficulty in this situation is, how can your company develop a high-quality product if your suppliers don't know how the product works? That may seem like an oversimplification, but it is a core problem that international companies face. Some companies deal with this risk simply by contracting with many suppliers and manufacturers, each of whom controls only a small component of the final product. Splitting up the supply source enables the international company to prevent supply competency from growing into a competing product.

We'll address this further in the next chapter, which deals with modes of entry in international business, but in essence, there is a strong strategic motive for owning production facilities abroad rather than outsourcing production or using contract manufacturers. Controlling production facilities removes the potential that your supplier in a foreign market could become a competitor later. When it comes to the acquisition versus outsourcing decision, the rule of thumb is, "If they don't join you, they might beat you."

WHAT STRATEGY IS RIGHT FOR YOUR COMPANY?

Choosing the right strategy will take not only an understanding of the market you are entering but also impartial understanding of your company's strengths and weaknesses. There are two basic factors that need to be considered: cost pressure and the need for local responsiveness. Some industries and products compete primarily on cost and cost alone. Products that are "universal" tend to fall in this category. Refined sugar, for example, is a universal product. It might be marketed differently in different markets, but the product is largely the same from producer to producer, so the competition is based largely around a low-cost leadership position. Some products are highly sensitive to differences in consumer preferences around the world, so differentiation based around different consumer needs is necessary.

The market for automobiles requires a great deal of local responsiveness in order to succeed internationally. Toyota learned this the hard way when they launched their first serious attempt to break into the heavy-duty truck market in the United States. Their T100 had a V6 engine instead of the V8 of the American-made competition in the heavy-duty truck market. In their first year, Toyota sold a mere 2,500 T100s in the United States. The lesson was hard learned, but well applied when Toyota made their second attempt at entering the market for heavy-duty trucks in the United States. The now popular Toyota Tundra is proof that they learned about U.S. preferences.

The factors of cost and local responsiveness are sometimes referred to, respectively, as the needs for standardization and localization. Basically, if a product is "standardized" from market to market, the product competes on cost, because the needs of consumers the product satisfies are practically the same from market to market. If the product needs to adapt to individual markets because the needs of consumers it satisfies are different from market to market, then that product needs to be "localized."

The different international businesses strategies formulated in response to the pressures of cost and local responsiveness correspond to different advantages and disadvantages. We will explain four basic strategies (although the terminology that describes them isn't widely agreed upon) and how they fit into the matrix of cost pressure and local responsiveness. You'll have to see where your company, market, and industry fit into the matrix before deciding what strategy will work for you. (See figure on following page.)

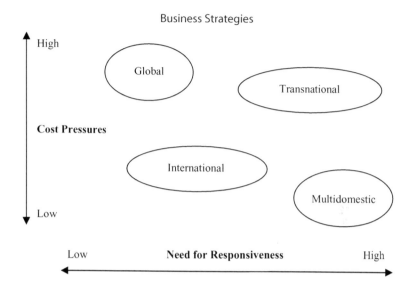

International Strategy

An international strategy is one with a "home office" in one country that controls foreign operations to a large extent. This typically works best with a product that doesn't require much customization for foreign markets. In order to be effective, an international strategy usually follows a sort of "colonial" structure, in which product decisions, research, and development are all centrally located. The foreign operations then serve as distribution points for the product and slightly tailor the marketing of the product for the country. Production can be divided by national market, which leads to relatively higher operating costs, because of manufacturing duplication. Many times, this strategy is predicated by a background in exporting. An international strategy is basically an exporting strategy, but you're exporting a factory and a floor of your office, too. Once a company has successfully exported to a new market, it can start developing its own sales and distribution infrastructure within that market and realize additional gains by owning and controlling more of the process. Many times this is the goal of an agreement with an export management company (EMC), which helps first-time exporters get their product to market abroad and often works as a consultancy in setting up international operations. We'll discuss EMCs in depth in later chapters, but for now you should at least know that there can be many milestones in your international development, and that there are many resources available to move you from one to the next. An international strategy is often the starting point for the nascent venture going abroad for the first time. It's a fairly intuitive strategy to take a successful product abroad and to bring it to a new market, then developing the delivery of the product in that market, only afterward considering actually changing the way you produce. Until that point, you only need to produce more.

An international strategy works best, as seen in the diagram, when cost pressures and the need for local responsiveness are both low in the firm's industry. Take, for example, bringing a successful consumer product into a new market that has little local competition, and where consumer preferences are already in line with the product. Microsoft uses what would be considered an international strategy for these reasons, creating a product in Washington State and then having their Paris office simply translate it into French.

When we say that cost pressure and the need for local responsiveness are low, that certainly applies to some technology markets. But an international strategy doesn't mean that product has to be complicated. 3M historically used an international strategy in its initial entry into new markets. It started by setting up minimal operations, hiring local employees, and selling a limited product line—sometimes just a single product. By the time sales of the selected product (e.g., Post-It Notes) gained traction, the company had a much better understanding of the foreign market and how to operate within it. Then it expanded the product line offered in that market. Once sales reached a viable level, 3M set up production facilities in that country or region. Note that the whole time, although giving some degree of freedom regarding the marketing of the products, headquarters decided what products would be carried, what markets were entered, when to grow the new operation, and how (or if) the products themselves were customized for the local citizenry. It was not until after new production facilities had been set up that local input was accepted for these decisions.

An international strategy can be a good starting point for your business. This strategy, in part because of its simplicity, is almost certainly the most comfortable way for your business to enter the international market.

This strategy shifts little (if any) control of your company's product into foreign hands. Without changing your production process or design life cycle, you can reach new clients without the uncertainties of producing abroad. For many companies, an international strategy is a first step toward some other ultimate strategic goal, but there are exceptions (if it's good enough for Microsoft, it might be good enough for you). Throughout this book, we repeat the need for your business to "learn" in the international environment. An international strategy allows for an incremental learning process, expanding your business, function by function, into your foreign markets. The other strategies, without an international strategy preceding them, are the equivalent of learning to swim by jumping into the ocean.

Global Strategy

Typically, this strategy is used for standardized products in situations in which each market has roughly the same requirements for the product. It entails locating business functions in key locations chosen for cost-savings purposes and efficiency of operations. This strategy is more efficient than international strategy in terms of controlling costs but allows for less customization for the local market. Essentially, if your company sells a highly standardized, "universal," product, your company can set up the most efficient production network by using the advantages of different national economies together. Create a competitive advantage for yourself by offering your product at the lowest cost, using the fastest product distribution, and having the fewest product defects. Many firms pursuing a global strategy practice Total Quality Management (TQM), setting up corrective loops in their quality assurance process to constantly improve the quality of their products and to decrease the incidence of defects.

The weakness of the global strategy is that if your company tries to expand into different product lines, if market forces change unfavorably, or if a cultural issue arises in one of the countries you operate within, your business will have a hard time trying to compensate by changing its structure or product. Just as an international strategy allows removal from a nation (other than your host country) with relative ease, in the same way a global strategy needs to be restructured in response to the same sorts of pressure. Suppose you allocate all production to Malaysia, because it has low-cost labor and expansive production capacity. But then a new trade agreement is signed between the United States and Malaysia, increasing the tariffs on goods imported from one country to another, changing your cost structure dramatically. If you own the production assets (factory, land, etc.) in Malaysia, but it no longer fits your cost structure, you'll have to divest yourself of the Malaysian holdings, find a new production facility elsewhere, and end up still vulnerable to the same sorts of cultural pressures.

This potential downfall of the global strategy isn't always an impending danger, but it is still a danger. Businesses pursuing a global strategy actually have protection against some losses and have various degrees of bargaining power with the governments under whose regulation they operate. A global strategy company can always move jobs elsewhere. But global strategy is the least responsive to changes in taste and the changing preferences of local consumers in different markets. The global strategy is very similar to the early vertically integrated companies like Ford. In the rapidly changing global market, "any color they want—so long as it's black," just doesn't cut it anymore.

An efficient global strategy and a company with a focused product line go hand in hand. Gillette has employed a global strategy because of its focused product and the standardized nature of the razor market in which it competes. By creating an efficient production system, Gillette has been able to capitalize on the economies of scale in the international market, the cost savings of strategic, centralized production facilities, and the global brand it has developed. This model is fairly safe for Gillette, because the market for razors has remained largely stable for a long period of time, and Gillette's dominance has come as the result of its ability to change with the business environment. Not all businesses, however, are similarly suited to the global strategy.

Multidomestic Strategy

A multidomestic strategy is essentially a conglomerate of national businesses in the same industry. National units are allowed a great deal of autonomy in this strategy; localizing marketing, distribution, and product development has a lot of advantages in an industry with significant need for local responsiveness. Problems can arise, however, because individual national units have little, if any, incentive to work together; they are largely independent operations. This often leads to heavy duplication of resources and costs in different markets. Compared to an international strategy, a multidomestic strategy means a significantly longer time to get a new product to market. However, a multidomestic strategy is the most locally responsive, an advantage in businesses in which products can be "over-standardized." It's an old rule that "you can't please everyone." The attempt to make a global product by considering the needs of multiple markets may lead to the creation of a product that doesn't satisfy *any* market.

The multidomestic model works very well with a service industry, as in the case of global financial services, management consulting, or advertising companies, in which services must be tailored to local environments. There are some hefty advantages to the multidomestic strategy in certain conditions. If your company is entering disparate markets in which consumers differ widely from country to country, it might make sense for your business to pursue a multidomestic organization. The autonomy provided in this strategy can foster a more entrepreneurial spirit and greater product innovation in each national unit, and each unit can focus directly on its direct, local competition within the marketplace. The problem is that even if one national unit is very innovative, growth in competence or product development is difficult to translate to other national units. Furthermore, this structure can encourage the development of a certain amount of territorialism between units in different countries and cultures. This strength in product development in each local market is also the curse of the multidomestic firm, because each autonomous unit tends to believe it is always right about its local market. Thus transferring knowledge from one national unit to another requires combating this territorialism in addition to crossing cultural gaps between national environments.

Unilever pursued the multidomestic strategy for a long time in the European market, tailoring each national unit to the specific needs and tastes of that nation's consumers. In some cases, Unilever tailored only the marketing, so that the same product had a different brand name in each country that it was sold. In the early 1990s, Unilever had 17 subsidiaries in

Europe alone. For a long time, this strategy worked, but as the marketplace changed and Europe became a more unified market, Unilever needed to adapt its strategy. However, even though Unilever has consolidated its production facilities in Europe and is now pursuing a more unified European market strategy, it still sells the same products under different brand names in different countries, because the brand name recognition from its multi-domestic strategy period still applies. To Unilever's thinking, the value of those brand names (which is the company's biggest strength in the marketplace) outweighs the potential value of being "pan-European."

The multidomestic strategy certainly does have benefits in markets that are driven by consumer preferences, as opposed to cost-based competition in firms pursuing the global strategy. But inflexibility, along with the levels of coordination required between units, can be a serious hurdle for your business and can require a great deal of cross-cultural literacy on the part of your company's upper-level management if the company is to be effective. Whereas an international strategy is "comfortable," because very little control is given away by the company's headquarters, a multidomestic strategy entails giving away much control. However, a company that can tolerate doing this will have a diversified portfolio of holdings and will find some stability in the structure. One of the financial benefits enjoyed by multidomestic firms is that underperforming national units are "covered" by other high-performance units. Furthermore, such a company can divest from a single, unstable market with relative ease. Recall that the global strategy, for example, makes leaving an unstable market with essential production functions very difficult. The difference between a global strategy and a multidomestic strategy can be summarized this way: a global strategy works for a company that does one thing really well, and a multidomestic strategy works for a company that needs to do one thing well in many different ways.

Transnational Strategy

The goal of a transnational strategy is to be able to respond both to cost pressures and to local consumer needs. It eliminates the duplications and inefficiencies of the international and multidomestic strategies while increasing local responsiveness in relation to the more stringent global strategy. Some academics have argued that the transnational strategy is ultimately the only way for an international corporation to build long-term competitive advantage, although this has recently been disputed. In theory, the transnational business is the perfect balance between cost-reducing standardization and the localization that meets the needs of varied consumers in different national markets. Does it sound too good to be true? Unfortunately, for a lot of firms, it is.

Pursuing a transnational strategy is very difficult for many reasons. First, it requires a lot of decentralization that most companies, for practical and political reasons, are uncomfortable with allowing. It also requires that knowledge not merely disseminate from the home office. Rather, it expects that competencies developed in one market will be applied elsewhere. This requires both a high level of cooperation between all offices and an incentive structure supporting such innovation. This global learning improves the overall efficiency and effectiveness of the entire business, but in order to attain to it, it will be best to view it as a goal, not as an expected starting point. But the good news is that any of the other three strategies can serve as a stepping stone to help you reach this point.

Caterpillar faced this situation, and with a great deal of success. Low-cost Japanese competitors and product requirements that varied widely from market to market made the global and multidomestic strategies unviable. Construction regulations and codes vary from city to city, and much more so from country to country. Trying to sell Caterpillar products globally was very difficult, and products required a great deal of customization for each national market. Caterpillar's solution was to establish a few large-scale, low-cost component production facilities, thus achieving economies of scale. Then the components were shipped to assembly facilities in each of Caterpillar's national markets. Based on the components used, the national facilities could assemble "custom" equipment for each market. The components were interchangeable, and their mass production in a few key locations allowed for cost control; in that sense, component production was essentially a global strategy. The assembly plants that customized Caterpillar's equipment for the needs of each national market increased localization. Because each national assembly facility was responsible for designing equipment to meet local consumer needs, assembly plants were essentially following a multidomestic strategy. By implementing this production process, Caterpillar was responding both to cost pressure and to the need for local responsiveness. The increased coordination of international efforts has proven to be very good for Caterpillar's bottom line. Today this combination of strategies at different points of the product life cycle, along with extensive coordination across all operations, is what earns Caterpillar the designation of successful transnational.

As we've said, a transnational strategy should be the goal. This is because a transnational strategy balances the two main pressures in the international market, allowing your business to be truly global. The flow of information is so strong in a transnational firm that you maximize the learning, competencies, and growth opportunities for your entire firm. That's not to say that there aren't markets and industries that justify other strategies. Earlier, we said that although some academics argue that the transnational strategy is the "best" strategy to pursue, others dispute this claim. But there is little disagreement that the transnational strategy is the most difficult to design and follow. There are many reasons to engage in any of the other three strategies for international business, but part of your vision for your company's growth should be a plan to go from national strategy to transnational. The biggest challenge is determining what needs to come in between those two strategies.

WHAT STRATEGY WORKS FOR YOU?

The nascent international expansion has two main opponents: complication and risk. Many firms stay domestic when they know there are opportunities available to them elsewhere; they fear the complication of international business and the risk that goes with it. Knowledge of the business environment in your target national environment may ease worries over complications in the new culture and, if your company starts small in international expansion, you'll learn a great deal in a short period of time. The knowledge you gain will help reduce some of the complications in expansion and allow your company to consider increased investment. Knowing the size of your company's future in that new market may alleviate worry over the risk of failure. If you see how large an opportunity international expansion presents to your company, the risk–reward analysis of international expansion is almost always going to favor going abroad. Once you've worked past these hurdles, it's time to choose a strategy. There are a few simple questions you need to ask:

What is my industry?

What existing competition is already present in the market I wish to enter?

How is my industry defined in that market?

As emphasized earlier, the nature of your company's product or service is a big determinant in choosing an effective international strategy. A technology product requires ease of use, and that typically means local customization, so you'll want to consider a multidomestic or transnational strategy. A commodity product, on the other hand, is usually a price-driven market, making a global or international strategy probably your best bet. Further, if your commodity product has a lot of competitors in the market, a global strategy will help you control costs and give you a cost leadership position. Similarly, if your technology product faces well-established competition in various national markets, a multidomestic strategy will give you the highest local responsiveness and help you break into the marketplace.

Each strategy has its advantages and disadvantages, so you'll need to evaluate which strategy is needed and valuable for your company, industry, and market. Let's look at some examples of strategies pursued by international corporations and how the strategies met the needs of the company, industry, or market.

GLOBAL ALCOA

Aluminum is aluminum, wherever you go. At least that seems to be the thinking behinds Alcoa's global strategy. Alcoa is a perfect example of a commodity producer who markets a cost-competitive product all around the world. By producing aluminum and related products at a low cost and developing long-term relationships with its clients, Alcoa has been able to maintain its position as an international industry leader for decades.

MULTIDOMESTIC MTV

MTV's original international expansion would be described as an international strategy—and it failed. Entertainment industries face a very high need for local responsiveness. That might seem fairly intuitive, but MTV initially thought it could export some of its programming and significantly reduce its production costs. When this failed, it moved toward a much more multidomestic strategy, differentiating programming between national markets. In India, for example, MTV developed a program about cricket, something that wouldn't play as well in America. Recently, MTV has been trying to cut some of the duplications of functions in its international operations in order to cut production costs globally.

INTERNATIONAL XEROX

Xerox pursued an international strategy for a long time, selling the same high-end copiers abroad. But when low-cost competition developed, that strategy was no longer viable. In Xerox's early days, it had few competitors or competing products, so it was able to produce its product and essentially export it around the globe, hiring local sales teams to tailor to the market without altering the product. In the 1960s this strategy allowed for aggressive expansion, and Xerox had a majority market share in many of its national markets. When this strategy worked, it worked because Xerox had low cost pressure and the product was so new that it didn't need much customization in order to be a differentiated product—there wasn't anything else like it!

TRANSNATIONAL FORD

Although Ford, like many automobile producers, has struggled with going transnational, it might be the best example of an American car company pursuing a transnational strategy. Ford components are manufactured all around the world and partially assembled in various locations, including Mexico and the United States. Continuation along the transnational path is viewed by many industry analysts as Ford's best hope for future competitive advantage in the struggle with automobile producers from abroad.

STRATEGY EVOLUTION

The Greek philosopher Heraclitus argued that no one can step into the same river twice, for both person and river have changed. In the business world—and even more so in international business—everything is changing, all the time. Your strategy will need to evolve with market conditions. Your company will need to adapt to organizational changes as you grow globally (see figure below). And you'll need to understand whether it is you or the river that is changing at any given moment.

Markets change rapidly, and there is (and has been) a sort of snowball effect surrounding these changes. As trade barriers decrease and individual firms take their companies into new nations, so does the competition. Competition continues on a new playing field. When markets open up to foreign investment, new companies are born to capitalize on the opportunity; if they are successful, their success breeds their own competition. As trade agreements are signed between one country and another, additional nations follow suit so that their trade balance remains competitive. Your strategy may start well-planned and enjoy initial success. If so, good for you! But you'll have to continue to adapt that strategy as your company continuously faces new challenges.

Strategy Evolution

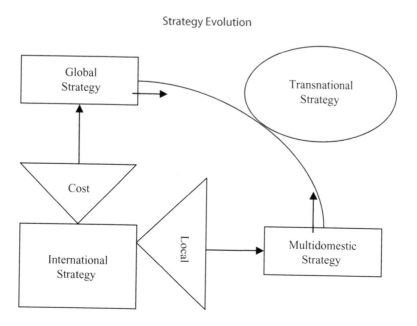

In the next chapter, we'll focus in detail on specific modes of entry into the international environment. For now, though, let's assume that your company is a successful domestic firm. Then you start exporting your high-quality product abroad. Meeting success there, you decide to start setting up operations, or you acquire existing operations in new national markets. You start by simply hiring a sales and marketing team for your existing product in that market, having your new local employees direct how the product is sold in this new market (an international strategy). And all is well.

Then a competitor (we'll call them Dinosaur, Inc.) enters the same national market with a significantly larger acquisition. Dinosaur will either undercut you on cost or localize its product more than you are in order to take your market share. So you respond by trying to further cut costs or to be more locally responsive, moving to a global or multidomestic strategy. Let's suppose that Dinosaur achieves better economies of scale and is undercutting your cost. By having local production, of whatever scale, Dinosaur passes on savings to the consumer to steal your market share. In response, you develop a more efficient production process with better quality management, increasing your production capacity with a new facility. In so doing, you protect (and perhaps even expand) your market share. Now you've moved toward a global strategy, and if you continue, you'll secure your cost-leadership position. So far, so good.

Then new government regulations are imposed on your industry in that national market, and you are forced to completely redesign the product in order to meet the new legal requirements. The new focus on local responsiveness requires more collaboration between your home office and your foreign subsidiary. The global strategy that had previously given you some advantage is now a liability, because your production process isn't geared to adapt easily; you'll need to change the process and the product in order to compete under the new regulations. Now you're moving toward establishing a transnational strategy, and your business depends on your success.

ORGANIZATIONAL DESIGN AND STRATEGY

Each strategy necessitates certain institutional supports and systems in order to pursue the direction your company wants to go. There are several elements that change from one strategy to the next. In order to understand the institutional side of these strategies, we'll introduce a little new vocabulary and context to measure them, and then we'll explain how the different strategies compare across these dimensions. Some of these elements will be addressed in a later chapter dealing with human resource management in an international enterprise, but it's important to see even now how the structure of an organization ties into the organization's international strategy.

The Need for Coordination

The way that production processes are organized determines the level of coordination needed. If the production process is spread out across multiple countries, coordination becomes more urgent. Similarly, if your company is engaged in very disparate markets—even with a single product—you'll need effective coordination of your marketing efforts in each national market. A multidomestic firm has reduced the need for coordination because of the relatively autonomous nature of each national unit. A firm employing a global strategy has a very great need for coordination, because production is often split at various stages; in order for a product to move smoothly from one stage of its life cycle to another, each link in the chain to market must be aligned.

Integrating Mechanisms

The controls put in place for coordinating production are integrating mechanisms for your company. There are two types of integrating mechanisms: vertical and horizontal. Vertical integrating mechanisms almost always appear in the form of quality assurance, whether for physical product or for design. Horizontal integrating mechanisms are usually involved in knowledge transfer. Take the example of the multidomestic firm: in order to be effective, many strong horizontal integrating mechanisms should be put in place. These include incentives for knowledge transfer, such as compensation for managers based on overall company performance, and simple formalization of communication, such as a pan-regional committee of managers. Many companies take great pains to make sure that managers at individual national units meet regularly with their foreign counterparts to increase cooperation and skills transfer. This is very important, especially in the case of integrated product launches. For example, firms that have diverse operations in Europe and national offices in multiple countries often use border-crossing teams to develop and coordinate product launches.

Performance Ambiguity

The causes of poor performance can be difficult to trace. When many units are collaborating extensively, it's difficult to see where value is being lost. Whether it's tracking the origin of a product defect or a breakdown in design, or communication with customers at different points in the production process, it becomes difficult to see where a problem is occurring in a complex international production system. This, in turn, leads to ambiguity and uncertainty about which national units are underperforming. This isn't an organizational structure component so much as it is a serious issue that you must face structurally. Your organization's structure will need to be designed to reduce such problems. For example, a multidomestic firm has low performance ambiguity; if an independent national unit is functioning poorly, it is typically its own fault. Quality assurance measures in global strategy firms can significantly reduce performance ambiguity, because the quality assurance between different stages of the production process should alert your company of breaks in the product's value. A transnational firm has the greatest performance ambiguity—just another one of the difficulties in pursuing that particular strategy.

Cultural Controls

Organizational culture is the system of beliefs and values that prevail within a given organization. Strong organizational culture means that these beliefs and value are highly correlated within an organization. Strong culture does not always equate to "better" culture. Sometimes a shared value has a negative impact on the organization. This might be a company that is highly formal and slow-moving, or one that isn't too little risk-averse. Optimally, a strong organizational culture means a more predictable organization, something that decreases uncertainty. The question then is how your company can maintain a strong, coherent organizational culture while operating in vastly diverse national cultures.

The value of diversity is stressed in nearly every modern organization, from corporations to colleges, and some research indicates that diversity is profitable for the companies that successfully support it. But when you hire a manager from a collectivist society (refer to Chapter 2's discussion of cultural dimensions), how well will he or she work with an individualistic manager from your home office?

Cultural controls are the answer to these questions. Some measures are as simple as personality tests administered to potential managers, or the arrangement of informal contacts between international counterparts. The transnational strategy for international operations is usually supported with many cultural controls that encourage employees in all national units to feel a high degree of commitment to the organization. The use of extensive cultural controls helps all your company's employees feel as if they truly are part of the same company.

PLANNING TO GO GLOBAL

The strategies that this chapter has outlined describe many roads to international expansion. Each strategy has its own strengths and weaknesses, and each corresponds to certain industries and markets, and to certain stages in your company's development. Although this chapter stressed the strategic potential of the transnational firm, you need to pursue a strategy that works for your company—not just in some ways, but in all. Young businesses don't have the crutch of corporate tradition, but they might also lack the sophistication required to expand in the global market. Larger, more mature corporations might be too set in their ways to aggressively expand abroad—and even if they do expand, they might be too slow to adapt to their new markets successfully. Before you make decisions about where and how to produce, and about what markets to enter and how to enter them, it is important that you plan out long-term strategic goals for your company's expansion, adjusting them when the changing environment calls for changes.

There is no silver bullet that kills the bugbears of international operations. Markets change too rapidly, and different markets have different requirements. But this chapter should have given you a framework to help you start planning to go abroad. In the next chapter, we'll discuss specific modes of entry; after that, we'll talk in detail about how your company can successfully expand internationally. But remember: strategy must come first, or stability will be lost, and opportunities will pass your company by.

KEY POINTS TO REMEMBER

- Expanding your business into the international sphere can bring your company the success you're striving for by allowing you to take advantage of favorable foreign business environments, diversify your company's portfolio of skills through experience and adaptation, and harness local strengths (whether inexpensive foreign labor and materials or talented, well-educated employees) in service of your company's vision.

- Keeping your focus on success may require duplicating resources, but avoid it whenever you can. Use tried and tested assets to help get new, untried ones on their feet, and then move them into their own spheres to leverage their capabilities.

- Unless you're acquiring a business partner through acquisition or merger, be careful not to end up equipping and training your suppliers to be your own competitors. Your success in your new business environment will bring your competitors back home running into the market you've opened, and the last thing you need is host-country competition that knows your new market better than you do.

- Considering your target country and the business you want to do in it in light of the markets you want to enter can help you decide which strategy is right for you: international (your home office manages your international offices and global product), global (your international offices work together to produce a global product), multidomestic (your international offices work separately to produce regional products), or transnational (your international offices work together to separately produce regional products). Whether it's necessities of economy or localization that drive your business, choosing the right strategy can lead to benefits in both spheres as a transnational company.

- When choosing your international business strategy, ensure from the start that your offices are coordinated, your quality assurance strengthened by knowledge transfer, and your workforce unified by cultural controls that support your chosen strategy.

Modes of Entry in International Business

Now that we've discussed some of the conceptual framework for international expansion of your business, it's time to talk about more concrete methods to actually start going global. This chapter will demonstrate various modes of entry into international operations, how they fit in with the four strategies discussed in the previous chapter, and how to decide which mode of entry is right for your business, industry, and market. The most important consideration when deciding how to enter a new foreign market is figuring out what your company's strengths are and deciding how they will help you compete.

If your company's core competency is developing brand-name products and marketing them, then licensing your product would waste your company's competency by turning over product marketing to another company that might diminish the strength of your brand name. Each mode of entry has advantages and disadvantages, and each works for different strategies and competencies.

No matter what else is considered in choosing an entry mode, no businesses, and particularly a small business, should consider comfort. Various modes of entry have varying comfort levels, partially because of the amount of uncertainty associated with each. It is important for you to choose a mode of entry that fits with your company's industry, market, and strategy, not just the mode of entry that your company's management is most comfortable employing, whether for personal or even financial reasons.

Just as we said about strategies in the previous chapter, modes of entry will likely change as your business changes, as you recognize additional opportunities, and as your company expands into more and more national markets. Depending on geographic distance, legal restrictions, or local product requirements, your company may need to use different modes of entry in each national market you choose. Each market is different from the one before, which means that adapting to each is your best hope for successful expansion.

MODES OF ENTRY

Exporting and Importing

The way that many, if not most, businesses begin expanding into international markets is by exporting products and services, which means that someone on the opposite end is importing those products into a different market. Because this relationship is really a whole system, we'll discuss both methods at the same time, although in the context of exporting. Importing is the same process as exporting—just from the opposite viewpoint—so if your company is considering importation, keep reading.

Exporting is almost certainly going to require expert help. You can do this in two ways: internally, or externally. You'll need some knowledge of export procedures in whatever market you're going to, as well as someone to manage clients within that market. Your company can hire someone for this purpose, or it can cultivate internal staff (although this may be the most difficult and time-consuming option). You can also turn to outside resources, hiring the necessary expertise from external companies, such as an export management company. Export/import procedures can vary widely from one nation to another, so even if your company has some experience exporting to one market, that doesn't mean that working in a second market will be the same.

Exporting brings with it some distinct advantages. It doesn't require entirely new business structures abroad, and it doesn't require significant foreign direct investment. Exporting is thus a relatively comfortable mode of entry. As mentioned before, this comfort level can be a serious problem for some small businesses. Many small businesses never get past the point of exporting, missing opportunities for further expansion in international operations. Exporting almost always means that some potential profit is being lost in the transaction to the importer and the financial intermediaries involved in the transaction.

In Chapter 7, we'll talk about some of the paperwork of international transactions, providing detailed transaction information about exporting and importing, so we won't go into much detail here. But remember that exporting involves four parties—your company, your company's bank, your buyer's bank, and your buyer—and that the two links in the middle are cutting margins for both you and your buyer.

All this is not to say that exporting can't be profitable, but keep in mind that exporting might simply be the first step in your company's international business goals. If you choose export as a mode of entry and then find that your new market is viable, the next step in your expansion might be taking steps toward an international strategy. After all, if you can sell your product to someone in a foreign market, and he or she can turn around and sell it for a profit, couldn't you make more money by selling it in that market yourself? Although it's not quite that simple, exporting shares profit with others; you should consider how your company might be able to recapture profit for itself. It's difficult to go from exporting to anything other than an international strategy in terms of developing strategy. Doing anything else would require a great deal of reorganization—keep this handicap in mind when choosing a mode of entry and an overall international business strategy.

Turnkey Projects

Turnkey projects are a way of selling your company's competence. A foreign company or investor pays you to set up a manufacturing facility or other means of production for its use. This type of arrangement is called a "turnkey," because when the project is completed, you hand the client a key to its new facility and walk away. This is a great way to learn a lot about a new market, but it is time-consuming, because it limits potential risk (and therefore profit)—after all, it's your client's facility, not yours. But your client will need the facility to adapt to its market, and in building it, your company will be taught the regulations of your industry within that market and the legal requirements of the host nation, and your client will guide you through tailoring your production facility to the needs of the local market. Your client doesn't want you to build a factory that gets shut down for violating code, or one that builds products that consumers in that market don't want, so it will have to teach your company how to meet those requirements. Your client has a vested (and invested) interest in your meeting the demands of the local environment, so you can count on it to teach you a lot about it.

In a turnkey project, the buyer usually comes to you. After assessing its reputation and credit in its national market, you can start building. Your client will help you keep in line with local requirements and regulations, so that's one less thing for you to worry about and one more thing to learn. The important strategic consideration, as is the case with many of the modes of entry, is to ask yourself, *Am I building my own competition?* And it's literal competition in the case of turnkey projects, not just knowledge transfer. If your client wants you to build a factory for widgets in its market, odds are that its market is ready for widgets to be sold there. So why build your client a widget factory when you could build yourself one? You didn't just show it what you knew, you gave it a ready-made production source to do it. If you eventually try to compete against your former client directly, it will have your technology, as well as better knowledge of the local market.

One reason to engage in turnkey work is that perhaps your client is wrong. The benefit of the turnkey project as a foray into international business is that if it fails, it's not your investment that's lost. This is another area where comfort comes into play. Turnkey projects are more comfortable than establishing your own facilities—but they may turn out to be short-sighted decisions. One of the major disadvantages of a turnkey project is that you have no long-term interest in a country in which you have invested considerable effort and money. Although the project may be profitable (assuming you priced it correctly), your return on such things as developing relationships with and inside the country, gaining the knowledge to work in that country, and learning about the nation's supply, labor, and transportation environments is very limited. Such benefits are hard to put on a balance sheet, but they are very real. Unless you can acquire other turnkey projects in the same nation, much of the potential benefit offered by your hard-earned knowledge and experience is lost.

Of course, there are reasons to engage in turnkey projects—not least, because they might be the only way to enter certain markets. Countries that regulate foreign direct investment or that limit foreign ownership of domestic companies—as well as state-owned or state-controlled industries—may not let your company in except through turnkey projects.

In terms of strategy, turnkey projects are similar to exporting, except it's much more difficult to progress to any of the four international business strategies outlined in the previous chapters, unless turnkey projects are your whole business. It's nearly impossible to use turnkey projects as the final step preceding any of the four strategies without some other intermediary step. Perhaps a turnkey project could lead to a partnership or joint venture; but it can be difficult for your company to go from building a factory to stepping into the driver's seat of a global international business strategy.

Licensing/Franchising

Although licensing and franchising are two separate processes, we'll deal with them together because they are fundamentally the same from a strategic viewpoint, simply corresponding to different industries. Licensing is used in situations involving manufactured or engineered products, when a company sells the right to manufacture a product to a foreign company. Franchising grows the face of a business and can be useful in developing a brand on a global scale—but it turns over the control of operations to the individual franchise owners.

The difference between the two, for our conceptual purposes, lies in how differentiation occurs. When a foreign company wants to license a product or technology, it usually intends to use it as you do. When it wants to franchise from you, it typically intends to customize for the local market—McDonalds has wildly different menus in India and Chicago! IBM software licensed to foreign companies, on the other hand, tends to be the same software, just in a different language.

In terms of the comfort level for these modes of entry, the risk is almost completely on your foreign buyer's side, which can make this attractive. But there are two strategic problems. Franchisors make money when more people buy more franchises and succeed. Bad franchisees, however, can seriously diminish the value of your brand in the market in which they fail—and if that market isn't compatible with your franchise's business model, the risk of failure is very real. The risk with licensing products, technology, or processes is simple knowledge transfer. When someone else knows how to do what you do, he or she might find a way to do it better; this is one of the most serious strategic issues in any mode of entry. It's important for the long-term health of your business that you minimize the potential for creating your own competition. Licensing technology, depending on the nature of your industry, might be the most sure-fire way to create competition for your company, within the market of your licensee and elsewhere. So although these two options certainly appear to be comfortable to managers, they both have a serious potential to threaten your business in the long term.

As potential international business strategies, licensing and franchising are both closest to multidomestic strategy. In both cases, a process is controlled in the market where the licensee or franchisee is located, with relatively little control kept in the home office. The licensee is free to do with the products what it will (save for competing directly against your company, because of legal covenants contained in the licensing agreement), and the franchisee is free to customize to the local market in a way that it thinks effective. Both licensing and franchising represent a fundamental tradeoff in any business, and one integral to the multidomestic strategy for international expansion: your company cedes power abroad, and it receives money in return. The strategies of licensing and franchising can be profitable for firms, despite their potential strategic weaknesses, and that's a balance your company will need to find. We'll discuss later in this chapter how licensing can be used as a means of diversifying risk and recovering research and development costs through strategic alliances, an important issue if your company is thinking about licensing technology.

Joint Ventures

If your company is thinking about expanding into a vastly different market from the one you currently operate in, a joint venture might be the best way to gain new experiences and competencies in that market by partnering with a firm that has already been successful in that market. Joint ventures can be a little precarious, but if you find the right partner to complement your company's strengths, then a joint venture can be the perfect move. Establishing a joint venture has many difficulties. In finding a partner, you need to find someone who won't eventually become your own competition, or at least to limit the potential of this risk. Also, your partner will need to be someone whom you feel you can trust: typically a firm of a reputation and size in its national market similar to yours in your own.

Although there are disadvantages to joint ventures, there are nations where joint ventures are the only available mode of entry—Malaysia, for example. To engage in business in Malaysia, you need to join hands with (pay money to) Bhumiputras (the Sons of the Soil). In deciding whether or not to enter Malaysia or a nation with similar requirements, you need clear understandings of what will be involved in the joint venture, whom you will have to pay, and the conditions under which the joint venture will be operated. Your best sources of such information are other U.S. firms that have undertaken a joint venture in the same place—learn from their experiences!

The most important thing to consider in a joint venture is simply, who is getting what? Many joint ventures between U.S. and Japanese companies in the late 1980s and early 1990s actually made U.S. companies less competitive because of the way the deals were structured and the way responsibilities were divided. U.S. companies ended up with the assembly and marketing of products such as consumer electronics, but the component production and actual product design were located in Japan. This meant that U.S. engineers weren't involved in product innovation—or at least not as extensively as they should have been—making U.S. technology firms less competitive when the technologies progressed, and essentially putting the health of their products' futures at the mercy of the Japanese halves of their joint ventures. The assembly and marketing jobs that stayed in the United States were stable, but the product design jobs in Japan were higher-paying and were more crucial to the products' life cycles and the joint ventures' overall futures. Product design is probably the most important part of the joint venture agreement, and your company needs to pay close attention to it in every negotiation.

Another aspect of the joint venture is knowledge transfer. Your partner will have to learn something about your company in order to work with you. But you need to be careful just how much your partner is learning, because if it learns how to make your product, and you don't know how to sell in your partner's market, your partner will lose you as soon as it can. In a joint venture, you and your partner need to need each other in order for the business relationship to continue. If that one condition is met, a joint venture can be very useful for both parties.

In terms of the way that international joint ventures fit into the four potential international business strategies, joint ventures can vary widely. A joint venture may be a nuanced form of international strategy in which each partner sells the fruits of the joint venture in its own national market. It may be part of global strategy if the joint venture is some sort of component production facility that each company draws on for efficiency. And it may be a type of multidomestic strategy, if neither partner exerts too much control over the decisions made by the joint venture's management. The one strategy it cannot be is transnational, because by definition, transnational strategy must involve one entity, not two entities meeting at a common point. Further, many joint ventures, depending on what business functions are performed by the joint venture, can operate so independently from either of the original two parties that the coordination that defines transnational strategy is almost certain to be absent.

Acquisitions

As mentioned previously, acquisition is one of the simplest, quickest, and most common forms of growing international operations. It's easy because a deal can be (and almost always is) negotiated quickly, and acquiring a company means that operations are already in place, which greatly speeds up the time required to get products to the market. We've mentioned earlier that one of the problems in acquisition is that American companies have historically overestimated the amount of value that can be gained from an acquisition, which often translates into overpaying for an acquired foreign company or subsidiary. But apart from this stumbling block, acquisition is still a great way to expand.

The first hurdle in acquisition is finding a healthy target. Finding a company to acquire that is in a position to be bought can be difficult; your first resource is industry contacts in your new market. If your company has any partners or relationships already established within your target market, these can generate potential acquisition targets, or may actually be such targets themselves. If you've been using a foreign firm to distribute your product within a given national market, acquiring that firm may realize additional gains for your company. That would qualify as vertical foreign direct investment and could potentially drastically improve your product's profit margin by removing an extraneous party from your product's life cycle in the market.

Acquisition as a process almost always requires the aid of outside resources—typically management consultants and investment bankers (and lawyers, but what big deal doesn't need a lawyer?). One of the problems that acquiring companies often encounter is that these types of specialists don't normally take into account subjective qualifications of an acquisition, such as organizational fit. Your company and your future French subsidiary may have vastly different cultures and structures and divergent hiring practices and norms, and these types of differences often turn out to be "hidden costs" in acquisitions. This is partially because the experts your company hires to negotiate and evaluate an acquisition are financial experts. They probably will do a great job giving you a company valuation of your acquisition target, because that is what you're paying them for. But therein also lies the complication: you're not paying them to research cultural differences between your company and your target. And these types of outside aids have their own worries, such as potential legal challenges your company might make if the acquisition goes poorly. The normative judgments of organizational fit are harder to defend in court than straight numbers are, so outside talent is likely to confine itself to those safer numbers. Similarly, many times the managers that are involved in acquisition negotiations are above operational level, meaning that they make the deal that other have to make work. This conflict isn't as common as it was fifteen or twenty years ago, but it's an important thing to remember for smaller companies making a first-time acquisition.

Acquisitions have a serious psychological stumbling block to contend with: the sunk-cost fallacy. It takes time and money to evaluate a target and negotiate an acquisition, and the managers involved with it have a vested interest in completing it, whether it's a good idea or not. Once time and money have been invested in the acquisition process, walking away from the deal seems less and less possible to the managers involved. This also drives the speed of acquisitions. Once a target has been acquired, managers involved in the negotiations have to contend with the fact that a competitor may buy the target company out from under them if they do not act quickly enough. Losing a valuable acquisition is personally and professionally damaging, so managers rush to close deals in order to avoid this potentially embarrassing outcome.

Acquisitions, mergers, and green-field operations are the only potential modes of entry that can immediately lead into any of the four international business strategies. Acquisitions tend to be the fastest and the most straightforward, and these two advantages are part of why acquisition is such a popular way for businesses to engage in international operations. It simply depends on what you acquire. An unrelated company that your management thinks has a profitable future may be acquired to hedge against domestic economic turmoil, and that would probably make that particular acquisition a form of multidomestic strategy. Buying a facility that will significantly reduce the cost of goods sold can be part of a global strategy, and so on. The versatility and ease of acquisition make it one of the most rewarding ways to engage in international operations, assuming that the acquisition is a good one and that your company avoids the mistakes we've mentioned.

Green-Field Operations

Perhaps the most difficult option your company has for expanding internationally is the green-field operation. This option requires developing new production facilities and building a foreign subsidiary from scratch. The difficulty of doing this shouldn't keep you from considering it, though. A successful green-field operation means that nobody else is taking a cut of the profit from your new international unit. Typically, companies who employ the use of green-fields do so in two ways: limit size (and thus potential loss), and compete in a market very similar to existing, familiar markets.

The first strategy is intuitive. By creating a small, new operation, your company can learn fast and limit risk merely by limiting the size of the initial investment. This is the way the 3M has typically engaged in international expansion, as we've discussed. A little office that imports your company's product from domestic operations and sells to a new market can learn quickly, because it isn't quite built up yet. Whereas changing the priorities of an acquired company can take time, your new operations don't have any habits to break, and as needs are encountered, you can build your operation to meet them. A caution here, though, is that one of the first things that you must set up in your green-field operations is developing a new human resources management system. This should seem obvious: if your new operation is small and only has two salespeople, they had best be the right two for the job if your new operations are going to be successful. Furthermore, your human resources managers are the people who hire your employees and who hear their concerns about the new enterprise. They are the simplest form of getting feedback about the success of your new venture, and the best way to instill an organizational culture in it.

Canadians aren't Americans, but they still drive Fords. If your company wants to expand into a market that is highly similar to a market in which you are already operating successfully, the potentially painful learning curve for green-field operations is shortened, because your company has already gained some of the requisite experience. This is the case for a lot of recent expansion in South America, where each national market is unique but where cultural climate is often similar from one country to the next. A green-field operation is less risky if your company doesn't have as much to learn before it can start moving products and production.

How can green-field operations fit into the international business strategies? You can build them into any of the four, just as you can with acquisitions. The strategic benefit of green-field operations, however, is that green-field operations are much easier to fit into a transnational strategy. Whereas an acquired company needs to build integrating structures and controls, a green-field operation can be designed to have them from day one; since operations are new, adaptation, not trying to change the existing culture of an acquisition, can come easily. This relatively easy method for transforming into a transnational strategy is simply another benefit balancing the somewhat higher investment of time and money required by green-field operations.

Mergers

Mergers tend to be messy: that's the simplest way of explaining it. A merger between companies requires extensive negotiations, a lot of tradeoffs, and, in some cases, near-impossible integration of operations. Different accounting standards in the United States and abroad can by themselves make the process difficult. The United States uses Generally Accepted Accounting Principles (GAAP), but many other countries employ International Financial Reporting Standards (IFRS). The nuanced differences between these two accounting systems, which we'll revisit in later chapters, can mean that one merged company from two corporations originally located in two different countries can result in highly discrepant valuation. Stock prices of the merged company in the different national markets will likely reflect this—an awkward position for a company to be in with its shareholders.

One of the most complicated aspects of mergers in general is the valuation of "goodwill"—in essence, how much is the name of each company worth? This was a major disaster in the merger of AOL and Time Warner, and that was between two companies in one national market. Imagine trying to evaluate goodwill in a completely different national market where your company may have little experience. Certainly the brand name of your merging partner or its company reputation is worth something, but it can be extremely difficult to tell exactly what. What's more, what will its reputation be worth in your national market?

These complications aside, companies do merge, and from a strategic standpoint, merging has some merit, even if it can be plagued with organizational difficulties. Mergers are similar to joint ventures but remove the potential for creating competition. In fact, mergers often combine a company with what was previously its competition, meaning that there can be strong strategic gains in merging toward consolidation in an industry. The relevant question with joint ventures was, *Who is getting what?* but with mergers, the question is, *What does each party bring to the table?* Mergers that combine market access, consolidate production, share technology, or generally involve two companies with complimentary core competencies can be both desirable and effective.

One final caution about mergers in the international business environment: think back to our discussion on culture in Chapter Two. Different cultures are bound to have communication, and a successful merger requires either a similarity in culture from the outset, a great deal of cross-cultural literacy, or significant amounts of time and money expended in working toward integration. A truly successful merger will likely need at least two of the three.

Mergers can fit into any of the four international business strategies, but if properly orchestrated (and, typically, after some period of adjustment), they can lead to a successful transnational strategy. In fact, many mergers between international firms are designed to do exactly that.

MARKET ANALYSIS IN AN INTERNATIONAL CONTEXT

Choosing the right mode of entry, and finding whatever other parties are necessary for that mode of entry, entails knowing the strengths of your company, the nature of your industry, and the strategy behind each method. But in addition to choosing how to enter and how to organize your company for strategic purposes, you must also find out which markets and industries to enter. Beyond how your company is going to make money when engaging in international operations, you need to plan where your company will make money.

There are numerous models for market analysis, the most prevalent of which is Porter's Five Forces Model for industry attractiveness. The model's dimensions are the bargaining power of buyers, the bargaining power of suppliers, the barriers to entry, the threats of substitutes, and rivalries. We'll discuss this model in brief and then begin using it to examine modes of entry and foreign markets. Many people are, or at one point were, familiar with this model, but we'll be using it a little out of the norm when we examine how attractive a particular market is for a given business.

The bargaining powers of buyers and suppliers have basically the same dimensions. When looking at entering a market (the model was originally designed for industry analysis, but it is still effective on the market scale), the bargaining powers of buyers and suppliers have many factors that define them. The degree of consolidation of buyers and suppliers is one of the simplest measures. When entering a foreign market, this is important, because depending on what companies have entered the market, it may be a very different industry landscape than the one your company is already used to. A highly competitive and very concentrated domestic market can be a great reason to enter a foreign market that has fewer competitors. One of the other parts of bargaining power is expendability. How easy would it be for your suppliers to sell to your customers, or for your buyers to make your product themselves? If your company is expendable in the value chain of a particular market, then that market probably isn't very attractive for your company. This is important in the international business environment, especially as it relates to knowledge transfer. If your company knows how to do something that buyers in a foreign market can't do or aren't willing to learn how to do, it decreases their bargaining power in relation to yours, which can make the market more profitable and more attractive.

Barriers to entry are the technological, capital, or legal requirements that prevent companies from entering an industry. These are especially important in international business. Capital and technology flow more freely today than they ever have before, and it appears that the trend will continue. But other legal requirements can prevent your business from expanding into a foreign market, or can protect it in a market you've already entered. Many countries still have various restrictions on foreign ownership (such as specifying a maximum percentage of a domestic venture that a foreign entity can hold). Conceptually, this is the way that barriers to entry always work. The barrier exists for your company too, but once you get to the other side, the barrier prevents competition to the same degree that it prevented you. The harder for your business to get in, the easier it will be for you to keep other businesses out.

The threat of substitutes is perhaps the most basic part of Porter's model. If your product is interchangeable with another product, and that substitute is easy to acquire (inexpensive, little difference in performance, strategically viable), then buyers will buy the substitute instead of your product. This is one area where your market research is important. What are potential buyers already using to satisfy whatever need your product satisfies? Will buyers be motivated to switch to your product? At what cost will they consider doing so? This thinking even applies if no direct substitute seems to exist within the market. Substitutes can rush in to a market as a response to your company's market entry, so remember in your analysis that the force is called "the threat of substitutes" not "the presence of substitutes." Your analysis will need to include substitutes that could *potentially* weaken your position.

Rivalry is the most difficult aspect of the Five Forces model to explain. It's the level of competition in an industry and market. This may sound straightforward, but it can be difficult to measure, and harder still to predict. A market with high rivalry tends to be less profitable, for it is defined by a high number of competing firms, aggressive pricing, and product differentiation, and it can be the result of high fixed costs (which often act as a barrier to market exit) or of low market growth. Rivalry often occurs when there is not yet an industry leader. The important thing to think about when examining rivalry in the context of international business is that if an industry within a particular national market is characterized by a high degree of rivalry, your entry isn't likely to decrease the level of rivalry in the industry. Environments with high levels of rivalry can lead to destructive competitive practices within an industry, and it's best to avoid them when possible.

Each of these five forces is important in analysis, but now let's connect the Five Forces Model back to the modes of entry. It will almost never be the case that you find a market with weak buyers and suppliers, no viable substitutes, passive competition, and high barriers to entry, unless you're buying a salt monopoly in the sixteenth century. Realistically, most markets you look at will have points in their favor and points in opposition. This affects the proper mode of entry and the associated international strategy that we've previously discussed. We'll discuss this in some detail to help you understand how strategy, mode of entry, and market analysis all interact in the life and health of your company's international operations.

Suppose you find a particular national market for your product (a highly specialized piece of equipment requiring a very expensive production facility) that has few potential competitors but also few potential customers. The raw materials for the product are relatively cheap and basic, with many potential supply lines, and with little cost for switching from one supplier to another. Do you enter the market? If so, how, and with what strategy?

The product is highly specialized, which tends to imply that there are few substitutes; if it takes time to learn how to make it, there also seems to be a knowledge-based barrier to entry. Production facilities are expensive, and they are specialized. So the investment necessary to start production or to customize an existing production facility to make this product is high, and that means that the barriers to entry are very difficult to pass. In this example, the bargaining power of the suppliers is low (cheap, and many sources), but bargaining power of buyers is high (few potential buyers). Rivalry is assumed to be low because there are few potential competitors. So this market is fairly attractive (the barriers to entry and high bargaining power of buyers are the worries, but the other forces are in favor of entering the market). Now, how do you enter?

In this example, acquisition of a would-be buyer seems the best. Of course, this would require additional analysis (the example is arbitrary, after all). But consider the situation: it's very difficult for someone else to enter your industry in the market because of the barriers to entry and the low threat of substitutes, and you have more bargaining power than your suppliers do. By acquiring a company in that market to distribute your product, you can integrate more parts of the value chain into your company, and the potential buyer you acquire will be more competitive in its industry and market—especially if you only sell to yourself! In this case, your firm would be pursuing an international strategy, buying a distribution channel in a market and producing the product elsewhere with little need for customization (because there aren't many viable substitutes).

Each mode of entry corresponds to a strategy, and to conditions in the Five Forces Model. Mergers and joint ventures are attractive in industries with high levels of rivalry, because those markets have low concentration, allowing combining to give your company an edge in a field with many competitors.

Green-field operations are attractive when barriers to entry are low, because if it's easy and cheap to set up new operations, it becomes a more viable option to start from scratch than to seek out an acquisition. If the bargaining power of buyers is high because of high concentration, then exporting can be the best mode of entry; your company can probably be replaced easily, so investing in production facilities in that market is dangerous (your product's health depends on keeping one or two large clients in that market).

In addition to tying mode of entry to general international strategy, remember to also make sure that it fits the conditions of your industry and of the national markets you're considering entering. The whole process needs to be integrated in order for your company to be successful in international operations.

SCALE AND TIMING OF ENTRY

Two additional conditions affect your company's entry into the international business environment: timing and scale of entry. Apart from deciding the *how* (mode of entry), *why* (strategy), and *where* (market analysis) of international expansion (all of which are interrelated), you must decide *when* and *how much*.

Scale of entry is a very important consideration, regardless of what mode of entry your company chooses. If you're going to export, you'll have to decide how much of your company's resources you will commit to finding buyers abroad, to hiring export professionals, and so on. The question of how hard to push is a big one in any aspect of business. You'll have to decide how to balance the potential risks and rewards of international expansion, deciding what level of commitment to make from there. Many businesses going abroad follow a gradual pattern of escalation in their international operations, starting with a small initial investment or a single client abroad and then expanding operations after initial success. This is an important consideration in international expansion for first-timers. A mistake on your first try (a bad exchange rate, a bad client, troubles with customs, and so forth) shouldn't stop you from engaging in international operations. Don't let a one-time mistake stop your business from expanding globally. The problem is learning to tell the difference between a one-time mistake and a market that is fundamentally bad.

More than once in this book, we've used the example of 3M's international strategy of setting up small-scale, green-field operations selling limited product lines in new markets. This mode of entry has historically worked very well for it in its international expansion. The initial scale of its entry was never very large, especially when compared with the entire scope of its operations. But 3M never shied away from increasing its investment once its initial operations met certain revenue and growth milestones, decided in advance for each new market. Rather than making these expanded investments when it felt like it, 3M set levels in advance that would signify that the time to expand had come, which leads us into the timing of international expansion.

Timing of entry and timing of expansion from entry level are very important in the international business environment. One of the mistakes that some American managers have made in recent years has been turning to international expansion to save a dying small to mid-sized company. Although there have been some success stories, international expansion shouldn't be your company's last hope. The challenges it presents can seriously hurt your company if you haven't planned properly ahead of time. The most important consideration when considering the timing of your company's international expansion is simply, *When is the market ready?* If you see a growing market that your product or services will sell well in, and if you have the experience and capital to invest in that market and build up operations to capture profit, then it is time to expand. Historically, the companies that have performed best in new international operations have been the ones who have done it before. Expanding internationally should be done as soon as the market can accommodate such growth, not when your company is desperate or when such expansion feels "comfortable." The general principle of timing is that although you might trip yourself up your first time out, it's the only way to learn how to play. The ultimate value of the experience your business gains from going global in a world increasingly characterized by global markets almost always means that you gain something from international expansions, so long as you plan and learn from your previous mistakes.

STRATEGIC ALLIANCES AS A GENERAL STRATEGY

By 2002, IBM had formed over five hundred different strategic alliances of various degrees of complexity. These alliances have since propelled IBM into the 21st century in industries in which high research and development costs and rapid innovation and technological obsolescence can be crippling. IBM has partnered with direct and indirect competitors in a wide range of initiatives for a number of reasons and has employed various modes of entry in order to expand its customer base on a global scale. This strategy is very complex and very difficult and is one of the best ways to remain competitive in a number of industries in today's rapidly changing and growing global economy.

Strategic alliances can employ any or all of the modes of entry previously outlined and can apply in nearly any industry or market. Forming a strategic alliance can mean creating joint ventures; licensing technology; distributing ownership through green-field operations, acquisitions, or mergers; and exporting products to a foreign distribution network.

In order to form a good alliance, the parties involved (not necessarily just two companies) must need each other, and must gain something from the partnership. Merck, Fujisawa, and Bayer all actively license each other's products in the pharmaceutical industry. Why? Because the costs of research and development, and the time and expense of getting new pharmaceuticals through regulations, are all immense. In order to make feasible the innovations the industry needs, each of these three companies licenses to the other two, who then distribute the new drugs within their respective markets. Merck drugs are licensed to Fujisawa for marketing and distribution in Japan, and the same goes for Bayer's drugs in Europe. In this case, the strategic alliance takes the form of licensing as a mode of entry, but there is a much larger coordination of purpose and a higher degree of cooperation at play here.

In technology-based industries, strategic alliances have a very significant role in shaping the industry in the long run. Strategic alliances that share technology help to create broader standards of technology on a global scale, which then allows technology firms in these strategic alliances a more level playing field with lower switching costs (decreasing the barriers to entry by making industry standards more comprehensive).

Perhaps most important for you and your company is that strategic alliances are not just for the IBMs and Mercks of the world. Many strategic alliances take place between large corporations and small, innovative businesses. A lot of high-tech startups use strategic alliances to bring their new technology into the marketplace through a large company's distribution network. In this case, the strategic alliance vastly improves the small company's credibility and legitimacy, making it easier for it to invest in further development and expand sales. The large firm tends to get exclusive rights to an emerging technology, which helps it expand its market share and keep ahead of its competition. For a lot of startup investors, such as venture capitalists, a strategic alliance with a larger company is the first step toward selling the startup, and a major payday. And such alliances have paid off. Nissan and Renault, for example, built a strategic alliance in order to compete in world markets.

Of course, strategic alliances have very serious potential risks. In our discussion earlier of joint ventures, we mentioned how certain distributions of responsibilities in U.S.-Japanese joint ventures made American companies less competitive. One of the major problems with strategic alliances of any kind is that one party may become overly dependent on the other (or others). This threat leads to the loss of skills. If your product development is being done by your ally, your engineers lose some of their skills, and you lose some of your engineers (or you at least stop hiring new ones). This dependence means losing old competencies and personnel, a phenomenon typically called "hollowing out."

Furthermore, many strategic alliances face high costs of coordination in integrating mechanisms. In the previous chapter about strategy and elsewhere, we have talked about how hard it is to cross cultural barriers with subsidiaries. If it's difficult for your headquarters to integrate a newly acquired foreign subsidiary, imagine how much more difficult it would be if the foreign subsidiary were owned by one of your direct competitors. Competitive corporations that enter into strategic alliances are concerned both about giving too much away to their partner and about getting too little from them, and this fundamental mistrust can lead to fruitless alliances.

Inflexibility is another concern in strategic alliances and cooperative agreements in general. Most of these agreements have protective measures in them, and even a "balanced" agreement will likely be thrown out of balance by changes in the industry, environment, or either partner. General Electric's strategic alliances with Japanese companies almost always included covenants prescribing where in Japan GE could sell its products and how fast it could bring them in. This constrained GE's potential expansion.

But the most important factor in creating a successful strategic alliance is a complementary partner. More important than timing, scale, industry, market, or overall strategy is finding a partner with whom you work well. Many strategic alliances, such as IBM's, revolve around projects that don't represent a significant portion of overall operations, which means that the self-interest of each partner shouldn't lead to potentially destructive direct conflict. Many strategic alliances create a situation referred to as "co-opetition," where two direct competitors in a single industry cooperate for the purposes of the strategic alliance. This balance is easily broken and can quickly dissolve into simple competition, which can hurt both parties.

One of the newer developments in international business is the creation of large, conglomerate strategic alliances between a great portion of industry powers. Sematech is a strategic alliance between a number of producers in the semiconductor industry, many of whom are direct competitors. These industry-spanning alliances help to share knowledge and standardize products in a state of co-opetition. This development is integral to staying competitive in some of today's rapidly expanding and innovative industries. Such alliances are a sign that in the face of uncertainty, and rapid change, banding together may be the only way for businesses to survive.

THE FOREIGN CORRUPT PRACTICES ACT

In many countries, bribery and corruption are prevalent, if not downright rampant. U.S. companies often have to compete with foreign domestic firms who are participants in such corruption. Regardless of the mode of entry your company chooses in international expansion, your company will have to deal with foreign officials in one capacity or another, and in cultures where bribery is prevalent, you'll have to decide how to act. Apart from ethical considerations, the Foreign Corrupt Practices Act governs the legality of such conduct. Under the act, U.S. businesses cannot offer bribes that direct business to anyone. This includes bribes seeking awards of government contracts to particular companies and bribes seeking to handicap competition within the market. The act does allow for facilitation, or "grease" payments, typically small bribes to a mid- to low-level ministerial or clerical officials to hasten the performance of their duties. In a culture where such practices are common (as in the case with many African nations), a small bribe to a customs employee to ensure that your company's goods make it through customs in a timely fashion might qualify as a permitted "grease" payment. Of course, this type of payment, even if protected under the Foreign Corrupt Practices Act, may be illegal under the laws of the country in which you are operating. As a general rule, bribery does not pay, and many companies find it much more advantageous to avoid highly corrupt nations than to risk jeopardizing a corporate image with a bribery scandal.

STRATEGIC SUMMARY

This section has introduced various strategies for taking your business global. We've covered particular modes of entry into foreign markets and the overarching strategies of cost- and differentiation-based competition around the globe, all important considerations and alternatives for your business to consider when expanding internationally. We've talked about the general environment of international business, about cultural gaps, about international finance, and about international business strategy. The next four chapters will look specifically at various issues in international business, but at this point, you've learned the importance of planning in international expansion, what problems to be aware of and how to navigate them, and how to match your company's strategy to your company's strengths, its industry, and its market.

KEY POINTS TO REMEMBER

- Your modes of entry into international business will depend on what you want to do and how you want to do it. Exportation and importation is a common first step. Turnkey projects move from exporting products to exporting your company's expertise. Licensing takes international partners on board to sell your products, and joint ventures take international partners on board to promote your combined products and expertise. Acquisition takes the joint venture a step further by incorporating a business partner as a permanent part of your company. Green-field operation creates new extensions of your company in other countries, and merger goes one up on acquisition by creating a brand new entity out of formerly separate companies.

- Deciding which mode of entry requires astute analysis of your target market that evaluates the bargaining powers of its buyers and suppliers, its barriers to entry, and its level of rivalry, including threats of substitute products.

- Because entry into a new market brings with it many chances for failure, making small bets at first can pay off later in improved market understanding. The potential of a market lies in its actual performance, not in analyses conducted of it. Try out a few products in small ways, building your presence gradually until the market has confirmed its present and future profitability for your company.

PART

IV

TRANSACTIONS, SUPPLY CHAINS, HUMAN RESOURCES, AND PROFITS

Communications and Paperwork

Is your business ready to expand beyond domestic borders by considering international markets and manufacturers? Building an import-export business in the United States, if done with the appropriate amount of information and foresight, can capitalize on some of the billions of dollars in goods that are imported and exported in American business. Although many large corporations are heavily involved in importing and exporting, small and middle-sized businesses are increasingly joining the ranks of international traders as well. In the age of globalization and the Internet, international trade is becoming more democratized and streamlined. Through international trade, businesses are expanding their consumer bases while remaining competitive in domestic markets. However, successful trade businesses do not happen by luck or by accident. Whether exporting or importing or both, companies need to understand the many factors and procedures involved in international trade in order to capitalize on the benefits of the international market.

This chapter briefly outlines the basics of international trade in exporting and importing goods and services, giving overviews of international trade transactions, financial paperwork and support resources for import-export programs, basic procedures for importing and exporting, and sources of assistance for first-time and established import-export businesses in the United States.

TYPICAL INTERNATIONAL TRADE TRANSACTIONS

Before discussing the resources available for import-export businesses and the procedural details of running one, let's start with a general overview of international trade transactions. International trade transactions are complex processes involving many elements that include buyers, suppliers, regulations, financial institutions, and, perhaps more than anything else, paperwork. To a new importer or exporter, this process may seem overwhelming, but if importing and exporting are properly understood and executed, both exporter and importer stand to benefit from increased access to markets and goods from other parts of the world.

The process of an international trade transaction can be initiated by an importer, someone looking for materials or products who places an order with an exporting company. Trade transactions can also be initiated by exporters after they have conducted thorough analyses to ascertain the potential benefits and risks of a target market. Based on market analysis findings, an exporter will develop a marketing plan and, with that plan clearly in place, will move on to negotiations with a foreign buyer. Sometimes trades are initiated by third parties (usually representing either the exporter or the importer) who act as "scouts" seeking out new products or markets on behalf of businesses.

The typical trade transaction process engages four primary parties: the exporter, the exporter's financial institution (usually a bank), the importer (buyer), and the importer's bank. Secondary parties, such as independent carriers responsible for the delivery of traded goods, are typically involved in international trade. Although the configuration of a trade transaction can vary greatly depending on the financial arrangements of the involved traders, a typical international trade transaction follows several basic steps. Here's an example:

- An American company wants to expand its business and export its products abroad. Subsequent to comparative analyses of several market options, the company contacts a potential buyer in Germany.

- The German company, looking to diversify its product offerings, is interested and orders some of the American company's products. The two companies agree to a letter of credit transaction, and the specifics of prices, shipment, timing, and so on, are negotiated. The German company applies for a letter of credit at Deutsche Bank.

- Deutsche Bank approves the German company's application and sends the letter of credit to the Bank of America, where the American exporter does its business. As the advising bank, the Bank of America reviews the letter and notifies the American exporter that the letter was received and can be opened.

- The goods are shipped from the United States to Germany on an independent ocean freighter. The ocean freighter provides the American company with a bill of lading.

- Following the conditions of the letter of credit, the American company provides the appropriate documents to the Bank of America: a bill of lading and a time draft. The American company turns over the ownership of the exported goods to the Bank of America.

- The Bank of America sends the documents to Deutsche Bank, which accepts the documents and agrees to pay for the goods within 120 days, as indicated on the American company's draft.

- The Bank of America buys the time draft from the American company immediately, so that it will not have to wait four months to receive payment for its exported goods. Meanwhile, Deutsche Bank notifies the German company that payment is due within 120 days.

- After 120 days, the German company has paid Deutsche Bank for the goods; in turn, Deutsche Bank pays off the draft at the Bank of America.

Even in this simplified scenario, there were many different steps and involved parties, but there were also a significant number of documents creating a paper trail for the financial transactions performed.

PAPERWORK FOR IMPORT AND EXPORT FINANCING

In each phase of an import-export transaction, financial documentation is necessary to provide the appropriate legal and communicative links among all parties needed to maintain the flow of goods and payments. Although much of this paperwork is now electronic and streamlined, it is still important to understand the purposes and procedures of documentation in international trade. In this section, we will outline three essential forms of financial paperwork used on import-export transactions.

Letters of Credit

Letters of credit (called LCs, for short) often play a crucial role in international trade transactions. LCs, which are usually issued by banks, transfer the responsibility of payment from the buyer to the financial institution; this shift of obligation allows buyers the flexibility they require in paying for imported goods, and it guarantees exporters faster payment for goods sent. Although there are many contexts in which LCs are used, international trade transactions rely on commercial documentary letters of credit.

Once an importer has applied for a commercial documentary letter of credit at an *opening bank* (such as Deutsche Bank in the scenario above), the bank writes a letter of credit on behalf of the importer. The LCs are usually sent to the exporter's bank, known as the *advising bank*, which then notifies the exporter that once the necessary documentation has been provided, the exporter will receive payment. Depending upon the requirements stipulated by the LC, the paying bank can either be the advising bank, in which case the payment will be received quickly, or the opening bank—which may cause a slight delay in receipt of payment. Once the payment has been made to the exporter by the advising bank, the importer is responsible for paying the debt to the opening bank.

Because international trade transactions use commercial *documentary* letters of credit, it is crucial that the exporter follow the stipulations of the LC and be able to furnish documentary evidence of having done so. Typically, these stipulations involve conditions, types, and quantities of products; shipping methods; and shipping dates—all of which must be met and produced to the advising bank with appropriate documentation *before* the exporter can receive payment. To avoid unnecessary delays in payment, it is crucial that the exporter verify the stipulations of the LC, making sure that there are no discrepancies between the importer's requests and the exporter's ability to meet those requests in the manner described by the LC. In addition to being documentary LCs, most international trade LCs are *irrevocable*: once an exporter has been notified of the LC and it has been opened, the importer cannot cancel or change the conditions of the LC without the exporter's permission.

Drafts

Unlike letters of credit, documentary drafts for collection (also called *bills of exchange*) do not involve the presentation of specified documentation before payment is submitted. Instead, the exporter's bank "drafts," or writes, a collection request that states the amount and due date of payment and sends it to the opening bank, who then collects payment from the importer.

There are two primary types of drafts that specify the conditions of payment. *Sight drafts* are drafts that, once accepted and signed by the importer, must be paid immediately—in other words, upon sight of the draft. A *time draft*, on the other hand, allows for a specified delay between receipt of the draft and submission of payment, usually an increment of 30 days.

Bills of Lading

The agreement between the exporter and carrier, which documents payment agreements between the importer and the exporter or between their respective financial institutions, must also be documented. Bills of lading (B/L) serve as the shipping contract issued by the carrier as a receipt that goods have been received by the carrier and, in most cases, as identification of the owner(s) of goods being shipped.

In their function as certificates of ownership, bills of lading are arranged in two basic ways: *straight* or *to order*. Straight B/Ls specify the name(s) of the recipients—i.e., the importers or the opening bank; only the named parties may accept the goods upon their arrival. "To order" B/Ls are more flexible; the language of to order B/Ls allows for the goods to be transferred upon arrival to another recipient. For instance, in the scenario above, Deutsche Bank could be named as the original owner but could then endorse ownership of the goods to the German company once the company signs a promissory note agreeing to pay for the goods within 120 days. Typically, goods that have not been paid for in advance, such as transactions involving letters of credit, are shipped under to order B/Ls.

SOURCES OF FINANCIAL SUPPORT FOR EXPORTING

Because international trades usually require large payments or long-term carrying costs, and because of the inherent credit risk in international trading, the financial institutions of the exporting and importing parties are a consistent part of any trade transaction. Exporters who allow importers to buy on credit rather than by paying in advance need working capital in order to ship their goods before importing companies pay for them. This capital comes either from export company funds or from commercial bank loans. These loans can come from private banks or from government agencies.

Although export credit is common, international trade—as with any business venture—is not without its inherent risks. Faced with the possibility that importers might fail to pay for goods received, particularly in instances when letters of credit were not issued, exporters will purchase export credit insurance policies. This insurance protects not only from commercial liability, but from political liability as well. For instance, if an exporter arranges a trade agreement with a buyer in a politically volatile country, and that country suddenly experiences political upheaval, such as war, trade might be interrupted and the buyer forced to default on payment to the exporter; or the shipping of goods could be intercepted and lost, or destroyed. In such an event, an exporter's credit insurance will cover a percentage of the losses.

There are several agencies that provide financial support through credit loans and insurance to exporters in the United States. Below are several common examples of government-supported agencies; keep in mind, however, that some institutions in the private sector are also able to offer export credit and insurance.

United States Export Import Bank

The U.S. Export Import Bank, also known as Ex-Im Bank, was established in 1934 by President Franklin D. Roosevelt and became an independent agency in 1945. The bank provides loans, guarantees, and insurance to exporters. As part of its official congressional charter, Ex-Im Bank does not compete with private sector institutions that can also provide export financial support but does provide support in credit risk situations that would otherwise prevent the export of U.S. goods, including matching the financing of foreign countries, which allows exporters to remain competitive in foreign markets. Ex-Im Bank assists both large and small companies. Information on its programs and application materials can be found at www.exim.gov or at one of its seven regional branches.

Small Business Administration

The Small Business Administration (SBA) provides loans for working capital and international trade guarantee programs. Also an agent of the federal government, the SBA was established in 1953 to encourage the establishment and development of small U.S. businesses. Included in its programs is the SBA International Trade Loan program, which grants loans through participating SBA lenders (see http://www.sba.gov/smallbusinessplanner/plan/getready/SERV_INTLLOAN.html for details). Visit its Web site at www.sba.gov for up-to-date information on programs available through the SBA.

Foreign Credit Insurance Association

A third federal government agency, the Foreign Credit Insurance Association (FCIA), provides export credit insurance. Established in 1961, the FCIA is an association of insurance companies sponsored by Ex-Im Bank. Although Ex-Im Bank itself provides coverage for political risk, the FCIA provides exporters with insurance policies against commercial risk. Currently, the Great American Insurance Company serves as the insurer for all of the FCIA's policies. To learn more about the FCIA, see www.fcia.gov.

EXPORT STRATEGIES

First-time exporters should carefully consider a strategy before initiating export transactions. In this section, we will suggest issues and concerns to consider while developing a strategy for initiating the export of goods and/or services. Although for the purposes of this text we do not offer an exhaustive strategic approach, we have gathered some essential elements of strategic planning for exporting.

Consider Hiring an Export Management Company

A company that does not have an in-house export department may contract the business of exporting out to an export management company. EMCs specialize both in assisting companies in establishing export operations and in serving as either temporary or permanent export departments for manufacturing firms. EMCs may work on a commission basis, earning payment from manufacturers based on the amount of sales in a foreign market, or they may buy the manufacturers' products outright, offering them for resale internationally. Typically, an EMC works with more than one firm at a time (so long as the EMC's clients are not competitors and will not present a conflict of interest); many EMCs specialize in a particular industry, a particular region of the globe, or both.

From a manufacturer's perspective, the decision to employ an EMC must be carefully weighed. An EMC is often better prepared to identify international markets and sell to them, to be aware of potential problems in certain markets, and to be knowledgeable about potential global contacts and partnerships for marketing particular products. However, potential exporters should note that because of the wide variety of EMCs, a decision to choose a particular company cannot be taken lightly. Beginner exporters should compare many EMCs to be sure that an EMC will be able to market a particular product to an appropriate location. For example, many EMCs do not market to Canada, so companies hoping to take advantage of Canadian markets may need to do some additional searching for an EMC.

Finding EMCs may be somewhat difficult; there is currently no central governing body or association of such companies. The Federation of International Trade Associations (FITA) is currently registering EMCs on its Web site at www.fita.org, but because not all companies may be registered with FITA, potential exporters should consider seeking out EMCs through other avenues as well, such as through publications within a particular industry and through a U.S. Department of Commerce Export Assistance Center.

Find a Niche in the International Market

Although it may be tempting to try to distribute products widely in order to maximize profit opportunities, it is often best for export programs to limit their initial ventures in order to take the time to better understand the market, to develop appropriate relationships, and to maximize future profits as an export program develops. After analyzing market analysis, exporters should select a single market—or a very few markets—to serve as the initial "pilot" for exported products. The export of goods to any such focus markets should take place on only a limited basis. Trying to market too much product in too many places not only creates sudden burdens on resources, but it also prevents an export company from gathering important information about an international market that can help guide for adjustments, leading to improved business in the future. Selling a limited product in a narrow market at first may lead to a better understanding of the local industry and consumer base, which may provide recommendations for product labeling adjustments or other locally inspired customizations that contribute to increased product sales and/or profit margins.

Spend Time Building Local Relationships

In addition to limiting initial export markets, any company exporting to a new location should devote substantial time to local networking. Not only does networking build foreign relationships, it also improves understanding of the local market (and thus of the best means for entering that market). This strategy also allows for the localization of company representation. Exporters should consider hiring local employees to market exported products. Local residents are more familiar with an area's language, customs, and consumer patterns. Indeed, such local expertise can bring with it large potential benefits for an export business. Similarly, developing substantial networks within a local market may reveal opportunities to save on transportation and manufacturing costs through local manufacture of exported goods.

Hire Help

Even if a company decides not to hire an export management company, emerging export programs need time and dedicated attention if they are to be successful. One of the worst decisions a company can make is to expect current employees to balance the work of exporting in addition to performing their domestic responsibilities. Hire (or appoint) employees to devote their full time and attention to researching markets and tracking export business, and be sure that upper management is fully involved in the exporting program.

Beware of Legal Uncertainty— and Protect against It

International trade transactions always involve certain legal uncertainties. As we've discussed, purchasing export credit insurance is a good way to protect against commercial and political risks in international trade. Also consult with EMCs or other export assistance resources to become familiar with the laws regarding your product type to avoid potential disasters of products failing to meet the legal restrictions of a foreign market.

When Appropriate, Consider Countertrade

Occasionally, exporters do business in developing countries that cannot, at that time, support currency convertibility. In other words, some countries cannot support the exchange of foreign currency or have some restrictions on converting currency. When nonconvertibility policies exist, exporters may have trouble arranging for payment of goods. In these instances, a countertrade may be negotiated to cover the cost of traded goods. Although the definitions and conditions of countertrades vary from case to case, they are basically bartered exchanges of one business's needs for another's—a reciprocal trade of goods and services. Countertrades can be negotiated in several ways; often, exporting programs involve a combination of countertrade types.

BARTERING

The most basic, though not the most common, form of countertrade is *bartering*, which involves the direct swapping of goods (or services) between two negotiators.

COUNTERPURCHASE

A *counterpurchase* trade entails a mutual trade of purchasing rights; for instance, a company from the United States will agree to purchase products from a foreign company, and instead of receiving cash payments, the foreign company will grant the U.S. company exclusive rights or discounted rates to its own products or services.

OFFSET TRADING

Much like counterpurchasing, *offset* trading offers exporters greater flexibility—an exporter must purchase a certain percentage of product materials or production elements within the importer's own country, stimulating the importer's local economy even as the exporter enjoys the advantages of being able to determine which goods or services to purchase in exchange for export sales.

SWITCH TRADING

Typically following on the heels of a counterpurchase, *switch* trading involves using a third-party clearinghouse to aid sales of surplus products (known as "counterpurchase credits") obtained through counterpurchase agreements.

COMPENSATION

Also known as *buybacks*, *compensation* trades occur in cases when a company contracts to supply the equipment (sometimes an entire manufacturing site) needed for production in a foreign country; that country can compensate the equipment-providing company or nation by offering free access to the products being produced. For instance, a U.S. company may agree to build an agricultural equipment manufacturing plant in a developing country; in exchange, the country can agree to give free agricultural machines produced by the plant to the U.S. company for a specified number of years, or until the debt is paid off.

Develop an Export Marketing Plan

Developing marketing plans takes time and resources, but if done thoroughly, this can help stave off potential pitfalls and identify opportunities for development. An export marketing plan should include specific details about the targeted market, about how the market's needs could be addressed by the export program, and about what resources (financial, material, informational, personnel-based, etc.) are necessary for the export marketing plan to work successfully. Essentially, an export marketing plan needs to include the "marketing mix": product, promotion, pricing, and placement (or distribution) decisions for the export program. The plan not only serves as a guide for what should happen and when, it also serves as a common point for all involved parties in the export program, so that everyone participating in the export process shares the same practices and expectations.

Export marketing plans should be brief but clear and should be in line with the exporting company's existing missions and overall goals. Although an export marketing plan needs to be concise, it also needs to cover a range of valuable information that provides a chronological map of the export marketing process. Below is a list of general issues to include in an export marketing plan; each item should be carefully researched and detailed with concrete support and logical rationales, but the plan should also be flexible enough to allow for necessary adjustments according to changes in the market, availability of resources, and so on.

- Company background: mission, goals, current resources
- Projected benefits and risks of export program
- Market research results: customer profiles, current demand, competitors
- Rationale for product and market choice
- Marketing, financial, and organizational goals
- Resources necessary for reaching marketing, financial, and organizational goals, including the plan for pricing exported products
- Agenda for making the marketing plan operational

Clearly, a large amount of preparation is necessary before entering into import-export transactions. From early screenings of potential markets to initiating a final marketing plan, willingness to invest time and resources, coupled with the flexibility needed to conform to the needs of particular markets, can increase the possibilities of a successful export business. Of course, once an export plan has been developed, it must be put into practice.

EXPORT PROCEDURES

In addition to the financial transactions, the physical procedures of transporting goods from one country to another also require careful planning and coordination. Transportation service is a major variable in export transactions; goods need to arrive on time and in good condition—important factors that are often left in the control of an independent carrier. Although understanding export procedures helps reduce the risks involved in shipping products internationally, even experienced export companies need advisory support. This section briefly discusses some standard procedures of exporting, but it also expects that first-time (or veteran) exporters will seek out additional advice on export procedures. Because every international trade transaction occurs in a unique set of circumstances, taking advantage of export assistance to help tailor procedures to a particular exporter's needs is a wise course of action.

Foreign Freight Forwarders

Choosing an appropriate transportation service can make the difference between a successful export transaction and a financial disaster. To aid export companies in this process, foreign freight forwarders have been established as independent agencies to handle such export shipping logistics as documentation and booking with shippers. Freight forwarders are able to assist exporters with shipping in various ways, some of which are outlined below.

Shipping Methods

International transportation entails several options for shipment, each with its own set of logistics and procedures.

AIRMAIL

For international mail order business transactions, airmail is one mode of shipment worth considering. The U.S. Postal Service has a schedule of rates that vary depending on the shipment speed, the weight (and sometimes shape) of the item being shipped, and, in some cases, the distance the item will need to be transported. In 2008, prices range from a minimum of $0.72 for First-Class International to a minimum of $29.95 for Global Express Guaranteed (arrives in 1–3 days). Note, however, that a daily maximum value applies to international shipments that may require you to provide a customs declaration. For up-to-date pricing information, see the U.S. Postal Service Web site, www.usps.com.

AIR FREIGHT

For much larger export shipments, air freight companies can be contacted directly (through the specific airline). However, many businesses elect to use air freight through the services of a freight forwarding agency, which can transport goods to an airport and complete the necessary documentation.

OCEAN FREIGHT

The most common and cost-effective method for large-volume cargo shipping is "steamship" service (an archaic expression, since no ocean vessels are powered by steam any more). Waterway shipping is available even to export businesses near shallow water through lighter aboard ship (LASH) vessels, which use barges to tow shipped items to deeper ports. Roll-on, roll-off (RORO) ships, which allow vehicles carrying cargo to be driven on and off the ship (rather than being lifted by crane) are also an option. Though usually cheaper than air freight shipping, ocean freight can take significantly longer.

SURFACE SHIPPING

For exports to Canada and Mexico, shipping via roadways or railways is common.

Shipping Documents

As might be expected, a significant amount of documentation is involved in international shipping. Shipping documents can be completed by freight forwarders or directly by the export company. These documents track shipments and aid customs clearance. Below are three basic documents that need to be provided before shipment.

EXPORT LICENSES

An export license signifies that a particular export transaction has been approved by a government agency. Requiring and issuing licenses to exporters is a way of regulating what products are being exported and, more importantly, to whom. Not all exports require export licenses, and many license applications are approved in a short period of time. To find out whether your shipment requires a license (and how to obtain a license), contact the Trade Information Center (TIC) or a local Export Assistance Center.

BILL OF LADING

As discussed in the export paperwork section above, B/Ls function as contracts between exporters and carriers, as receipts indicating that goods have been accepted by carriers, and as identification of goods' ownership.

INSURANCE CERTIFICATE

Much like drivers must be able to demonstrate automobile insurance coverage, exporters need to provide evidence that cargo is insured, for most carriers are not responsible for lost or damaged items except in cases of loss attributable to the carrier's negligence.

Export Assistance

Neither beginners nor experienced exporters need fear that they have to go it alone in the export business. There are many organizations that will advise and support them. In addition to the financial and insurance support provided by Ex-Im Bank and the FCIA, and shipping assistance from foreign freight forwarders, a number of government and private agencies are available to provide advisory information on export procedures. The U.S. Department of Commerce and the Internet are two rich resources of consultant agencies and firms that can help exporters to get started with their export programs. The table below includes a selection of these resources:

Organization	Services	Contact Information
Trade Information Center (U.S. Dept. of Commerce)	Comprehensive resource regarding export processes.	1-800-USA-TRADE www.ita.doc.gov/td/tic
Export Assistance Centers (U.S. Dept. of Commerce)	100+ centers around the United States run by trade specialists that offer trade and marketing advice.	www.export.gov/eac/ index.asp
U.S. Small Business Association	Extends export loans and provides export consultants.	1-800-U-ASK-SBA www.sba.gov
International Chamber of Commerce	Publishes books on international trade.	212-206-1150 www.iccbooks.com
National Customs Brokers & Forwarders Association of America	Provides information on customs brokers and freight forwarders.	202-466-0222 www.ncbfaa.org

IMPORTING

Although the earlier sections of this chapter treat importers as buyers in foreign markets for goods exported from the United States, many U.S. businesses serve as importers of whole products or of raw materials for production. Once a product is selected through careful market analysis, importers, like exporters, must take the time to investigate potential transaction partners in foreign markets.

Sources

When looking for potential sources from which to import a particular product, companies should begin by finding the product (or similar products) and researching its manufacturers (U.S. law requires most imported products to be labeled with their origin countries' names).

Although a good way to get in touch with manufacturers is travel abroad, many companies do not have the resources to spend extensive amounts of time investigating foreign manufacturers in person. However, many countries have representative chambers of commerce located in the United States, such as the Swedish American Chamber of Commerce and the Caribbean American Chamber of Commerce and Industry in New York. Offices such as these can help importers identify and contact sources of imported goods from their respective countries. Importing companies should also consider seeking out sources at domestic trade shows, which may present representatives of foreign companies seeking to export goods and/or services. Also, companies should also use Internet databases and networks such as Kompass, an electronic directory of businesses in the United States and around the globe. The Internet also hosts the sites of trade promotion organizations (e.g., the China Council for the Promotion of International Trade), import-export service firms, and the World Trade Centers Association—all of which can, whether for free or for a fee, put companies in touch with foreign manufacturers wishing to export.

After gathering appropriate contact information, be sure to send inquiries and request quotes from multiple manufacturers—perhaps even in multiple countries—and then *visit* top choice companies in order to gain the best possible understanding of available options and opportunities. From this information, an importing company can choose its suppliers. In general, the best supplier is one who is responsive and enthusiastic about exporting, who is established in a politically stable country, and who demonstrates business savvy through good business communication practices, good financial status, and good quality assurance.

Customs Broker Houses

Once a supplier has been chosen, the real business of importing can begin. As with exporting, the importing process is laden with regulations and paperwork that help the U.S. government to keep track of all products crossing U.S. borders and being sold by U.S. businesses. Fortunately for importers, customs broker houses can take on much of the responsibility for these procedures. Like freight forwarders in export transactions, customs broker houses are independent businesses that aid paying client firms in the import shipment process. Customs broker houses, among their primary services, use their broad knowledge of import regulations and tariffs to clear clients' imported products through U.S. Customs upon arrival. Some customs broker houses also arrange transportation of products that have reached the United States.

Import Quotas

In order to restrict the amount of foreign goods available for sale, and, in some ways, to support the sale of competitive domestic goods, countries set import quotas to restrict the amount of certain goods that can be brought into the country during a particular time frame. These quotas may be established worldwide, or sometimes only on goods imported from specific countries. Some products, such as illegal drugs, have a *zero quota*. Companies should be aware of the quotas existing in the United States on their imported goods, for once a quota has been filled, the product in question cannot enter the country until a set period (e.g., twelve months) has elapsed. When this occurs, companies have the option of leaving products in bonded warehouses or other places where products can be stored duty-free until the quota period passes and the products can enter the country once more. However, in many instances, time-sensitive products in excess of quota are abandoned or sent to other countries, resulting in dramatic profit loss.

Tariffs and Duties

Tariffs and duties, interchangeable terms, are taxes on imported goods. Perhaps one of the most crucial elements of the importing process is understanding how the tariff system works. Not knowing how much must be paid in taxes could be disastrous for the profitability of imported goods. To determine appropriate tariffs, U.S. Customs uses a system called the Harmonized Tariff Schedule of the United States (HTSUSA), which is a version of the Harmonized System, a tariff code used globally. You can refer to the HTSUSA to determine the tariff for your products of interest. The pages will look like the sample shown on the following page. This sample is just one page from Supplement 1 of the 2008 HTSUSA. It covers certain types of fabrics. The complete schedule covers the full range of products traded internationally. The full schedule is available on the Web site of the United States International Trade Commission (http://www.usitc.gov/tata/hts/bychapter/index.htm).

Harmonized Tariff Schedule of the United States (2008) Supplement 1
Annotated for Statistical Reporting Purposes

XI
60-3

Heading/ Subheading	Stat. Suf- fix	Article Description	Unit of Quantity	Rates of Duty		2
				1		
				General	Special	
6001 (Con.)		Pile fabrics, including "long pile" fabrics and terry fabrics, knitted of crocheted (Con.):				
		Other:				
6001.91.00		Of cotton		18.5%	Free (BH, CA,CL, IL, JO, MX, P,SG) 5.6% (MA) 8% (AU)	70%
	10	Over 271 grams per square meter (224) ...	m² kg			
	20	Other (224)	m² kg			
6001.92.00		Of man-made fibers		17.2%	Free (BH, CA,CL, IL,JO, MX,P,SG) 8% (AU) 5.2% (MA)	79.5%

The HTSUSA, adopted in 1989 to streamline global comparisons of products, assigns each imported product a unique 10-digit commodity number, allowing cross-referencing in any language. The over 8,000 commodity codes are organized into classes (in headings and subheadings) and given standardized descriptions and rates of duty. Duty rates are divided into three columns, each with a separate duty rate; these are determined according to the country from which the particular product is imported. Most countries fall under the "normal trade relations" status, whereas others (such as developing countries) are assigned preferential status, and thus lower duty rates. When the United States does not share normal trade relations with a nation, as is the case with Cuba and Iraq, tariff rates are usually much higher than those from countries enjoying normal trade relations status.

Because duty rates can vary drastically, it is essential that importing companies understand how to appropriately classify their products when reporting them to U.S. Customs, as well as how those classifications can alter the duty rates. Because of this, it is a good idea to seek out the advice of clearinghouse brokers even before selecting the exact product for importation, for even the slightest of product alterations can alleviate heavy tariff burdens. In cases in which product classification is unclear, U.S. Customs can provide written classification of a product in advance to prevent a major catastrophe when the product reaches U.S. borders.

KEY POINTS TO REMEMBER

- The process of import-export transactions is complex; it involves many third-party financial institutions, government agencies, and independent carriers, as well as significant amounts of documentation. Understanding this process takes time and experience, but companies engaging in international trade must understand the ins and outs in order to capitalize on its potential benefits.

- However complex international trade transactions may be, no import-export business has to handle the entire process through in-house staff and resources. Independent agencies such as export management companies, freight forwarders, and customhouse brokers are available to lighten the workload of import-export procedures. In addition, advisory centers such as the U.S. Export Assistance Centers are rich resources of information regarding international trade.

- Using these abundant support resources, companies wishing to engage in international trade programs should develop a thorough and implementable marketing plan. This plan should be clear and concrete, yet flexible enough to allow for customization after entering a foreign market.

Global Production, Supply Chains, and Logistics

As we've discussed in previous chapters, the decision to do business on a global scale is quite complicated and requires careful consideration. Only by analyzing every element of the business model can you properly assess the risks of taking your business beyond the domestic marketplace. After all, international business has the potential to improve the success of your business profoundly, or to make you wish you had never considered the possibility of international business in the first place.

DECIDING WHERE TO PRODUCE

One such element of business, production, is one of the greatest determining factors of whether or not a business will become and stay competitive. The fact of the matter is, without reliable, intelligent, and cost-effective modes of production, you simply cannot generate revenue at a rate that will allow you to stay on top of the market. This chapter outlines the fundamentals of production and provides you with the information necessary to decide on and find a production source that meets the needs of your business.

At the heart of the production question is the idea of location. Where you are in the world makes a huge difference. For example, if your company is based in the United States but you are interested in selling products to India, you not only have to consider the laws, customs, and consumer climate of the United States, you also have to consider the same set of concerns as they apply to India. Furthermore, if you opt to manufacture the products in Mexico and buy the raw materials from Germany, you need to familiarize yourself with issues having to do with all four countries. In fact, it is not at all uncommon for international businesses to be involved with dozens of countries—and, in the case of large transnational or multinational companies such as Microsoft or Coca-Cola, it is standard practice to consider each and every country in the global marketplace.

Actually, depending on the nature of your company, it is often wise to follow the lead of larger businesses and broaden your understanding of numerous international markets. Even if many of the markets you investigate are far beyond your reach or interest at this point, you may encounter a viable market in a place you had never considered doing business. The old maxim that knowledge is power applies as much to business as it does to any other pursuit: the more you know about the world, the more you can manipulate it to your advantage. Though this sounds a bit sinister, there is nothing wrong with identifying a niche and capitalizing on it—that's what drives capitalism.

It is also important to remember that all the factors that affect production fluctuate on a daily basis. If you take a moment to think about low production costs for clothing or plastic goods, for example, the first place that likely comes to mind is Asia—perhaps more specifically, China. Obviously, China and other Asian countries do not have a monopoly on cheap goods—other countries elsewhere in the world have developed a similar reputation. Nevertheless, countries such as China and Indonesia have a relatively long history of producing goods at remarkably low prices. But this will probably not be the case forever. As China continues to industrialize and use the sorts of technology that its thriving economy allows for, it may very well shift its production focus to other areas. Of course, the moment that transition takes place, countries dependent on China's production will have to look elsewhere, and other countries at a similar point of transition might seek to take China's place. If all this talk about shifting economies and radical transitions makes the global marketplace seem volatile, it should! As new technology changes the ways goods are produced and the strengths and interests of nations wax and wane, the way international business is conducted changes, too.

Though it's true that such drastic transitions seldom (if ever) take place overnight, the business world is constantly evolving. Consider America's focus in the 20th century in terms of industry. The United States, among other things, spent a lot of time, energy, and money becoming a formidable force in the automotive industry. For a long time, companies such as Ford, GMC, and Chevrolet were considered the industry standards. Is this because Americans, as a people, are inherently talented when it comes to designing and creating car, trucks, and other vehicles? One look at the meteoric rise of foreign car companies such as Toyota and Honda should tell you that that is clearly not the case.

So why did the United States excel in the automotive industry for so long? It was in the right place at the right time. Although it's true that Americans provided a great deal of innovation and worked hard to establish their position in the industry, it was more than likely that they would succeed. During the 20th century, the U.S. population saw the automobile transform from a luxury to a necessity. Consequently, as perception shifted, demand skyrocketed. A similar phenomenon occurred with the personal computer; computers are now considered a necessity, and the electronics industry is booming. And when the demand for cars went up, car manufacturing followed suit.

But the United States was not the only country to embrace the automobile as a staple of modern living. Argentina, Switzerland, Japan, and many other countries in various stages of industrialization witnessed a large portion of their population learning to rely on the car as much as Americans did. Why, then, did the United States dominate the industry for much of the 20th century? For one thing, it was among the victors in both World Wars. This meant that it had the resources and international clout necessary to ramp up production and saturate the market with American-made cars. Meanwhile, car manufacturers in Germany and Japan, for example, faced serious production challenges as they struggled to rebuild and revitalize their countries. The United States identified a need and had better means of fulfilling it than any other country at the time. That was the recipe for success that helped nurture the U.S. economy throughout the 20th century.

Despite the indisputable benefits that won wars, suppressed competitors, or forged alliances offer a firm, there is something to be said for simple geography. Where a country is in the world—or, alternately, where a company chooses to produce goods in the world—will inevitably affect production.

That is why certain nations in antiquity prospered as much as they did. The Fertile Crescent (the expanse of land near the Mediterranean Sea), after all, did not earn its name because of lack of wealth, culture, and prosperity. People in the Fertile Crescent were able to take advantage of the numerous resources available to them: the Euphrates, Tigris, and Nile Rivers, the Mediterranean Sea, and a landscape that supplied them with all the essentials of life. Because the environment was hospitable and resource-rich, they were able to transfer much of their energy from basic survival to the more efficient production of goods. With such advances, ancient peoples could enhance domestic and international trade, and, over time, amassed enough wealth and power to exert control over much of the surrounding area.

Similarly, the location of a modern nation makes a massive difference in its likelihood of becoming a major production center. Many countries in the Middle East, for instance, are blessed with substantial oil reserves that they use to churn out countless barrels of oil every year. Middle Eastern countries can produce oil barrels relatively cheaply, because they have the necessary resources right at their fingertips. Generally speaking, a nation's production falls in line with the resources it can acquire natively.

Of course, one look at the global marketplace will reveal a lot of exceptions to this rule. Although ordinarily it makes little sense for a country that has none of the natural resources necessary to produce a product, it does happen. Let's consider a hypothetical scenario. Say Iran is the primary supplier of crude oil to a neighboring country, Turkmenistan. What if another country—let's say Tajikistan, a country far less oil-rich than Iran—wants to take over some or all of Iran's oil supply to Turkmenistan by importing oil from Iran, refining it domestically, and selling it to Turkmenistan. Under what circumstances might this happen? At first glance it seems foolish: Tajikistan would have to buy the oil from Iran at the regular rate (or inflated rate if Iran knew about the scheme and wanted to prevent the loss of one of its consumers), take on the transportation costs, and pay workers to produce the oil. All of those additional costs would have to be passed on to the consumer, Turkmenistan, in order to make a profit. At that point, one must question why the Turkmenistan wouldn't go directly to the source and pay a lower price. The reason could be one of many. Perhaps there is some sort of political strain between Iran and Turkmenistan. Perhaps Turkmenistan is hoping to forge a stronger relationship with Tajikistan. Perhaps there are economic incentives evident to all countries involved. When contemplating production, one should never assume that companies or countries will operate in accordance with tradition or a prescribed plan.

BUYING VERSUS MAKING

By now, two things should be apparent: the location of production can have an enormous impact on business, and choosing where to produce is a complex decision that should be weighed very carefully. Deciding whether to make or to buy a given product is another piece of the production puzzle, and it will drastically affect your business model.

Buying

As you might guess, there are benefits and drawbacks to both sides of this quandary. First, let's examine the option to buy your goods from another supplier. As we saw in the previous example concerning the oil market in the Middle East, sometimes buying from another country with the intent of selling to yet another country can foster strategic advantages. But often a company's motivation to buy from another country is neither politically nor strategically motivated; it is borne of necessity. If there is not an abundant supply of wood in a business's vicinity, it will be impossible to produce the wooden components of an entertainment center, for example. If a certain resource is essential to the production of a company's goods, the company will need to explore buying.

As discussed in our hypothetical oil production scenario, one of the greatest drawbacks to purchasing goods from another country instead of making them yourself is the cost involved. A lot goes into the purchase, transportation, preparation, and eventual sale of an item—all of which takes money.

It's easy to forget about the costs of shipping when you send e-mail for free and personal letters for less than fifty cents. But if you've ever tried sending a large package through the mail, you know that transportation costs can become a real concern. Sometimes the cost to ship a package represents a large percentage of the value of the package or even exceeds it. At a certain point, it may not seem worthwhile to send the package. Imagine this problem on a much larger scale, if you were sending not one package, but thousands or even millions!

While we are addressing the idea of transportation, take a moment to think about the other factors involved in the movement of goods from one place to another. If the distances are particularly great or the production sites are not on a major airline route, the cost of shipping rises considerably. And when a firm is dealing with shipments on a large scale (perhaps sending millions of packages) transportation costs can really affect profits. Depending on factors like customs and tariffs, a number of "hidden fees" and hassles may also come into play. If that weren't enough to think about, consider the matter of reliability. Businesses have to pay for reliability— electing to use a less trustworthy mode of transportation may save money initially, but terrible loss can ensue if a shipment is somehow lost or damaged. Transportation should never be underestimated; it should be scrutinized as heavily as any other component of business.

Time, money, and the complexity of organizing the purchase of goods from another country are directly related to the notion of transportation. You will need a workforce sufficient to accomplish a variety of jobs: receiving products, storing products, recording information about products, communicating the status and nature of the products, and preparing products for delivery or further manufacturing, among other things. And you will need a team of reliable managers to ensure that all that work is completed properly and efficiently. Taking into account the laws governing minimum wage and the difficulty of retaining employees in lower-level positions, the task of staffing an operation of that magnitude can seem quite daunting. Furthermore, you may require legal counsel to handle some parts of the transaction, regardless of whether or not you encounter any "problems" with the purchase of your goods, such as payment disagreements or unethical behavior. Thus, before undertaking this option, you must be certain that employing all these people, transporting goods from one place to another, and orchestrating all other aspects of the operation does not undermine the profitability of your enterprise. Making this decision relies on the use of cost-benefit analysis, an idea we'll investigate later in greater detail.

With all these potential drawbacks, you may be asking yourself what would motivate a business to choose buying over making. Besides the obvious answer—some businesses have to purchase from others because they simply cannot make the goods themselves—there are a number of very good reasons to decide to buy from another firm.

A business may opt to purchase rather than make because it is cheaper to do so. Making can be quite expensive. Often, even considering the costs of staffing and transporting goods (among other things), a business can increase profit margins by leaving the production up to others. One possible reason for this situation is that different countries have different resources and different production environments. In some countries, the pollution created by the manufacture of products is monitored more extensively and punished more severely than in others. If a business does not have to worry about any adverse environmental effects as a result of its operation, it can often produce goods more cheaply. Though this may have ethical ramifications, it is one way that production costs can be reduced.

Also consider the price of labor in a developed nation such as the United States compared with that in a developing nation such as Somalia—by law, Americans are required to pay substantially more to their workers than employers in places such as Somalia are required to pay. This reduction in the cost of labor can lead to substantial savings on the part of the company buying the foreign goods. Nevertheless, like the pollution situation outlined before, there are sometimes ethical considerations. On one hand, you must reflect on the lives and rights of people in other countries: Is it morally right to pay other workers so little? Are those workers treated humanely? On the other hand, you must consider the consequences of your actions on your home country: Are you damaging the domestic economy? Are you putting fellow citizens of your country out of work? These are very real considerations that should be contemplated thoroughly before proceeding to make a decision. There is, after all, more to business than just the bottom line.

Making

The other side of the coin, making instead of buying, presents its own set of potential challenges and benefits. Let's start with the benefits this time. There are times when making a product domestically is actually cheaper than producing it elsewhere. This is often the best possible scenario, because a company doesn't have to settle for higher production costs, and it is spared the headache of conducting production operations (staffing, transporting, etc.) in another country. Without the added expenditures of time, money, and effort on foreign production, a company can focus more resources on other aspects of the business, and, with some skill and a little luck, profit can be maximized and the business will thrive. Thus, when you see products in the United States with large "Made in the U.S.A." tags, be aware that there are financial incentive for that sort of production, too.

But what if it is not cheaper to make goods in your business's home country? Why do companies still choose to produce domestically? One possibility is patriotism. The owners of some companies transform their love of country into a business model of sorts. People choose to embrace patriotism as a central tenet of their business for many reasons: a desire to keep jobs in their country, an aim to improve the nation's economy, and a sense of duty, among other things. Government-sanctioned incentives (financial or otherwise) may also support keeping jobs in a given country.

Beyond patriotism, a company may choose to produce at a loss or with a thinner profit margin based on a certain strategy or strategies. Perhaps a company believes that its primary supplier of coiled rope, for example, is experiencing a risky amount of political unrest. If there is a coup, that country's production of coiled rope is likely to be slowed down, at best, and, in an extreme scenario, stopped permanently. Or what if the cultural differences (including language barriers, methods of communication, and certain prejudices) seem too vast to conduct efficient, reliable business? Or what if a gigantic hurricane is currently threatening (or regularly threatens) the coast of a country where most necessary manufacturing takes place? Is it wise to proceed as if nothing terrible will happen even when all signs indicate the opposite? Though any sensible person will answer "no" resoundingly, you might be surprised to learn how many business disasters could have been avoided with a little observation. A business owner should be ever-vigilant and should never risk an interruption of production if at all possible.

Another benefit to keeping production local and within a company is that the heads of the company—or the people who are hired to assess the company as a whole—can monitor production more closely and more easily. Even if all workers are making an effort to complete their tasks honestly and efficiently (a situation less prevalent than we'd like to hope!) the employees may be making mistakes unknowingly. Because workers with specialized duties tend to work exclusively within the parameters of their jobs, it is difficult for them to have a big-picture perspective of the entire operation. Essentially, it becomes increasingly difficult for the higher-ups to get very involved with production as the distance between a firm's home base and the site of production increases. For this reason, it is helpful to have people such as the CFO (Chief Financial Officer) or COO (Chief Operating Officer) close by to point out any problems or to make recommendations for improvement.

The problem of long-distance supervision is further worsened when production sites are not only far from home, but numerous. Imagine trying to coordinate six different factories in eight different countries where language, culture, geography, legal environment, and worker mentality are vastly different in each factory. Because it is almost always of the utmost importance to ensure that all products are identical and defect-free, the task of coordination and oversight becomes all the more critical. In fact, the golden standard of production in many industries, known as Six Sigma, was developed to ensure that products were created to such exacting specifications. The production system draws on fields such as statistics and resource management, and one of its components, Six Sigma quality, is relied upon to create fewer than 3.4 defects per million opportunities. In order to maintain such high standards, management needs to be directly involved with the production process, fixing problems before they develop—quite a tall order when management is hundreds, if not thousands, of miles away!

Though the downside to self-producing is usually encapsulated in the idea of cost (i.e., you may be able to buy goods for less than you can make them), there are other factors to keep in mind. Perhaps most importantly, as discussed in the section on buying, choosing to outsource production to another country can help to forge strong business alliances. Imagine that you own a microprocessor company, FastWires, and you are considering expanding into the cell phone market. Though you can make microprocessors cheaply and efficiently in your own country in your own factories, you know nothing about the plastic molding that will be required to house the circuitry. You decide that it will not be cost-effective to start up and operate a production line in a different industry (plastics), so you contact another company, PerfectlyPlastic, which can do the job at a reasonable rate. After working with PerfectlyPlastic for awhile, you may find that they can perform other tasks for you as well, and, because a trust and partnership has been established, they may offer to reduce their prices to keep you, their valuable customer, coming back for more. Alternatively, PerfectlyPlastic may one day expand into the world of silicon, and who better to do business with than FastWires, a company they already know and trust? In the world of business, knowing the right people and establishing strong bonds can take you much farther than the current sale; creating a strategic network is the lifeblood of business.

Thus, as you can see, the disadvantages of making are often the advantages of buying, and vice versa. There are no hard-and-fast rules for choosing which strategy to adopt—you will have to assess the situation and make your decision based on experience and knowledge. The good news is that there are tools at your disposal to help with the decision making process. You can and should research any company with which you are considering doing business, as well as its host country. You may wish to consult legal counsel before you even begin drawing up contracts and other transactional documents. And before taking any conclusive steps, you must perform a cost-benefit analysis.

COST-BENEFIT ANALYSIS

Now that you're aware of some of the production options out there, you need to know how to select one. Because hard-and-fast rules are difficult to come by in the business world, you will need to use a system versatile enough to work in any situation. One such system is cost-benefit analysis. Though cost-benefit analysis can be done either formally or informally, it is easy to understand the concept in a general sense by thinking about a piece of paper with two columns: good and bad. This is, admittedly, a simplification of what can be a very complex discipline, but it may prove useful to think about this idea in everyday terms. The fact is, we engage in cost-benefit analysis all the time. If you go to the grocery store and see your favorite candy bar, you have to decide whether or not to buy the candy bar. On the good side, you might include the following items: it will taste good, it will whet my appetite, it's not very expensive. On the bad side, you might include this list: it's not very healthy, it won't help with my diet, I won't be able to buy something else with that money. (The last item on that list actually speaks to a larger concept, opportunity cost, that we'll discuss later.) At any rate, a quick look at those two lists shows you that there are some compelling reasons for both buying and not buying that candy bar.

How do you know which decision to make? Sticking with our candy bar example, we clearly cannot make a sound judgment based on the number of items on one list versus another. In this case, the number of items on each list is the same, but even if they were vastly different—say ten items on the good side and one item on the bad side—we couldn't use the number of items as the sole criterion. Even though the money we could get by robbing a bank could bring with it many benefits, bank robbery's illegality outweighs them all. Thus, rather than adding up the number of items on each side, you should carefully weigh the importance of each item—the candy bar may be cheap, but buying it may mean not being able to afford the eggs you need to make your spouse a birthday dinner, or it may mean adding another hour to your workout routine.

Now let's consider an example more relevant to the production side of the business world. Suppose a firm in Canada offers to produce aluminum cans for your beverage company at 2 cents per can, and a firm in Rwanda offers to produce the same product for 1 cent per can. What factors might influence your decision to go with one firm over the other? The first factor is probably the cost of the product—on a price-per-piece basis, the Rwandan firm is twice as good. But there are other financial factors: What sorts of tariffs will you be required to pay for each country? What will it cost to transport the goods back to your home country from each country? What will it cost to send quality control specialists from your country to each of the countries? Needless to say, there are many possible financial concerns that may color your decision to go with one firm instead of another.

Moreover, you should consider the political climate of the country. Often the political climate is particularly volatile in developing countries.

Also, where your company is located in relation to the other country makes a big difference—if your company happens to be located in the United States, for example, then doing business with Canada instead of Rwanda has some advantages, because both Canada and the United States are members of NAFTA. Many of these formal and informal alliances or networks exist throughout the world, including groups such as OPEC and the EU. In the best scenarios, trade barriers are minimized between nations in certain organizations, bringing down the overall cost of doing business.

So, in our fictitious beverage company, the price per product may be higher, but if the tariffs are exorbitant in Rwanda and the cost of shipping all those aluminum cans back to United States to be filled is too high, the final price per product may be roughly the same. If the production prices are the same, you must take into account other factors, such as the relative risk of production interruptions, the legal and political atmosphere of each nation, and other less tangible qualities, such as your impression of the way each country does business and the degree to which your company's ideologies align with each of theirs. After you have finished weighing all these factors, and anything else that seems pertinent, you will be left with an overall view of each country, at which point you simply choose the country that seems best to you. Still, however, the idea most important to remember in terms of cost-benefit analysis is that the accuracy of your judgment relies upon the accuracy of your assessments; if you cut corners in the decision-making stage, you will pay for it later.

COMPARATIVE ADVANTAGE THEORY

The theory of comparative advantage is a concept we have touched on throughout this chapter, although we have not yet discussed it explicitly. At the heart of the theory is the tendency of nations to produce those goods that they can produce most efficiently. The upshot of this idea is that even if a nation can produce an item more cheaply than another nation, it often will not, because it is ultimately more profitable to concentrate on the *most* efficiently produced goods. Sometimes this phenomenon creates counterintuitive situations in which a company can produce a product very efficiently in its home country but chooses to pay more to have the goods imported. Even though a firm may not make as much money as it could in one area of production, the ability to focus exclusively on the most efficient production areas is hoped to maximize profits in the long run.

In some ways, comparative advantage theory is just another way of looking at opportunity cost—an idea we addressed briefly in our candy bar example. An opportunity cost, after all, is essentially a hypothetical loss—it asks the question, "What are you giving up by doing this and not something else?" In the candy bar example, the opportunity cost is mainly limited to the financial component of the purchase. By spending, say $1.00 on a candy bar, you restrict the usage of $1.00 to the purchase of the candy bar, and nothing else. Though this is a very straightforward concept, the consequences are, at times, easy to forget. Because the $2.00 is being used for a purchase that is, arguably, frivolous, the money cannot be used for something else. That something else could be vital (perhaps the crucial ingredient in a birthday dinner, perhaps just enough gasoline to get home) or equally frivolous (it could be a pint of ice cream, for instance), but the drastic reduction in options is important to think about.

Consider an example rooted in the international business world. If a firm elects to deal with one manufacturing company to produce all its goods, it is automatically and necessarily excluding all other manufacturing companies. What are the consequences of this decision? Most obviously, if the firm has not researched its options well, it may be missing a better deal with another manufacturing company. As a consumer, you have probably had this experience: you buy an item at one store only to find it cheaper at another store hours later. With small personal purchases it is relatively easy to remedy your mistake—you simply return the item for a refund and buy the second item. When firms are engaged in international business, it is not nearly as easy to fix such problems, because it is not just one item being purchased, but thousands, if not millions. Furthermore, it is difficult to contend with the legally binding documents that frame such transactions. To borrow an adage from the world of carpentry, make sure you measure twice and cut once—in international business you won't get many second chances.

Another opportunity cost that may not be so obvious is time. The time (or effort, for that matter) that you spend doing something cannot be spent doing anything else. There are only so many hours in the day and so much money that you can afford to pay your workers, so the time that is spent conducting business operations had best be worthwhile! Because production is such a large part of a business's expenses, it is absolutely crucial that time not be spent on pursuits not likely to yield good products and healthy profits.

The history of international business is riddled with opportunity costs, causing problems for (or even destroying) businesses. If a technology firm spends too much time designing and creating a product that is unsuccessful in the marketplace, it will have a difficult time recouping the losses incurred by the unprofitable product. Likewise, if a company cannot effectively eliminate redundancies—which basically means doing something twice unnecessarily instead of doing two different, productive things—the company's overall efficiency will plummet. In light of these observations, the ever-present risk of missing a valuable opportunity or of investing too much time, money, and effort into a doomed product should always govern the way you do business. As with all elements of business, be sure to research what you don't know and meticulously scrutinize that which you do know lest you make an irreparable mistake.

Of course, the history of the international business world is no graveyard of failed businesses and boneheaded errors. Many of the success stories you know by name; you find products by these companies in your home, at work, and in virtually every corner of the world. Aside from a healthy dose of luck, there is a reason these companies are so successful: they produced something the world needed, in an intelligent manner. They used the strategies described in this book and found unique ways to make their business models outperform their competitors'. It is a delicate balance to strike, and a difficult one, too. But the good news is that there are concrete methods of attaining success in international business. One way of doing this is by looking to the businessmen and women who have reached the top and have continued to thrive there.

WIN-WIN SCENARIOS

This chapter has investigated the ways that you can make the production process work to your advantage. One of the central ways to accomplish this task is to seek out and take part in win-win scenarios. As the name suggests, these sorts of situations benefit both or all parties in a given business transaction. Naturally, a win-win situation does not necessarily entail complete satisfaction in all elements of a business partnership; it just means that in a crucial facet of the business dealings, both companies are happy with the outcome. Note that this does not imply equal contentment—one company may benefit more than another, and companies may benefit in different ways.

Let's take a look at a real-world example of a win-win situation. As e-commerce started to become more acceptable to Americans in the 1990s and early 21st century, many businesses sought a means of capitalizing on this emerging market. One of the more ingenious types of Internet businesses that cropped up at this time dealt in price comparisons for airline flights. Companies such as Travelocity and Orbitz founded businesses that did the job of shopping around for the best travel deals for customers. Thus, after a customer simply input the basic details of a flight—desired departure and arrival dates and places, number of passengers, and preferred number of stops—a Web site would supply the user with numerous options fitting those criteria. From there, the user could pick the carrier, time, and price combination that best met his or her needs. It was (and continues to be) a tremendous help to weary vacation planners. Also, because of the concept's great success, such Web sites are able to generate a massive amount of revenue through fees and advertisements. In this way, consumers save money, and the company makes money. It is a true win-win situation, and this circumstance likely accounts for much of the concept's success.

Other win-win scenarios involve trading certain goods and services for other goods or services. The important thing to remember is that business transactions don't have to follow conventional models whereby money is exchanged for goods or services. In fact, in antiquity the preferred (and often only) method of trade was bartering—one item was traded for another, without money ever entering the equation. Nowadays, the bartering transactions that take place are more complex, because virtually every object is linked to a monetary value. This valuation system makes it easy to trade one thing for another fairly. Of course, it gets trickier with goods or services that are new, or that are valued differently in some parts of the world.

What if one nation values a service such as unloading boxes very highly, whereas another nation, with no shortage of workers willing to work for next to nothing, does not value it much at all? How do companies in these two nations reconcile their varying estimations of the service performed? One answer to the problem is for one company to trade something that is valued as highly as the good or service being traded by the other company. This is a classic win-win scenario. If a company in Uganda needs a company in the United States to unload and organize boxes, for instance, but doesn't value the work much, the Ugandan company may be able to trade a product that has high value for the American company, but little value to the Ugandans. In this way, both parties are satisfied and both businesses prosper.

MANAGING A GLOBAL SUPPLY CHAIN

After you have decided where to produce and have made any necessary arrangements with other nations and businesses, you must decide how to produce. As any good manager knows, there are a lot of ways to manage a business—and there's not only one right way to do it. As with most things in the business world, management (and, consequently, production) must be handled on a case-by-case basis. Deciding to use a certain management style to drive production, or employing a certain production technique, may be completely effective in one situation but a complete waste at other times. One thing, however, is certain: the more you know, the more likely you are to make sound management and production choices.

One decision every business must make involves the ways in which different parts of an organization interact with each other and contribute to its larger production goals. There are basically two schools of thought on this topic: centralized and decentralized methods of production. Centralized production entails standardizing production processes across the board so that production is reliable, consistent, and easily understandable. With centralized production, a business can monitor operations accurately and institute global changes more easily. Decentralized production, on the other hand, advocates a more localized approach whereby every branch of a company works to optimize its own productivity, because doing so requires less supervision and coordination. Also, when production sites have greater autonomy, they can respond quickly to site-specific changes and needs. (See models below and on next page.)

Choosing either of these methods, like so many other things in business, will depend on the individual needs and goals of your business. Also, different industries tend to perform better under certain production models. McDonald's is a prime example of a centralized production model—everything is standardized, allowing food items to look and taste the same, regardless of which franchise you visit. Conversely, a film production company might employ a decentralized production model allowing different branches to respond to each individual film in the most effective way. In fact, it is relatively common for smaller firms to embrace this sort of decentralized model. One type of business, the micro-multinational (a small multinational company that uses ingenuity instead of financial muscle to succeed) is particularly well-suited to the decentralized model, especially in the high-tech industry. In order to make the final decision on this issue, you should research how other successful firms in your industry are handling their production. If they are successful, they must be doing production well.

Centralized Production Model Indicating the
Flow of Information and/or Resources

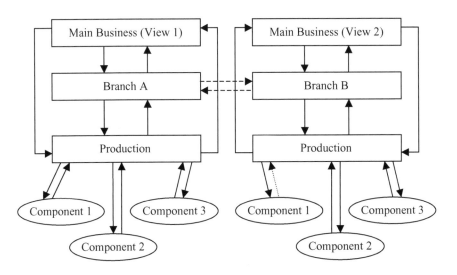

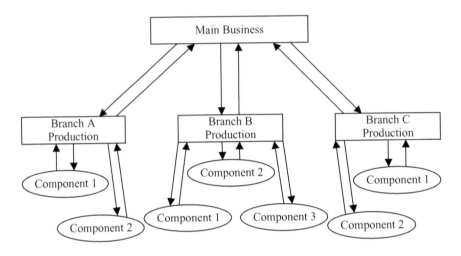

Decentralized Production Model Indicating the Flow of Information and/or Resources

When it comes to actual production, how efficiently you produce goods can make all the difference. Fortunately, as businesses move further into the 21st century, they can rely more and more on the technological innovation of others. Consider, for example, the first production plants. The technology they used was, by today's standards, extremely rudimentary. Although the machines offered much-needed supplements to human labor, they were not terribly efficient. Part of the reason for this is the linear nature of technology: you can't have a personal computer, for example, before you invent a television screen. Like science, inventions or discoveries tend to build on their predecessors. Though the first manufacturing machines were not terribly impressive, the ground they broke allowed other people to break new ground by improving them. Over time, this building-block methodology has created production aids that we never thought imaginable.

One result of the ever-growing technological sphere is that machines are no longer limited to one task. In the industry, this is called flexible manufacturing, and it allows complex machines to handle numerous production tasks as needed. For example, a multi-task painting machine at an automotive plant might be responsible for cleaning the metal surface, applying the primer, applying the base coat, applying the high-gloss finish, and drying the paint when needed. Compare that one machine's versatility with a machine you might have found in an early production plant, which might have been able only to apply the primer.

There are many benefits to flexible manufacturing. For starters, with only one machine instead of multiple machines, substantially less physical space is required. Production processes that once required an array of machines scattered about a large room can now be accomplished by one small machine placed in the corner of a workspace. Also, with fewer machines, repair costs and breakdown frequency are likely to decline— businesses can take the amount of money they would spend on numerous machines and invest in one machine that works better and that is made with higher quality parts. Further, with fewer machines to buy, a firm can allocate more money to other areas within the business. In this way, it is difficult to look at flexible manufacturing as anything other than a huge help to any business.

Ultimately, flexible manufacturing lends itself to lean manufacturing. Lean manufacturing encapsulates the positive benefits outlined in the previous paragraph, as well as a few others. All elements of production are more efficient: less space is used, less time is needed to complete tasks, less money is required to repair machines or buy other machines, and less human labor is needed. Flexible manufacturing and lean manufacturing work together to improve production at all levels.

Because lean manufacturing can really boost a business's bottom line, it is vital to strive toward it whenever possible. Achieving this goal is accomplished by finding creative and logical ways to reduce the usage of resources while maintaining (or increasing) the quality of goods and enhancing the overall efficiency of production. It is certainly a lofty goal, but it's one that every firm must pursue if it wants to stay competitive.

Of course, depending on your perspective, flexible and lean manufacturing may not be wholly good. Although anyone would have to acknowledge the sheer impressiveness of one machine doing the job of several machines and even more humans, there can be negative consequences for the labor force. As technological advances allow machines to perform increasingly complex tasks, businesses require less human labor to keep the production operation up and running. What do the workers do when their jobs have been replaced by machines? In the best-case scenario, workers are offered more advanced jobs, their work becomes less physically demanding, and they enjoy higher paychecks. But this is usually not the case. In reality, a decreased need for human labor often means letting employees go. From a financial standpoint it makes sense: why pay a human when a robot can do the work for less? Of course, anyone who has ever lost a job as a result of technological innovation probably has a different perspective. Is it right to lay off a hardworking employee just to save a little money? That is a complicated ethical question that has been answered differently by many companies. It is up to you to decide how to navigate these treacherous waters, keeping your employees as happy as possible while still securing healthy profits.

The idea of maintaining employee satisfaction while improving a business's financial situation has become quite a hot-button issue as more and more industries look to outsourcing to reduce costs. Like the use of machines for human labor, outsourcing is an easy decision if you don't take into account the human factor of business. As you know, however, disregarding the workforce inevitably leads to problems. You cannot expect a human being to work like a machine, and you cannot expect a worker to graciously accept the loss of his or her job to someone in another country. In the event that you opt to move production elsewhere, it is best if you do it from the start. If you need to shift production sites after staffing domestically, you must be tactful, respectful of workers' rights, and resolved as you make the transition from domestic production to foreign production.

CONCLUSION

In production, efficiency is the name of the game. A lot of decisions need to be made on the production end of business: Should you buy or make your products? With whom should you do business? How will you handle transportation? How will you manage production? What role will workers play in day-to-day business operations? How will you respond to an ever-changing global environment? These questions and many others can seem overwhelming when you first begin doing international business—and even when you're a seasoned veteran!—but if they are not seriously and carefully considered, your business is far less likely to succeed.

KEY POINTS TO REMEMBER

- A company doing international business can look anywhere in the world to meet its needs. Whether it's a workforce, raw materials, or expertise that is needed, if a business is buying, countries are selling. A company deciding where to produce might choose a country because of its location (and the natural resources available there), its demographics (and the workforce thus represented), or even its political climate (and its associated business climate).

- Buying goods avoids spending time on manufacturing, expending effort to acquire resources, and wasting money through lack of expertise, but it represents some costs as well. If you're buying, someone else is making a profit on your purchase—and isn't just the seller. Freight companies take their share, and government tarriffs can increase costs even further.

- Making goods removes profit-cutting middle men, shipping costs, and government penalties and can in fact sometimes take advantage of government incentives to produce domestically. But even though it can protect a company from political disruptions that might affect foreign suppliers and cross-cultural confusion that can hamper communications, it may also bypass profits for the sake of security.

- Choosing whether to buy or make goods doesn't have to be a blind decision, however. If the advantages and liabilities of doing business overseas or in a particular market can be felt, they can be measured. Comparing the potential gains of entering a certain market or adopting a particular strategy with the losses you might incur can become the basis for a safe, profitable operation that benefits all involved.

- Conducting a cost-benefit analysis can help you in any situation, including deciding your company's mode of entry into international business and its form within the global marketplace. The benefits of creating a decentralized business model might outweigh the costs—or vice versa. Using a cost-benefit analysis can help you decide.

International Human Resource Management

International human resource management (IHRM) can be defined as those human resource issues that arise from the internationalization of business, along with the policies and practices implemented to deal effectively with those issues. This, however, is a somewhat simplistic definition that glosses over the fact that most of the research done in this field is concerned with expatriate-related issues such as culture shock, compensation, and repatriation. Although other issues obviously exist, they tend to take a secondary role, because when a business opens an office in a new country, there is a definite need for managers from the "home office" to be transferred with the task of getting the new branch operational. Additionally, of the three approaches to international staffing, a topic we'll cover later, two make heavy use of expatriates.

WHO IS AN EXPATRIATE?

Many people have romantic notions of what being an expatriate is. They imagine traveling around the world, meeting interesting people, and spending afternoons in cafés. To be sure, some expatriates enjoy this existence, but for our purposes we'll concentrate on another type of expatriate: someone who is sent by an employer to a country other than his or her native country for a specific business-related purpose. Expatriates of this kind do get to travel the world, but they also have to go to work, and they struggle to adjust to new cultures just like anyone else.

The expectations for expatriates vary widely from business to business, as can the motivations for sending expatriates overseas in the first place. Sending expatriates across the world is expensive, and there can be significant drawbacks if this is done without appropriate care. Because of this, businesses generally do their research before committing their employees to assignments that can be years long, if not open-ended. How businesses choose to approach this problem can also vary depending on factors such as overall philosophy toward human resource management and the nature of the business that will be done overseas.

It is important also to keep in mind why businesses send out expatriates in the first place. Obviously, each company is going to have its own reasons for doing so, but most fall under the umbrella of maintaining control and financial security. Many companies use expatriates to keep management techniques in-house, rather than depending on foreign nationals, for example. They give the parent company the ability to control its subsidiaries more directly. Additionally, if the foreign country is drastically different culturally, using expatriates lessens the risk of local managers chafing under a management system that they find unusual and irritating. Again, each business will have its own unique reasons for using expatriates. What is of vital importance is how the company approaches the problem of international human resource management to determine when and how to use expatriates.

THE IMPORTANCE OF A GLOBAL MINDSET

Stated simply, a global mindset is a company-wide understanding that doing business on a global scale requires intricate understanding and acceptance of the world's political and economic structures, laws, and cultures. This applies to international human resource management in many ways. For example, it determines when and how a company will use expatriates in its foreign entities. It will also determine what kind of role those expatriate managers will play. Will they simply be surrogates for managers at headquarters, or will they be more autonomous, using their expertise of the foreign culture to influence their decisions?

To help us understand what a global mindset is and why it is of such great importance, let's look at two hypothetical companies: Company D and

Company G. Both companies are based in the United States, and both have various operations in Latin America and across Europe. Company D has a domestic mindset and sees globalization as a way of doing a larger volume of business (in the global market) through a centralized organization of decision making. Company G maintains a global mindset and sees globalization as a challenge to understand its business operations in an international, cross-cultural way. They do this in order to avoid cultural problems and to recognize, and take advantage of, new international opportunities as they arise.

Now, imagine that there is a major economic crisis in Argentina, where both companies have a presence. There is a good chance that Company D would not have the ability to fully understand the implications of such an event or to respond to it efficiently, because it would only see it from the perspective of a domestic entity. Company G, on the other hand, has an advantage because it has instituted a management structure, through its global mindset, that is more open to influences from beyond headquarters. Its managers can determine whether the best way to deal with the new development requires an adapted local response, a consistent global response, or a combination of the two. Company D may simply approach the development in the same way that it would a similar development in Asia or Africa, with little or no global-minded consideration for the unique nature of the situation.

As this simple example demonstrates, a global mindset is critical for a successful international business. The international human resource manager (IHRM) plays a crucial role in this process by educating a company's managers and by facilitating its expatriate program to take full advantage of the experiences and skills that expatriates will gain during their assignments.

STRATEGIES FOR HUMAN RESOURCES

How an international business decides to use its human resources abroad is usually a reflection of the degree to which it has adopted a global mindset. In this section we will look at three strategies that businesses use, often at different stages of internationalization, to achieve their human resourcing goals. First there is the ethnocentric strategy, which consolidates control in the home country headquarters and uses expatriate managers abroad to maintain this control. Next is the polycentric strategy, which can be thought of as the opposite of ethnocentrism; it is characterized by decentralized control, with each foreign subsidiary having a great degree of autonomy and often being managed by foreign nationals. Finally, there is the geocentric strategy, which can be seen as a compromise between the two: headquarters and subsidiaries are thought of as partners, and the most qualified individuals are used to fill foreign positions, regardless of nationality.

Ethnocentrism

An ethnocentric company is headquarters-oriented. All major decisions are made there, and all key management is located there. As a result, use of expatriate managers is usually limited to training the foreign nationals and reporting back to headquarters. They function very much as extensions, or surrogates, of management back home. Their objective is to essentially transplant the corporate culture of headquarters to the foreign location.

There are advantages and disadvantages to this strategy. Using expatriates from the home country can overcome a lack of skilled workers in the host nation, if such a shortage exists. It also produces strong integration within the company, which can be beneficial to a younger or smaller organization that is just beginning to branch out. This strategy is also very cost-effective in the short term. It is not sustainable as the company grows, but it will provide a company with a window of time to expand and grow into its new role as an international company. However, this strategy can also lead to resentment in the host country and local employees if the company asserts its culture too strongly. It can also lead the company to inadvertently become rigid, unamenable to change and to improvements developed in the host nation.

Perhaps the greatest danger when international businesses use this strategy is that of expatriate failure, with the high cost that accompanies it. Expatriate failure can be defined as expatriates returning home or resigning before foreign assignments are complete, or performing poorly while on assignment. There are many reasons for expatriate failure; the major ones are inability of employees to adjust, inability of spouses to adjust, and other family problems. Expatriate failure should be seen as a failure to train and prepare employees before the start of assignments. Another associated risk is that many repatriated expatriate employees leave the company within a year. Returning managers may have a hard time re-integrating to their home culture and the corporate culture of their company. In addition, former peers may have received promotions, and returning workers may feel passed over. Again, the failure of returning employees should be seen as a human resources failure on the part of management to ease the repatriation process of returning employees.

Polycentrism

The polycentric strategy can be seen as the opposite of the ethnocentrism. It is characterized by a strong orientation toward the host country. The idea is that because each country is different, each subsidiary in those countries should be managed by foreign nationals. To this end, a polycentric company would staff its foreign subsidiaries with foreign nationals instead of with expatriates from the home country.

The advantages of the polycentric strategy tend to address the main disadvantages of the ethnocentric strategy. A polycentric strategy eliminates many of the cultural barriers present when an expatriate manager is used. For example, there would be no language barriers between management and worker. A polycentric strategy also results in more autonomy for the foreign subsidiary. This addresses the problem of rigidity. When action is called for, a native manager will be able to instinctively respond in a culturally appropriate way, which will result in less conflict and a more efficient pursuit of profitable opportunities.

One of the most immediate advantages that company will see as it moves to the polycentric strategy is savings in management. Because management positions are staffed with natives of the host country, which are much less expense even if they are paid a premium salary, the cost savings can be substantial. In addition, because of expatriates' diminished role, there is less risk of expatriate turnover—and its associated costs—in the foreign subsidiary.

Although the polycentric strategy seems to solve many of the problems inherent in the ethnocentric strategy, it comes with its own set of disadvantages. Most of these disadvantages stem from the breakdown in communications that can occur when headquarters and a foreign subsidiary are staffed with managers from each respective country. Headquarters may even start to think of a subsidiary as an independent national unit. Add to this that the inherent autonomy of the foreign subsidiary will allow little physical presence and interchange between the two entities. This may serve to harden any differences between them, making them difficult to reverse later.

Geocentrism

The geocentric strategy can be seen as a compromise between the ethnocentric and polycentric strategies and, it can be argued, is the strongest of the three. To understand this strategy, try to imagine an international business that operates as if it were nationless. Political and cultural borders do not matter, because corporate resources can be moved without regard for borders. Additionally, any national or cultural differences, such as local law or customs, can be learned or managed.

There are two main advantages to this strategy. First, it deals with the polycentric problem of foreign subsidiaries becoming autonomous units, because those subsidiaries are now staffed with people most qualified for the positions they hold, regardless of nationality. Second, and perhaps most important, the geocentric strategy allows a company to create an international executive team with transnational ability. Headquarters maintains a firm understanding of foreign and domestic needs, and managers are moved around to best meet those needs.

The geocentric strategy is not without its drawbacks, however. First, a host nation may have laws that require that a certain number of managers be natives of that country. Additionally, many countries, particularly Western ones, have laws that make getting work visas difficult, time-consuming, and expensive. Another problem is that the geocentric strategy greatly reduces the autonomy of foreign subsidiaries. Managers at these subsidiaries may resist this loss of autonomy. Finally, the largest drawback for many companies trying to adopt this strategy is cost. Moving large numbers of highly paid professionals around the world can get expensive, quickly. Finally, cost and the visa and legal issues combine to create situations in which the company can become less responsive because of the longer lead time needed to operate in this way.

SELECTION OF EMPLOYEES AND OTHER HUMAN RESOURCES

So far we have looked at some of the ways that international businesses use their human resources and some of the reasons why they choose the strategies they use. Next, we'll look at some of the considerations of these companies when selecting employees and other human resources. These will include labor laws abroad, compensation practices, and cross-cultural literacy.

Labor Laws Abroad

As you might imagine, each country has its own unique set of labor laws. These laws can govern everything from the use of expatriates in management to training practices to anti-discrimination legislation and can differ greatly from those in a company's home country. Additionally, there is a growing list of international organizations, such as the United Nations and the European Union, that are developing standards with which your company may need to comply. Moreover, as more and more companies are internationalizing, many countries are beginning to take into consideration the laws of visiting companies' home countries as well as their own laws, essentially meaning that two countries' laws must sometimes be considered. These things make this area of IHRM one of the most complex.

So how can an IHRM deal with all of this complexity? It helps to break it down into three steps.

First, consider the general human resource challenges common to all international businesses, such as expatriate failure rate and training. We have touched on some of these already in this chapter, and we'll deal with more in the following pages.

Second, understand labor regulations on an international level. Remember that international organizations such as the EU and UN are becoming increasingly involved in this area of international business regulation.

Third, maintain a working knowledge of the labor laws and practices of each host country.

Because of the complexity inherent in this area of human resource management, it is often necessary to have local participation in the management process at a subsidiary. A local manager from the host country will greatly ease the process of remaining in compliance with the foreign laws.

Compensation Practices

On its surface, the problem of compensation within an international business may seem like a relatively simple problem. But evaluation of the added complexity of compensation on a global scale can make the picture much more complex. For example, consider that an expatriate's compensation package can include not only a base salary but also travel and standard-of-living bonuses. Or consider that managers doing essentially the same job in different countries will most likely be working under different labor laws, subject to different local tax systems, and living in areas with drastically different costs of living. Do you pay them different amounts? If so, what if one of the managers discovers the discrepancy and becomes disgruntled? These are just a few of the many problems faced by the IHRM.

These problems are usually correlated with the degree of a company's internationalization. When a company is just beginning its global operation, its compensation concerns will be of a more immediate nature, consisting mostly of paying enough to attract and maintain an expatriate workforce. But as its international operations expand, the company will quickly sense the need for a systematic approach toward international compensation.

Generally speaking, there are four goals that the IHRM should try to achieve with a compensation program. The first, and most general, is that the program should be consistent with the International Human Resources program as a whole, as well as with the company's structure and goals. Second, the program must provide incentives that will attract and retain skilled employees. Short-term savings brought about by low compensation will obviously lead to undesirable workforce quality. Third, the program should be nimble enough to facilitate transfer of human resources in an efficient manner. Fourth, and with all this in mind, the program should strive for overall equality and efficient administration, unburdened by an overwhelming and unfair bureaucracy.

Here are brief descriptions of the most common elements of expatriate compensation packages:

BASE SALARY

Base salary is usually the main component of the compensation package and is also used as a benchmark to determine the size of other compensation components. Because of this, it is also the most controversial.

COST OF LIVING ALLOWANCE

Cost of living allowances are usually paid to employees to offset any differences between the home country and host country that would result in a shift in their standards of living. For example, a manager sent from Wyoming to London would suffer a negative shift in his or her standard of living because of the higher cost of things such as gasoline, food, and entertainment in the host country. Such a degree of difference is often very hard to measure.

HARDSHIP PREMIUM

Hardship premiums can be thought of as added incentives for employees meant to counteract the hardships of moving, changing cultures, and creating distance from family and is affected by the overall length of an assignment. The degree to which these hardships exist is used to determine the size of such premiums.

HOUSING ALLOWANCE

If the company does not provide housing in the host country, it will often offer an allowance to help employees maintain their standards of living while on assignment. The company may also provide services to help employees sell or let their homes in the home country.

HOME LEAVE ALLOWANCE

Home leave allowances are given so that employees can more easily visit the home country during the year. This is considered useful in helping employees maintain home ties and in helping prevent repatriation problems.

EDUCATION ALLOWANCE

Education allowances help employees send their children to schools comparable to those they attended in their home country.

RELOCATION ALLOWANCE

Relocation allowances are meant to offset the cost of moving to and from the host country. These costs often include shipping and storage costs, as well as the purchase of new home goods such as furniture and appliances.

The Balance Sheet Approach

There are many different approaches that an IHRM can use to help solve the problems associated with international compensation for expatriates, but the one most commonly used is the balance sheet approach. The balance sheet approach aims to achieve equality between expatriates' purchasing power and standard of living in the home and host countries. To this end, premiums, allowances, and other incentives are used to offset any disparity between the two. Several factors go into determining how much compensation is needed to achieve equality, such as the costs of goods and services, housing, and taxes.

Although this approach is widely used, it is not without its drawbacks. Two worth remembering are that it can result in considerable compensation differences between expatriates in different nations, and that it can be overly complex and burdensome to manage.

Cross-cultural Literacy

As was discussed in Chapter 2, cross-cultural literacy can be defined as the ability to understand and learn about another culture in a functional relationship. An employee can be said to have cross-cultural literacy if he or she can be sent to Asia, for example, and, over the course of the assignment, come to understand and accept the many differences within that culture.

Because this is an essential quality for an expatriate to have, or at least to be capable of having, it is a key quality for IHRMs to look for when considering candidates for expatriate assignments. The two researchers Mendenhall and Oddou devised a system for expatriate selection that aims to measure employees' cross-cultural literacy to determine their abilities to successfully complete expatriate assignments. Mendenhall and Oddou's expatriate selection model is a four-dimensional assessment tool used to determine whether particular candidates are well suited to handle the cultural and personal challenges of a foreign assignment.

THE SELF-ORIENTED DIMENSION

The self-oriented dimension reflects the degree to which employees will adapt for purposes of self-preservation, self-enjoyment, and mental hygiene. Will they, of their own volition, take appropriate steps to ensure their own mental health, or will they maintain rigid mental states, succumbing to culture shock and depression and ultimately failing their assignments? This dimension can be measured using a variety of psychometric tests of qualities such as stress tolerance and personality type.

THE PERCEPTUAL DIMENSION

The perceptual dimension measures expatriates' abilities to understand why people native to the host country think and act differently from people from their home country. Will expatriates automatically respect the differences and try to understand them? Or will they make irrational judgments, such as of inferiority? Obviously, most candidates will fall somewhere between these two extremes. Psychological tests can be used, often in conjunction with consultations with employees' superiors, to gauge employees' perceptual dimension.

THE OTHERS-ORIENTED DIMENSION

The others-oriented dimension reflects expatriates' willingness to communicate and interact with locals from the host country. This is important, not least because this kind of interaction helps alleviate culture shock. Many difficulties that expatriates encounter can be solved with the help of locals—particularly local co-workers! Like the perceptual dimension, the others-oriented dimension can be measured using psychological tests.

THE CULTURAL TOUGHNESS DIMENSION

The cultural toughness dimension measures the degree to which the culture of the host country differs from the culture of the expatriates' home country, and, by extension, how tough it will be for expatriates to adjust to it. Only employees with high scores on their evaluations should be considered for assignments that will create a great degree of cultural toughness. If there is a small degree of difference, as, for example, between the United States and England, employees with lower scores can be considered.

The results of Mendenhall and Oddou's selection model should be used in conjunction with a consideration of employees' technical abilities and previous experience to determine whether employees are good candidates for expatriate assignments. However, it should be noted that this four-dimensional model is limited by its lack of consideration of employees' family situations, which can often be cause of expatriate failure, something we'll talk about in just a moment.

Selecting Those Most Likely to Succeed

The cost of expatriate failure can be enormous, both in terms of finances and of lost opportunity. An expatriate returning home from a foreign assignment has gained knowledge and skills that can be of great use to the company as it strives toward greater internationalization. But this opportunity will be lost if an expatriate has failed to complete his or her assignment or if he or she leaves the company. It is therefore of great importance that the IHRM minimize expatriate failure at the outset by selecting those expatriates most likely to succeed at an assignment. In the previous section, we have looked at several facets of human resource selection, with Mendenhall and Oddou's expatriate selection model being key to selecting those expatriates who present less likelihood of failure. But there are several additional steps the IHRM can take, in terms of training and pre-assignments practices, that can help maximize expatriate success.

THE EXPATRIATE FAMILY

One of the hardest considerations that an IHRM must make about an expatriate's potential for success is his or her spouse. It is also one of the most important. A great deal of research directly relates a spouse's ability to adjust to a new location with an expatriate's success. A spouse has to over-come many of the same challenges that the expatriate does but may not have the social network or sense of purpose that a job provides. Spouses can often end up feeling isolated, even resentful of their expatriate spouses and their spouses' employers. It is not hard to imagine the strain this puts on a relationship, and how this strain contributes to expatriate failure.

Further complications arise when considering expatriates' children. Though the strain that can be put on an expatriate by bringing children overseas is quite different from that of bringing a spouse, it is still very significant. In addition to the potential strain that children can place on a relationship, there may also be concerns about school, safety, and social atmospheres, depending on the ages of children.

Many IHRMs neglect this very important aspect of management because of the strong traditions in most Western nations of separating the work and personal lives of employees. Most managers are quite uncom-fortable asking about employees' spouses' emotional and mental states in a professional context. Though this concern is often valid, the special cir-cumstances of expatriate assignments and the strong connection between family and success make it appropriate for a more complete picture of an employee's personal life to be evaluated.

Spouse

There are many things that a company can do to ease spouses' transitions into a new culture, and thus improve expatriates' chances for success. Some of the solutions, such as offering employment, will not be possible for all com-panies, for financial reasons, but all options should be strongly considered.

The first, as mentioned, is offering employment to the spouse. This will provide a sense of purpose and ease the social isolation that spouses often feel, as well as providing added income and improving the standard of liv-ing for the family. The spouse will be earning respect and making friends in the workplace and will feel like a contributor instead of a tag-along. Again, this may not be possible for all companies, but alternatives can be found by forming relationships with other companies in the region so that the IHRM can at least put the spouse in contact with potential employers in the host country.

Another way that a company can help ease a spouse's isolation is forming a social network with other expatriate spouses in the area. The spouse will then have a group of people to plug into who are experiencing similar problems and frustrations and who will be able to sympathize and offer solutions.

Perhaps the easiest way that an IHRM can help prepare a spouse for international travel is offering language and cultural training. This is often a trivial expense on the part of the company, because it can take place in the home country before departure—and because the system is often already in place for employees. This spousal training will help alleviate the sense of isolation that spouses feel, as well as helping lessen the shock of moving into a new and unknown culture.

Children

Children are a major consideration for an expatriate before choosing to accept an assignment, so they should also be a consideration for the IHRM. After safety, which can be considered with living arrangements, the main concern of many expatriates for their children is schooling. This can be difficult in some regions of the world that do not have schools that teach in children's native language, but every effort should be made to make the transfer of children into a new school as seamless as possible. A child will always have some struggles to overcome when transferring to a new school, but if parents perceive that a foreign assignment is having a detrimental effect on their child's educational development, they may decide that completing an assignment is too great a risk.

Language and cultural training should also be offered to the children of expatriates, if their age is appropriate. This will aid in their education but also, just like with spouses, it will help alleviate their feelings of social isolation upon arriving in the foreign culture.

LANGUAGE TRAINING

Many companies based in English-speaking countries make the mistake of thinking that because the English language is also the language of international business, they do not need to provide language training to their expatriate employees. They assume that most of the business-related interactions that expatriates will have will be in English, and that interpreters will be available when necessary. Though these assumptions may be correct, they overlook the reality of the expatriate situation and suggest an ethnocentric mentality.

Foreign language training can benefit expatriates in many ways. First, it will enable direct interaction with local workers. This can help encourage local workers as well as helping to build rapport between them and expatriates. Appropriate training will also help in any negotiations that may take place. Even if a translator is available, having a working knowledge of the local language will help prevent miscommunication or unfortunate situations in which language barriers are exploited to cheat or take advantage of expatriates.

It should be noted, however, that an investigation of need should take place to determine the degree of language training that should occur. Some expatriates may rarely come into contact with local workers and may never be in a negotiation. In the course of such an investigation, both professional and personal considerations should be weighed. Being able to speak the local language can greatly ease expatriates' transitions into foreign cultures, contributing to their success.

CULTURE SHOCK AND HUMAN RESOURCES

If you have ever traveled abroad for a significant amount of time, you may have some idea of what culture shock is. You get off the plane, and for a while you are excited and full of a feeling of possibility. But soon the frustration begins to set in, because you can't understand the language and you don't understand local customs. Why do all the shops close in the early afternoon? Why do people eat dinner so late? Why did the waitress act offended when I tried to give her a tip? You may also be missing your family and friends and the sense of stability they give you. Your stay is suddenly not as pleasant as you thought it would be, and you may even be starting to feel depressed. This is just a taste of what some expatriates feel. Compounding their negative feelings are stress from work and a lack of control over the length of their stay. They can often feel like an astronaut in space: isolated and at the mercy of someone else to bring them home. As an IHRM, it is important to remember how serious culture shock can be, and how detrimental to the success of a foreign assignment.

Culture shock is characterized by feelings of homesickness, confusion, irritability, stress, anger, and depression. Whenever people travel from their home country, they take all of their knowledge of culture with them. This knowledge includes not just the types of TV shows they expect to watch, but also the appropriate ways to greet someone in a meeting and to interact with the opposite sex. If this knowledge and understanding conflicts strongly with the culture they travel to, something that is often the case, they are prime candidates for culture shock.

Culture shock generally takes place within a four-staged process consisting of a honeymoon, culture shock, adjustment, and mastery. The honeymoon can last from a few weeks to several months and can be thought of as the time when excitement and curiosity overshadow and distract from the stress of being in a foreign culture. Employees brush off the confusion caused by trying to hail a cab because of their excitement about the meeting they are going to, but eventually the excitement fades, and culture shock sets in. Suddenly, employees become annoyed or depressed because they don't know where to go to buy toothpaste. This stage can also last from weeks to months. At some point, though, expatriates enter the adjustment period and begin to recognize the importance of learning the norms and approaches of living in a new culture. Finally, expatriates enter the final phase, mastery. This stage is characterized by adaptation to the new culture, understanding of local customs, and ability to get along with locals. Employees who reach mastery have internalized the cultural differences of the home and host cultures and understand them.

These four stages can be very hard for an expatriate to go through and can take a great deal of time. In fact, many expatriates may never reach the fourth stage, because their foreign assignments may end before they reach it. However, there are a few steps that a company can take to minimize the impact of culture shock on employees and to lessen the amount of time it takes them to get through it.

Training For a New Culture

One of the most important ways that a company can help minimize the negative effects of culture shock on expatriates is by providing cultural training before their departure. A comprehensive training system contains four parts: cultural awareness training, visits to the host country, language training, and instruction on practical everyday matters that may be different in the host country.

Cultural awareness training consists of different methods of introducing expatriates to the destination culture and of increasing sensitivity to differences from the home culture. The training varies in degree based on the level of expected interaction and the relative difference between the two cultures. For example, if the expected interaction is low and the cultures' differences slight, the training should be relatively short and should consist of reading, watching movies, and perhaps listening to lectures. On the other hand, if the interaction is expected to be high and the cultural difference great, the training should last longer and should be more rigorous. In addition to less rigorous training methods, at this level, training can consist of active sensitivity training and role-playing.

Visits to the host country prior to the actual move can also be very effective in preparing expatriates for assignments. These are active exercises, but the short duration (usually around a week) and relative low stress levels make them ideal for easing employees into the new culture. In addition to this, these trips let employees meet future co-workers and get a sense of their future work environments. It should be noted, however, that there are risks associated with these trips. If the future location is generally unpleasant, a company may find itself unable to convince anyone to accept the assignment after the visit. Also, if employees begin to equate visiting a potential location with accepting the assignment, this facet of the training system will actually become a detriment to staffing positions.

As has been discussed, the value of language training should not be ignored. It is the single most powerful tool that expatriates will have for solving their own culture shock problems. It allows them to interact with locals and gives them an added sense of value when interacting with native co-workers. For business purposes, it may be appropriate to minimize language training if the stay will be short and interaction low, but if the stay is going to be long, language training should be given regardless of anticipated interaction levels, because of the risks of culture shock.

The final facet of training for a new culture is instruction on practical matters in the host country. This training, which can also go on into the actual assignment time, consists of giving the employee practical instruction on daily living in a society that may function in ways very different from their own. For example, how are children registered for school? Where must people go to pay certain registration fees? Questions such as these, if left unanswered, can lead to feelings of resentment and anger on the part of expatriates. When mixed with other feelings of culture shock, these feelings can be devastating to morale and success.

Aiding Adjustment to a New Culture

Obviously, assisting expatriates' adjustment to new cultures does not end when they depart. No matter how much training is given, expatriates will still experience difficulty in everyday life and work in the host country. There will be bad drivers and rude neighbors, just as there would be at home. For this reason, it is important for the company to continue to offer support throughout the duration of the assignment. This support can come as continuing training of the sort described above, as availability of liaisons in the host country, or as the maintenance of a network of fellow expatriates working with the employing company, or with other companies with whom it works. The value of this ongoing support should not be underestimated. Many companies, especially those just beginning their international operations, are guilty of an out-of-sight, out-of-mind mentality toward their expatriates' cultural adjustment. By not adopting a proactive attitude, they may inadvertently contribute to a failure rate that can have tremendous costs in both the short and long terms.

Repatriation

One of the great advantages of using expatriates is that you are simultaneously building a highly trained, culturally attuned group of managers that will strengthen your company and improve its international operations. Which do you think will work more successfully in international relations, a manager who has stayed at headquarters, or a manager who has spent two years in Japan, a year in France, and three years in Brazil? Thus it is a great loss when, as commonly happens, expatriates leave their employers after returning home from assignments. The reasons for this phenomenon vary but generally fall into the realms of reverse culture shock and dissatisfaction with the quality of their jobs when they return home. Whatever the reason, this should be seen as a failure of human resources to train expatriates for reentry into their home country.

The reasons expatriates give for leaving jobs after returning home include uncertainty about what positions they will hold upon returning or how their careers will progress, having to take lower-level jobs than the ones they had overseas, and returning to offices in which former peers have been promoted to higher positions. Repatriated employees are confused about their current positions, and they are uncertain about their futures. In addition to this, many expatriates, particularly those returning from long assignments, often suffer reverse culture shock when re-entering their home culture. They have learned new habits and adjusted to new customs, and they are troubled to discover that upon returning home, their former lifestyles and work environments frustrate them. This professional and personal disorientation often overwhelms them, and it becomes easier to find a new job rather than to adjust to their old one.

There are several practices that IHRMs can implement to alleviate much of the conflict and frustration that expatriates feel upon returning home. First, expatriates should be made aware as early as possible of the positions they will hold upon return. For shorter assignments, this can even be discussed before they depart. Second, every effort should be made to avoid the perception that returning expatriates are being shuffled into lower-level positions or are suffering decreases in their standards of living. A company cannot be expected to match all the perks of a foreign assignment, but special care should be taken in regard to status and pay. Finally, repatriation training should begin a short time before the end of the foreign assignment. This training should consist of reorientation meant to educate employees about future roles both in the company and in personal life.

Repatriation is the final step in a process that selects, trains, sends, and brings home expatriates. Failure to perform this final step can lead to the failure of the whole process, and a great deal of a company's investment may be lost.

ORGANIZED LABOR

Whenever a company or industry creates a large workforce, there is a chance that employees will organize in order to acquire bargaining power with management. Many companies ignore this reality and are often caught off-guard in the event of a walkout or other labor action. It is important that an IHRM understand the nature of organized labor and have a system in place to work with it and to deal with the consequences of its actions.

When a group of employees organize, management will often have to meet with them to determine terms of employment and compensation. Management and organized labor will then form a contract under which they will operate for a set period of time. When that time is up and the contract expires, renegotiations begin. If an agreement is not settled upon and negotiations fall apart, the labor union may strike in an attempt to force management to accept its terms. But because a union's members can vote out their leadership if they so desire, management may try to break the union by locking it out and hiring replacement workers. This often sows discontent among the members and weakens union leaders' position.

These actions, on the part of either party, pose significant risks. Workers give up their salaries and must survive on small stipends from the union, if even that. The company is also hurt, because production is often stopped completely, but overhead costs must still be paid. There is also the risk of the company losing market share while operations are on hold. For example, the UPS Teamsters strike in 1997 is credited with costing UPS a significant percentage of market share; during the strike, customers switched to using the USPS or FedEx. It is for these reasons that such heavy-handed tactics are relatively rare. Obviously, maintaining the delicate balance of this relationship is desirable, but it requires respect and dedication to finely tuned labor relations.

INTERNATIONAL LABOR RELATIONS

Labor relations are a difficult matter on the nation level, but on the international level they can become almost overwhelmingly complex. Each country's labor force has its own unique relationship with management. In countries like France, labor views management with a classist perspective, and all relations must take place with that in mind. On the other end of the spectrum are countries such as Japan, where conformity is much more the rule and where there is not such a confrontational view of management, but a greater sensitivity to perceived respect.

In order to operate in such mixed environments, international businesses must deal with each nation's labor force individually. Though there is bound to be significant overlap, many businesses have found it advantageous to decentralize labor relations so that each subsidiary has supervised control of its own operations, seeing this as the only way to maintain a strong position in such a fluid area of business.

It is not only businesses maintaining foreign subsidiaries that are interested in international labor relations. Companies that import materials or components from other countries are particularly vulnerable to fluctuations in labor relations in those countries. Because their relationships with labor in those countries are indirect, they cannot directly prevent strikes that could potentially bring entire operations to standstills. To prevent shutdowns from happening, many of them simply source their materials or components from multiple suppliers. Although this prevents truly efficient operations, it is sometime the only defense against the crippling shutdowns in the supply chain that can result from poor labor relations.

KEY POINTS TO REMEMBER

- When human resources goes international, a multitude of new considerations come to the fore. Employees are affected by events across the world, managers are sent abroad, and the international human resources manager must choose whether to enact ethnocentric (home office–centered), polycentric (foreign office–centered), or geocentric (company-centered) policies.

- Part of the IHRM's job is maintaining company policies in light of international labor laws. Pay scales must be adjusted, relocations funded, and cross-cultural literacy created—all while choosing the employees most likely to successfully make the transitions that are a part of expatriation.

- Expatriate managers often make the move abroad with their families. One of the most difficult parts of an IHRM's job can be preparing an entire family for expatriation. A spouse introduces certain considerations, and children still others. But language training, early and regular, can greatly ease the transition for all involved—as well as improving the manager's communication with foreign colleagues.

- The shock of entering a new culture can be alleviated by immersion—and immersion comes only over time, ideally deepened by a knowledge of the language. Brief trips abroad and cultural acclimitization that precede a trip can reap great rewards both before and after transfer, especially when paired with ongoing training in practical matters after arrival.

- The IHRM's job isn't done after expatriation. When expatriated managers return to the United States, they will experience another shock like the one they encountered when they left home. Many repatriated managers soon find leave for new work with another company in all the readjustment that follows a homecoming, but the IHRM's job is to keep them with their parent company as valuable sources of knowledge, experience, and expertise by fitting them back into their old corporate environment as seamlessly and as comfortably as possible.

- Whether working with expatriates or not, IHRMs working in an international business environment constantly deal with global issues. Labor relations in particular can make or break a company's profitability when it expands abroad, and IHRMs are the first line of defense when things threaten to go sour. Leveraging the strong points of the company's business model and mode of entry can mean the difference between profit, loss, and long-term success.

Evaluating Profits and Building for Future Growth

O nce you've started international operations, or any kind of new business expansion, you'll need to assess the health of your new venture and plan for that venture's future. It can be difficult in a new environment to tell how much progress you're really making. As previous chapters have discussed, the structure of many international agreements have time lags built into the collection of payment. Delays in acquiring information are important hurdles for your business, because if you want to be successful in international operations, you'll need to collect and interpret information about your foreign operations quickly. Adequate forecasting of product demand and an effective collections system are very important in the success and growth of your international operations. And, at the end of your fiscal year, you'll have to file financial statements and pay taxes, activities that are more nuanced in an international environment.

This chapter will explain some of the taxation and cash flow issues of international operation and give you some of the tools necessary to measure and plan for growth, including some potential strategies to reduce your overall tax liability. Specifically, we'll discuss some basic corporate tax issues, transfer pricing for firms that own foreign subsidiaries, international accounting standards, credit, and collection in the international environment. Additionally, we'll discuss how successful international businesses are dealing with the complex environment of world trade, as well as a few miscellaneous financial strategy issues. The important concern for this chapter is repatriation. Repatriation is the ability to move funds from a foreign subsidiary back to the domestic unit. Getting the bottom line abroad into the bottom line at home can be difficult for many reasons. The simplest reason is that some countries have repatriation limits, whether in absolute dollars or as a percentage of total subsidiary income. If you have successful operations abroad, you'll want to be able to bring the money home.

TAXES

Taxes are one of the most important factors in corporate finance decisions. Tax incentives for corporations participating in international operations can be very significant, both from domestic and foreign governments. Tax legislation that is business-friendly, that gives tax credits to foreign investors under certain circumstances, or that levies low effective corporate income tax rates is available in various countries. The barrier to finding and exploiting these incentives is that international tax law is incredibly complicated. Think of the U.S. tax code, a large and convoluted document. It's hard to find anyone who likes it, and it's harder still to find someone who knows *everything* about it. Then add another tax code for the other country you're doing business with or in, and a stack of trade relations treaties between the two nations. Corporate tax in the international environment may well be twice as complicated as it is in the domestic environment, if not more. And this leads us to the first problem with international corporate taxes.

One of the first issues in corporate taxation on an international scale, and historically one of the first problems with international trade, is double taxation—not the double taxation of corporate and individual income, but double taxation of corporate income alone (which could become triple taxation if you're a shareholder). If you own a foreign subsidiary in any way, you don't want to have the subsidiary taxed on the profits by its host nation and then have it taxed in the United States a second time. You want to have every dollar you make taxed only once.

Fortunately, the issue of double taxation is resolved, in large part, by agreements between countries. In many cases, developing nations have made bilateral or United Nations–sponsored treaties to resolve this issue so that no profits are taxed twice at the corporate level. The United States is also a member of the Organisation for Economic Co-operation and Development, or OECD, which forms exactly this type of boundary between tax administrations in each of the member states. The OECD contains most of America's largest European trading partners and Japan, although not China or India, which are covered by other agreements outside the OECD.

Generally speaking, it's likely that your company will only do business in a country where double taxation of corporate profits is not a significant issue, because the cost of business anywhere else would likely prohibit investment in the first place. The markets most likely to have negotiated some sort of agreement on tax issues are most likely the nations that businesses are most frequently investing in already. So if corporate income is not taxed twice, how is it taxed? What income and expenses belong to the subsidiary, and what belong to the home office? These questions become increasingly prickly for firms using a global or transnational strategy, in which production is spread across multiple national borders and can take place in countries where your company's product isn't even available on the market. This is just one issue associated with establishing production facilities abroad that you'll have to deal with in starting international operations. With the global or transnational strategic model, there is no true end value of manufactured parts. There is only an arbitrary one, which we'll discuss later in this chapter. So if the only price of components for your factory in Singapore is the price you pay from home office to subsidiary, but then you resell them at a higher price in Germany, then how does the "markup" get reported for your German offices, your home offices, and your factory in Singapore?

There has been a great deal of recent legal movement on this point in the last quarter of century: toward opening trade barriers by ensuring that double taxation of corporate income will not occur. However, this gives rise to questions about expropriation. Expropriation laws set how much (in currency or proportions) of the profit of a subsidiary in that country can be "sent" home, whether as payment or as dividend. Expropriation legislation sets the limit for how much money can be repatriated to the company headquarters. These laws serve two functions: to make sure that companies don't exploit different tax levels in an unfair way, and to encourage the reinvestment of profits made by a national unit back into the host country. In this way, expropriation pushes businesses that have made a foreign direct investment to continue investing within that national market.

The most important thing to remember is that you need to plan these matters with an accountant well versed with the tax laws of the United States and of whatever nation you're beginning international operations in—and having expertise on corporate tax law within that nation. Your American accountant is unlikely to have all the answers you need for these new environments. Many companies initially use tax consultants for this purpose, but you'll need continuing tax and accounting services as your operations grow and develop.

Exporting companies have much less to worry about in terms of tax issues. Corporate taxation for exporters is different than for purely domestic models, but the differences tend to be in your benefit. The United States currently offers various forms of tax incentives to exporting companies. The incentives are designed to encourage companies to export products abroad to alleviate a massive national trade deficit (discussed in previous chapters). The problem is that some of our trading partners view these tax incentives to exporting national firms as a form of government trade subsidy, not conducive to free trade markets, and perhaps inherently unfair. So some of these taxes have changed in recent years and will likely continue to change, generally trending toward reductions in trade barriers and subsidies.

When planning international operations, you should ask your accountant about depreciation, expensing, and general tax liability. Depreciation, or the rate at which assets "lose" value, and recognizing expenses financially (expenses that are then deductible from your corporate income, reducing tax liability) are two of the most important things in international accounting standards, as we'll discuss later in this chapter. Where you put your assets, including things such as property, plants, and equipment, determines where you get to depreciate it. Depending on the regulations between your home country and subsidiary host country, the question of "what gets reported where?" becomes very important in reporting your company's expenses (and thereby reducing your overall tax liability).

Although it probably won't last forever and isn't available to every company, there is one specific tax strategy that exporters in particular should keep in mind. Currently, a potential loophole exists for small exporting companies that are exporting to nations that have contested exporter tax incentives (largely European Union member states). That minor loophole is the ICDISC—the Interest-Charge Domestic International Sales Corporation. In order to use this, you'll need to consult with a lawyer and an accountant. It essentially allows you to capitalize on two different tax loopholes. Your company sets up an ICDISC as a separate legal and corporate entity, with itself as the sole shareholder. You "sell" your product to your ICDISC, and your ICDISC exports it abroad. The commission that your ICDISC takes for making the sale is then declared a dividend to your corporation, and it is taxed at the capital gains tax rate instead of the corporate income tax rate—and at the time of this writing, the capital gains tax rate is at a relatively low 15%. Again, we stress the importance of consulting with a lawyer on the choice of forming a new entity, and with an accountant on corporate tax planning and the benefits of the ICDISC for exporters. The reason we mention this is not so much to present this strategy as an answer to tax problems, but to encourage you to find tax liability strategies. Available tax strategies change all the time because of legislation, but they do exist, and by learning about them, you can begin to incorporate tax strategy into your overall growth strategy.

Apart from tax loopholes and differing tax legislation, we've mentioned in previous chapters that some countries are particularly receptive to foreign direct investment. The most common mechanism is a relatively low corporate tax rate. Tax rates differ from country to country, and some nations have adopted lower corporate tax rates as an incentive to invest within their borders. When making location decisions, taxes are an important part of the cost/benefit analysis process. You can research online and very easily find comparisons of corporate tax rates in other countries, which is a good way to start planning for tax liability in international operations.

Nobody seems to like taxes, but there are good ways to handle them, and there are bad ways. In the international business environment, the rules can change, and your company will need to learn how to handle taxes well in your new foreign operations.

Keep in mind that different countries have different auditing processes; you'll want to become well versed in the auditing process for the nations you operate in so that there aren't any surprises when they audit your subsidiaries. Audits are the last step in the cycle of taxes, and for businesses going abroad for the first time, this often overlooked part of life is something you need to think about from day one.

TRANSFER PRICES

One of the ways that companies can benefit from lower corporate taxes in other national markets is through the manipulation of transfer prices. Transfer prices are what one unit of your company charges another unit for some good or service. Suppose your company has a subsidiary in a country with lower corporate income tax rates. Now imagine that your national offices sell some input to your subsidiary, or that your subsidiary sells it back to your home office. The price you charge yourself (the transfer price) can be manipulated to capture more of your profit by reducing your overall tax liability. Suppose you have a foreign subsidiary that makes components, and that your domestic plants assemble them. If you "pay" your foreign subsidiary a high transfer price, then your taxable corporate income will be lower in the domestic market, and higher in the foreign market (with lower tax rates). Because the expense of paying yourself is tax-deductible in one place, with the revenue in a relatively lower-taxed nation, this means less overall taxation.

Manipulation of transfer prices is subject to various trade agreements and laws, so you'll need expert advice to find out whether or not it's a possibility for your company to use transfer prices to your advantage, and how much you can manipulate them.

Another benefit in the use of transfer prices is that it can shift your company's funds away from a currency that is expected to devalue in the near future, or to a currency that is expected to revalue. This motive for manipulating transfer prices allows your company to protect yourself from certain levels of foreign exchange risk.

An important role of transfer pricing is combating tariffs. We've said many times in this book that trade barriers, such as tariffs, are generally being reduced, but they are still prevalent in many countries. As nations engage in trade and open themselves to international direct investment, tariffs become a way to generate funds for the government, bringing with them other political benefits as well. Because of this, many countries still use tariffs extensively (including the United States). Take for example, ad valorem tariffs, or tariffs figured as percentages of the values of goods. If you need to send a good into a country that has an ad valorem tariff, you can set a low transfer price, thereby reducing the dollar cost of the tariff.

If the benefits of transfer pricing sound too good to be true, you're on to something. Governments tend to think of transfer pricing as, at the very least, violating the spirit of the law. They see it as being cheated out of income that ought to be theirs. Because of this, many governments pass laws defining what is acceptable or unacceptable manipulation of transfer price. You'll need to find out how strict the nation you are working in is on transfer price manipulation before you engage in the practice, or you may find yourself on the losing end of government penalties and regulations.

Note here that transfer prices are not to be confused with transaction costs. Transaction costs are the costs of performing a transaction, such as fees paid to financial experts evaluating an acquisition, or payments to banks issuing letters of credit on your behalf. Transfer prices, on the other hand, are internal to your firm.

Another way that companies have tried to extract money from subsidiaries to national offices for tax savings, or to get around repatriation laws, is the management fee. Technically, it is a kind of transfer price, because it is the cost of a service charged by one unit of your company to another.

This type of transfer price manipulation is extremely delicate and is the least favorite of many national tax administrations. When your subsidiary pays any form of "management fee" to its domestic parent, the subsidiary gets to write off the expense, which decreases its tax liability within that country. The fee goes home, and the government where your subsidiary is located will not be happy to lose out on some tax income. Most laws governing management fees as a type of transfer price are based around considerations of what the fair value of management expertise should be. When companies consistently decide that fair value is exactly the dollar amount that makes subsidiary corporate tax liability zero dollars, that gets discovered in the auditing process, and tax administrations can and will "reassess" corporate income. Be aware that there are regulations that govern this kind of behavior, typically with an eye toward curbing it. This is mitigated by one factor though—there's a lot of it. In 2000, it was estimated that about half of all international trade was intracompany—goods and services moving across national borders to get from one unit of a company to another unit of the same company—and that these goods and services were all done using transfer prices. Thus, if legislation on transfer pricing were too stringent, it could reduce over-all incentive to engage in international trade, and rational governments don't want trade to decline.

ACCOUNTING IN AN INTERNATIONAL CONTEXT

Accounting is sometimes described as the language of business. This is true, as far as it goes. But language, as we've discussed earlier in this book, doesn't always translate well. There are two major sets of accounting standards that you need to know: the U.S. GAAP and IFRS. The U.S. Generally Accepted Accounting Principles (GAAP) is set by the U.S. Financial Accounting Standards Board (FASB), which, in combination with the Securities and Exchange Commission (SEC), sets the way that American companies make financial reports, in terms of legal requirements and conventions. The International Accounting Standards Board (IASB) does the same for other nations, creating the International Financial Reporting Standards (IFRS).

These two systems are more alike than they are different, but the differences have a great deal of significance in terms of financial reporting compliance and company valuation in differing methods.

In terms of complying with local legal requirements, the financial rules that apply in the nation where you are doing business represent one of the most basic legal hoops your company needs to jump through. Abroad, you are likely to be operating in a country that uses IFRS, and you'll have to file financial statements using those rules and conventions. This might sound like your accountant's problem—not yours—but that isn't the case. Managers typically use figures from financial statements to forecast growth and to assess progress and profitability, so you'll need to be able to make the translation from one set of accounting standards to the other in order to make your financial analysis meaningful. Understanding the difference between the two can be tricky, and there is some movement (in a general sense) toward converging the two sets of standards, but as long as they're different, you'll need to know what the differences are. Furthermore, although there is a strong trend toward standardized accounting practices, IFRS is really a framework, not a code. Many countries use IFRS standards, but often with minor variations that are necessary to each country.

Apart from simple reporting requirements, the difference between accounting standards is also very important in the process of company valuation. If your firm is planning to acquire a target that prepares its financial statements using IFRS instead of GAAP, you'll need to be able to make sense of the differences. This is made especially important by the different ways that GAAP and IFRS treat goodwill.

How are GAAP and IFRS different? Here are some examples:

Issue	U.S. GAAP	IFRS
Reporting: The financial periods required in financial statements.	Two years of data for balance sheet, three for other financial statements.	Only one year of data for all statements.
Acquisition: The date an acquisition's market price is determined.	Usually the date of acquisition, but sometimes before, according to an agreement based on currency exchange fluctuation.	Always the date of acquisition. An upcoming convergence on this standard will unify to the IFRS standard by July of 2009.
Depreciation: Assets with components that depreciate at different rates from each other.	Component depreciation is allowed, but is not typically practiced.	Component depreciation is required if components differentiate from each other at different rates.
Equity: Reporting changes in equity.	Footnotes for each type of equity, or a separate statement.	A separate statement, at minimum, often accompanied by further information in the notes, or a specially prepared statement of all changes in equity.

This table is far from exhaustive, and at any rate some of these differences are moving toward convergence in practices. But these examples are nevertheless an illustration of the kinds of subtle differences in accounting rules that can make a difference for your company in reporting or valuing abroad. Obviously, some of these differences are in technical reporting disputes, whereas others can actually change the numbers significantly. Some of the more basic things, such as revenue and expense recognition, are more closely aligned between GAAP and IFRS—and moving toward further convergence. But differences between the two methods can lead to inaccurate calculations. Company valuation depends not only on the best possible, most detailed information, but also on knowing what that information means.

For example, when the German auto manufacturer, Daimler-Benz, applied to the SEC to get a listing on the New York Stock Exchange, the incompatibility of using two different sets of accounting practices was made clear. In an agreement with the SEC, Daimler-Benz would file GAAP financial statements and German financial statements. When it did this in 1994, the German statements said that Daimler-Benz had a profit of over $100 million. The GAAP statements recorded a loss of $1 billion. This level of discrepancy is unacceptable in an increasingly global business world, and in this instance, it led to highly discrepant stock prices on the NYSE and the other exchanges trading Daimler-Benz.

Additionally, the problem of accurate valuation can be a problem because accounting does have a certain level of subjectivity to it. Choosing a depreciation schedule, along with other leeway that companies have regarding when to recognize revenues and expenses—and other measures such as these—can change how "optimistic" financial statements are. Be sure to keep this in mind when valuing a foreign firm.

One final issue in international accounting is that the financial statements of a subsidiary (assuming that it has its own) are, by convention or law, prepared in the local national currency of the market it exists in. This means that your company would prepare your Japanese subsidiaries statements in yen and then use an exchange rate to put figures into American dollars. The exchange rate used varies for different statements. The balance sheet's exchange rate is the spot-exchange rate on the last day of your subsidiary's fiscal year. The income statement uses an annual average exchange rate from the fiscal year it covers. This is a minor hiccough, because, as discussed in the chapters about currency markets, spot-exchange rates can fluctuate a little from day to day. But over a year, exchange rates can fluctuate dramatically, meaning that the income statement can be less accurate in translation using the annual average exchange rate of a currency that appreciated or depreciated relative to the dollar over the course of that year.

When we say convergence of standards between GAAP and IFRS, it's important to know that there are many different national accounting standards, but that more and more countries are adapting their accounting standards to the IFRS model. And the IFRS model and GAAP are moving toward each other. For years, India had its own accounting standards, but over the last half a century, it has slowly pushed toward unifying these standards with international ones. Eventually, it completely satisfied IFRS adoption requirements, so that by 2005, an Indian company could be listed on the London Stock Exchange without having to file separate IFRS financial statements, its own being close enough to satisfy European security and exchange administrations. Obviously, this is an important criteria for multinational public companies. But having standardized accounting conventions has benefits for private companies, too, especially when it comes to attracting foreign investment or strategic alliance agreements. Foreign partners will want to see your financial statements before they consider making an investment in your business or participating in a strategic alliance, and they'll want to see those statements in the accounting language they use.

CREDIT AND COLLECTION INTERNATIONALLY

Accounts receivable are, in theory, the closest an asset can be to cash without actually being cash. Collecting payment is an integral part of the sales process, and that principle holds true for international operations. But credit collection is different in different national economies, not only legally, but in terms of reporting and cultural norms. Most companies have a general "pay slowly, collect quickly" policy toward accounts receivable and accounts payable, because a dollar today is worth more than the same dollar tomorrow. But apart from this general strategy of fast collections and slower payouts, there are also different national business norms that define appropriate timetables for payment disbursement and collection, just another part of the international business environment that tends to surprise companies taking part in their first international ventures.

Before making a sale or buying on credit, the first thing you'll want to know is, can I trust this company? Checking the credit history of a foreign firm can be difficult. Some information can be gathered by finding out that firm's reputation, but the traditional measures and credit reporting systems of other countries are often unfamiliar to American businesses, and are also less accurate or less comprehensive than American equivalents.

This is another area where advances in information technology have facilitated the expansion of international business. A great deal of individual businesses' credit reports are available through a variety of online databases. One of these can be your company's first source, followed by any credit agencies based within your foreign partner's country.

In terms of collections in the international environment, credit insurance of several kinds is available, and your company should consider it. Coverage is available for just about anything, from genuine cash flow problems in your buyer's company to a coup that disrupts trade. These insurance programs can be either offered by private companies specializing in business insurance or, as is the case for much political risk (the risk of political upheaval effecting business), by the U.S. government.

In previous chapters, we discussed some dimensions of the use of letters of credit in international business. The most important thing to remember is that the best collections come when dealing with companies that have favorable credit reports and history. A letter of credit should be created by you and the issuing bank and should be agreed upon before it is issued, because amending it later can increase the cost of the transaction substantially. Furthermore, if your company is just starting to use letters of credit or is examining credit insurance, keep in mind that there is a significant learning curve in the legal and paperwork sides of international operations, so if the transaction costs of your early efforts in international business seem very costly, keep in mind that those costs will decrease significantly as you become more familiar with all aspects of the international business process.

As discussed previously, comity and jurisdiction are important safeguards in international transactions. This is especially true in the case of credit and collections. In any sale or purchase made on credit, you'll want to know what authority or authorities can come to your aid if things go wrong, and where the dispute can be heard. Questions of jurisdiction are set either by treaty or by agreement between parties. Remember in negotiations that this is an important point, and one worth arguing over, especially when doing business with a nation that has an unreliable justice system. Often times, rather than arguing over it, it's best to establish that disputes will be heard in some other national court. The London court system is used frequently for this purpose, but there are others.

Collections strategy can actually use the changes in currency valuation to your advantage. If you have accounts receivable in a currency that is expected to appreciate in the near future, you can wait to collect it until the currency is worth more. This is called a lag strategy. A lead strategy is just the opposite: when you have accounts receivable in a currency that is expected to depreciate, you want to collect as quickly as possible to avoid the negative affects of the lower relative value of the payments. What should be coming clear to you at this point is that all of the financial issues in international business have both positive and negative aspects, each requiring precise understanding of the issue. And there are still other ways to use taxes and collection and accounting differences to your company's advantage.

TRANSACTION COSTS

Transactions costs are the costs of doing business within the cost of doing business. They are associated with moving funds in the international context. When your company puts funds into an international project, it will need to convert those funds into the local currency; the commission charged by foreign exchange dealers is a transaction cost. Similarly, just moving money to a bank abroad will often incur a transfer fee. Transaction costs are a significant part of international operations. The easiest way to minimize them is through transferring in volume. Consolidating transfers to larger sums, or converting currency in large quantities rather than in individual purchases, will end up saving you money during your business's monetary transfers.

Transaction costs can also be minimized by consolidating transactions, or netting. This is a simple process. If a subsidiary owes $2 million to its parent, but the parent wants to make an additional loan to the subsidiary for future operations of $1 million, than the netting solution is to just have the subsidiary repay $1 million. By decreasing the amount transferred, the company can cut transaction costs significantly. The transfer fees charged by banks are typically a percentage of the funds transferred, and the commissions paid to foreign exchange dealers are as well. Using tried and tested strategies can decrease can decrease them.

Multilateral netting takes the simple process of netting and extends it to large and diverse multinationals. It's a much more complicated process when a company is operating in a wide array of countries, especially if there's a great deal of interplay between them. But multilateral netting is (theoretically) the most efficient way for a multinational to reduce transaction costs: simultaneously reducing the number and size of transactions between different business units. The reason we say "theoretically" is that effective multilateral netting requires centralized and accurate financial decision making, because only a CFO with a "birds-eye view" of all the transactions between all the national units can make multilateral netting possible. Gathering that much information in one place is difficult for some multinational corporations, but there are methods for doing so—including one we'll discuss later in this chapter.

An important consideration in today's global business environment is taking a relationship-oriented approach to international banking needs. You might be able to reduce transaction costs on an individual transaction by bidding them out one at a time and choosing the financial intermediary with the most competitive bid every time, theoretically reducing your company's overall transaction costs. But the caveat to strategies for minimizing transaction costs by finding the cheapest banker is that banks vary in their speed of execution and the quality of the forecasting and currency market information that they can provide. Keep in mind the long-term benefits of establishing a relationship with a bank—because a good bank is worth its weight in (your) gold.

INTRACOMPANY LOANS

One way to finance your international operations is to do it yourself. Many large multinationals have increasingly used intracompany loans from parent to subsidiary or from subsidiary to subsidiary to finance new projects, to capitalize on tax benefits, or to move funds out of a country whose government restricts free movement of repatriated funds. One variety is a "fronting loan." In this case, the loan isn't made directly from parent to subsidiary but is channeled through a large international bank. A parent makes deposits in such a large international financial intermediary. The funds it deposits are paid interest by that bank. The bank then loans the deposited amount to a foreign subsidiary of the parent depositor, charging a slightly higher interest rate on the loan than they are paying to the deposit. The interest earned transfers money from the subsidiary to the parent, and the interest expense on the loan is tax deductible for the subsidiary. Here's what this looks like:

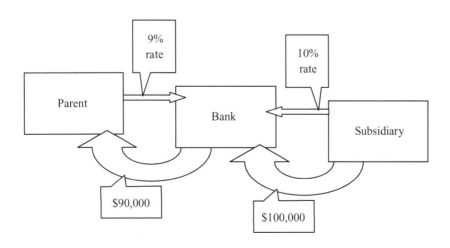

Suppose a parent deposits $1 million in an international bank. The bank loans the $1 million to that parent's foreign subsidiary. The bank pays 9% interest on the deposit and charges 10% on the loan. For simplicity, we'll assume that the subsidiary is located in a country that taxes corporate income at a 50% rate. The $100,000 that the subsidiary pays in interest is a tax deduction, meaning that the after-tax cost of the loan (with the relatively higher 50% rate) is $50,000. The bank pays the parent $90,000, keeping $10,000 for itself as a charge for the fronting loan. Because the after-tax cost of the loan is lower than the interest payment on the deposit, the company overall has netted $40,000 on the agreement and has effectively moved $90,000 out of your subsidiary as well as a $1 million investment into it. The use of a large international bank for the loan prevents some country-related political risk; national governments are unlikely to contest loans made through a large international bank, because doing so is apt to have a negative impact on their relationships with foreign investors and could negatively affect credit with international financial institutions.

THE RISE OF THE INTERNATIONAL FINANCE CENTER

A recent trend in international business for companies to establish their own international finance centers, functional business units whose sole purpose is focusing on international finance management, including corporate tax strategy, and valuing and translating financial statements prepared with different accounting principles. An international finance center can manage currency risk, focus on inflationary pressures in multiple domestic markets, and find the best capital at the best rate in a global marketplace for money by focusing on international finance management alone. This doesn't make such a center just a support system for your company's strategy decisions; international finance centers can effectively increase profits for your company in a number of ways. If you operate a small business and this sounds like too high a level commitment of resources for the scale at which you operate, you might be right. But for a growing company that is expanding in international operations, the establishment of an international finance center or the use of an international finance specialist (in the case of a smaller business) might not only be necessary, it might be the edge you need to compete in a global marketplace. Remember all the times we've told you that additional resources or special expertise will be needed. In order to be truly successful in international business, your company will need to get as much of that expertise in-house as it possibly can: hence the creation of international finance centers.

FINANCIAL STRUCTURES AROUND THE WORLD

Financial structure, or the mix of debt and equity used to finance a business, can have a lot of variation within any one country. But there are some larger trends regarding how financial structures differ from one country to another. Japanese firms tend to use more debt financing than Americans, and Italian firms have debt-to-equity ratios that are almost twice those of firms in Singapore. The financial structures are part of "business as usual" within these countries. Some academics argue that the reason that financial structures vary from country to country is that financial structures are adaptive to national capital markets and tax regimes. But for our purposes, it's not all that important why financial structures are different from nation to nation. When beginning a new international operation, should your new subsidiary conform to the typical financial structure in that country? In acquisition, should you reshape the acquired unit's mix of debt and equity to look like your own? These are topics that academics have spent a lot of time researching in recent years, and their findings have not yet been conclusive.

Generally, your company should always choose the financial structure for any business unit that minimizes the cost of capital for that unit. Sometimes that means adapting to the local market, and sometimes it doesn't. Don't be afraid of increasing the debt ratio in a foreign subsidiary to align with cultural norms. The reason that companies within a national market use more debt financing tends to be at least partially that the cost of debt is relatively cheaper. Furthermore, part of the price of debt is the value of the currency in which it is repaid. If you borrow in a currency that is expected to depreciate, you can repay it by converting higher value currency to that currency, thereby decreasing the cost of debt. An important consideration that ought to encourage your company to go international is the benefits to your firm's overall cost of capital. One factor in your firm's cost of capital is default risk—the likelihood that your firm will incur liabilities that it cannot meet, going bankrupt. If your company is diversified internationally in any form of participation (partial ownership, diversified products, etc.), your company will be receiving cash flows from diverse sources. If your international operations are successful, cash flows coming to your company from unrelated wellsprings will decrease your company's default risk, lowering your average cost of capital across the board.

USING MONEY TO MAKE MONEY: CENTRALIZED DEPOSITORIES

We've outlined several ways to move cash from one place to another, and there are practical reasons for that: cash is a primary resource and allocating it where it is needed is important. But there is also a strong strategic reason: centralized depositories. Every business needs to have some cash reserves on hand to use for emergency expenditures or for opportunities that won't wait long. Financial formulas provide us with estimates of the amount that a business should theoretically have on hand at any moment in order to service these needs. But cash reserves need to be put to work, in order to keep pace with inflation and currency valuation issues.

Businesses typically hold their cash reserves in money market accounts from which they can withdraw their reserves at any point, as well as in a variety of other short-term investments. The problem is that these money market accounts earn relatively low interest returns. Returns can be increased by holding larger amounts of money in these accounts (and thereby qualify for a higher interest rate). By putting all the cash in one place, the larger deposit earns a higher rate of return. It also can be put to better use, and earn a higher return, if a combination of liquid accounts (such as money markets) and slightly less liquid short-term investments (such as certificates of deposit) are used. Pooling money together has strong advantages, because you need to have some cash reserves, but you want the cash reserves to increase while you wait to use them. Centralized deposits, particularly if located in a financial center like London or New York, can achieve a better rate of return than individually held cash reserves by a group of subsidiaries. That's one of the strongest incentives for moving money out of subsidiaries and pooling it together. The centralized depository does have limits, in terms of regulation by governments that restrict moving capital out of your subsidiaries, but any successful multinational must work around them.

BLOCKED FUNDS: WHAT TO DO WHEN YOU CAN'T GET YOUR MONEY OUT

We've talked about assessing political, or country, risk in many places throughout this book: how to analyze it, how to calculate for it. But what do you do when your funds are blocked? Any number of political issues could upset the flow of trade, from riots to elections to reforms. If you can't find a way around government restriction by strategic use of dividends, transfer pricing, or fronting loans, what do you do? The answer is easy—put it to good use. In the face of blocked funds in one subsidiary, many companies have established research and development facilities within that national market. If you can't get operating profit across the border, research and development investment is a good option. You can't take the money out, so use it to spread benefits to other subsidiaries. Research and development costs must be incurred somewhere, but their potential benefits can be felt everywhere. You won't just be reinvesting in the future profits of the subsidiary where funds are being kept by regulation, only to turn a profit that's still trapped within a national border. Also, when political issues do arise—and they almost certainly will—don't be afraid to get involved with the local government. As long as you are providing a tax base and economic stimulation for their country, you are a constituent of that government. Developing some relationships with government officials and lobbying for yourself can be very beneficial in ensuring your company's safety from political fluctuations.

FOREIGN INVESTORS

There are two main reasons that businesses use equity sold abroad. The first is that it can be cheaper, depending on the required rate of return for investors in a given national market or the availability of investment capital within the market. The second is that sometimes they have to do it. Host countries prefer, and sometimes require through legislation, that you raise capital within their own markets. So your company will either be complying with the local regulations or enjoying the favoritism of a foreign government if you raise some capital through selling equity within that national market. In order to do this effectively, first research the cost and necessity of raising capital this way. In order to maintain healthy relationships with foreign investors, you'll need to market your shareholder services in a way that foreign investors want. In Japan, investors want to hear about long-term corporate goals and strategy. In Europe, there's more interest in the performance, capabilities, and stability of your company's management team. Many multinationals (assuming they have the resources to afford it) use local consultants or financial firms in order to research likely foreign investors, how to market shares to them, and what structures are necessary to maintain the relationship. And there's another reason that foreign investors are appealing: broader demand for your shares can boost share prices. Raising equity funds in a global marketplace has a lot of benefits for your firm, which is why more and more companies are trying to get listed on multiple international stock exchanges (which hearkens to the drive to standardize accounting principles). Global companies are a new phenomenon in terms of the geographical distribution of ownership, but they are gaining traction.

CAPITAL BUDGETING IN INTERNATIONAL BUSINESS

When it comes to evaluating potential projects, there are two special considerations for international business ventures. The first is that money that never comes back home isn't really your money. If you can't get money out of a foreign subsidiary because of government restrictions, tax liability, political risk, or currency exchange risk, it's not really yours. In planning an international operation, you need to take this into consideration when determining the value of a new international business. Calculating the risks and the limitations on funds that could transfer from subsidiary to corporate headquarters is an important nuance in capital budgeting that your company will need to learn. A lot of the "risk" factors are arbitrary estimates that you'll have to research to determine what is reasonable. The other important factor when you're crunching the numbers on your new international venture is that you can research the market as long and thoroughly as you like, and it will still surprise you. Furthermore, the importance of establishing your company or your product in a growing international market has such strong strategic benefits to position your company for the future that the numbers don't have to work out perfectly for international expansion to be a good idea. Obviously, this is an area where a lot of discretion is involved, so it's really up to your company to develop guidelines for how good an opportunity has to be to spur action. The strategic value of international operations does mean that lower projected values of an international project are acceptable, and many companies recognize this. What they don't always recognize is that the extensive environmental variables and the internal meddling of transfer pricing and tax strategy can seriously alter the normal measurements of effectiveness. The simple rate-of-return ratios that companies typically use to evaluate the performance of a business unit can be drastically manipulated by shifts in the foreign currency market, or a fronted loan, or any of the international finance tactics that we've discussed. So assessing the health of a foreign subsidiary ought to "adjust" the numbers in order to make them meaningful. This is also true for evaluating the performance of managers at foreign subsidiaries. Because many managers have compensation tied to performance, they managers will feel mistreated if the real reason they performed "poorly" was because of a fluctuation in currency value.

PLANNING FOR FUTURE GROWTH

Throughout this book, we've tried to stress that the international business environment is constantly changing. The changes show general trends in many cases, but the general rule is to expect the unexpected.

In discussing cultural issues, we talked about how culture is an adaptive mechanism. Cultures are, to varying extents, changing around the globe to adapt to a smaller and smaller world. We discussed the international monetary system, how the policy of major international financial organizations is changing, how currencies fluctuate and affect the world economy, and how foreign direct investment trends are changing the ways that companies use resources around the globe. Discussing strategy options and potential modes of entry for your firm, we stressed the importance of strategy evolution, changing and adapting your company's plans and methods as experiences are gained and new opportunities present themselves. We examined how political and legal factors influence international business through regulation and processes, and the ways that these are changing. In this final section of the book, we looked at issues that are more specialized to international business, including global supply chain management and international human resources, two topics that are essentially new phenomena in the business world.

This book has not tried to be a complete guide to international business, but by showing you the kinds of changes and forces that are at work in the international business environment, and by giving you the tools and the conceptual framework to approach it, we hope to have given you the confidence to go global.

The idea of change is forbidding to new arrivals, but there is one thing about it that managers ought to take comfort in: change is good. Shifts in the way business is done mean new opportunities. Some companies have been engaged in international business for a long, long time. If they've succeeded, it has been because they have continually adapted to a changing world. But change temporarily levels the playing field. There are opportunities all around the world, whether presented by reductions in trade barriers, advances in transportation and information technology, or any of the other trends behind globalization today, and all you and your company have to do is find and capitalize upon them.

KEY POINTS TO REMEMBER

- Plan ahead to handle taxes in international business, and understand the tax liabilities you will be expected to fulfill.

- Remember that exporting incurs fewer tax problems than operating in a foreign nation does, and that loopholes such as Interest-Charge Domestic International Sales Corporations (ICDISCs) can help you take advantage of doing so.

- Be versed in the auditing processes used in the nations where you will be operating, whether the U.S. Generally Accepted Accounting Principles (GAAP) or the International Financial Reporting Standards (IFRS).

- Credit insurance can help you collect on international obligations.

- Minimize transaction costs by leveraging high-volume transactions and by netting—remember that you can finance your own expansion by loaning funds to your foreign subsidiary.

- Use company international finance centers to help provide you with international expertise, giving you an edge in international operations—use your money to make money. Focus on creating a financial structure for your business that minimizes the cost of capital for each unit.

- Research and development efforts can provide value for your company when funds are blocked—remember that money that doesn't come back home is not your money.

- Remember to expect the unexpected, and plan for it. No matter the business climate, always look for opportunities.

Appendix A:
Where to Get More Information

There are many sources of information you may find helpful as you prepare to enter the world of international business. In this section, we have provided a number of sources where you can find more information. First, we provide a partial list of where you can find information from government sources. Following that list is a section on academic sources and a section on private sources. Finally, we provide information on the print and online sources used in the preparation of this book.

GOVERNMENT SOURCES

CIA World Factbook
URL: www.cia.gov

On the Central Intelligence Agency Web site, there is a resource available to the public called the CIA World Factbook. It contains basic demographic sketches of every country, with maps and some basic cultural facts about each nation. This can be a good reference if you already know what foreign nations you are planning to enter. The information is not geared specifically toward businesses, but it can provide a good foundation of information for an unfamiliar national culture, economy, and environment.

International Monetary Fund: Country Reports

URL: www.imf.org/external/country/index.htm

The International Monetary Fund country reports are less general than the *CIA Factbook* profiles of countries. They are focused primarily on economic rather than demographic factors. The site has an index of countries, and each country's page has various reports, with new ones frequently added or updated.

Business.gov

URL: www.business.gov

This Web site is a good place to start when researching what your business needs to know about international business. The site is designed to provide a wide array of information about compliance and business processes in international trade. The site is run by the United States Small Business Administration (mentioned later in this appendix), and is designed as a reference site for American companies. Unlike the Small Business Administration, Business.gov is solely an information and reference source, whereas the SBA provides services beyond information.

Export-Import Bank of the United States

URL: www.exim.gov

The Export-Import Bank of the United States provides financing for U.S. goods and services exported abroad. There are six regional offices, which you may contact directly once you find which office serves the state where your business is located. The financing is competitive with the market, but as a government agency the Export-Import Bank has a vested interest in helping American-owned companies succeed in exporting.

The Export-Import Bank serves companies large and small but has specific structures in place to serve small businesses. The Export-Import Bank is also a wealth of information on foreign markets and can help to identify potential prospects for international marketing efforts of your company's product or service. Some of the information available on the bank's Web site or in its offices is categorized according to industry, target market, or both. But the most comprehensive services and information require you to deal with the bank's regional offices directly.

Department of Commerce: International Trade Administration
URL: Trade.gov

The Department of Commerce collects a wide array of data, much of which can be useful to your business. For the purposes of international business, the most useful is likely to be that collected by a subunit of the Department of Commerce, the International Trade Administration.

At the International Trade Administration site, you'll find that there are different organizations within the ITA. The one that we've mentioned in this text, and that will be able to help your business expand into international markets, is the United States Commercial Service. As mentioned earlier in this book, the U.S. Commercial service is able to perform some basic market research for your company, help network with foreign buyers, and provide counseling in the exporting process to your business. Think back to every time in this book that you were told to "consult an expert." The U.S. Commercial Service can be that expert. Additionally, the International Trade Administration will help your business comply with international trade standards, with regard to both the legal requirements of the U.S., and the legal requirements for your company abroad.

United States Small Business Administration
URL: www.sba.gov

The U.S. Small Business Administration provides a vast array of information and resources for any small business. Some of the available resources are tailored specifically to international business, although the SBA is not quite as focused on international trade as are some of the other resources mentioned here. If you are part of a small business, you may already be familiar with the Small Business Administration, and you should research how they can help your business compete in international markets, specifically.

International Organization for Standardization (ISO)
URL: http://www.iso.org/

If you are going to manufacturing abroad, selling abroad, or buying abroad, you will want to be aware of the international standards that apply to the products and services of interest. The most widely used standards in international business are those set by the International Organization for

Standardization (ISO). This is a rapidly changing area that impacts international business. The ISO has over 17,000 standards on a wide variety of subjects. Some 1,100 new standards are published each year.

Foreign Agricultural Service
URL: http://www.fas.usda.gov/

The Foreign Agricultural Service of the U.S. Department of Agriculture offers a plethora of information for businesses in fields related to agriculture, including not only individual commodities but also such areas as biofuels, wine, and wood products. The FAS offers data and answers questions about trade, and in sections of its site you can learn about getting export assistance.

ACADEMIC SOURCES

Many academic organizations have resources for, and actively seek partnerships with, international businesses. These resources provide various supports, largely information-based, that can be valuable to your company. We provide two examples here, but you should check with the academic institutions that are convenient for you to find what programs they have available to your disposal.

Bradley University: The Turner Center for Entrepreneurship
URL: www.bradley.edu/turnercenter

The Turner Center for Entrepreneurship provides free counseling and low-cost training for businesses in central Illinois. The center has different units that focus on small business development, international trade, and startup firms. The counseling the center provides can be valuable to planning and executing international trade operations, especially for companies entering international markets for the first time.

University of Illinois Urbana-Champaign:
Illinois International Trade Center
URL: www.itc.uiuc.edu

The Illinois International Trade Center offers counseling services and international trade seminars (similar to those offered at the Turner Center for Entrepreneurship). Also, it grants access to a trade reference library that will help your business in the early stages of researching international markets. Further, the ITC can help you find financing sources for exporting, a valuable service.

We present these two sources as examples, but you should be aware that many universities have such resources available to businesses, and you should look into institutions convenient to your business's location. Even these two examples are not exhaustive of the universities that sponsor them. Bradley also has an organization specifically devoted to trade in Asia, and the University of Illinois has many organizations that can aid in international trade. The best part about these resources is that much of what they provide in information is free, and the services tend to be priced below what your company would have to pay at a private institution.

PRIVATE-SECTOR SOURCES

International Chamber of Commerce
URL: www.iccwbo.org

The International Chamber of Commerce, just like national, regional, or local chambers, is an organization that your business might consider joining once already engaged in international operations. The chamber's stated purpose is to further international economic growth. As a member, there are many privileges (and dues). But if your business joins, it may be easier to find other companies in similar industries or markets, who can share their expertise and experience to help in your company's international expansion.

Your Bank

We do not include any particular bank as an example here because the most natural choice is to turn to your current bank. You'll need to work with a bank in the case of importing and exporting, for foreign exchange in many cases, and in many other international business functions. If your current bank has these capacities already, it is probably best to work with them, at least in the early stages of international operations. Find out through your banker what services are available through your current bank (as a healthy banker–business relationship can be a big help). If your present bank does not offer the international services you need, they may be able to help you locate another bank that does offer the services you need. In any case, you should thoroughly research the banking options available to you. The time required to locate a bank that is a good fit for the needs of your business, both now and down the road, is time well spent.

PRIVATE INFORMATION SOURCES

There are many subscription fee databases available on the internet today. We give one example here, but there are more out there. Paying a subscription fee for information is something you should only consider once you have already exhausted free information sources, because there's no sense in creating an unnecessary expense for your business.

ISI Emerging Markets
URL: www.securities.com

The information available on this site is specific to emerging markets all over the world. There are databases on industry standards and norms in these markets, financial reports on companies within these markets, and news pertaining to these markets. The database is user-friendly in finding information based on searches for what is relevant and current in your industry, and the authority of the sources that the database draws from is high. The information is useful and of high quality, which is why the owners of the site are able to charge businesses a subscription fee to use it.

Stock Exchanges

Stock exchanges are the locations where ownership of businesses is publicly traded. If you would like to know more about these exchanges, here are locations where you can find more information about the five largest stock exchanges.

New York Stock Exchange (NYSE)
URL: http://www.nyse.com

American Stock Exchange (AMEX)
URL: http://www.amex.com

NASDAQ Stock Market (NASDAQ)
URL: http://www.nasdaq.com

London Stock Exchange
URL: http://www.londonstockexchange.com

Tokyo Stock Exchange
URL (English): http://www.tse.or.jp/english/

There are stock exchanges in many, many nations, from Australia to Zimbabwe. Some are well respected despite their comparatively low trading volumes. The very small exchanges (such as the Khartoum Stock Exchange or the South Pacific Stock Exchange) have little influence on the world economic environment and are likely to be of only marginal use for most international businesses.

Commodity Exchanges

Commodities are also traded on exchanges. The major commodities traded include agricultural products (such as grains and grain derivatives, animals and meat, coffee, wine, and wood), fuels and biofuels, emissions and other environmentals, industrial metals, precious metals, rubber, and plastics. Not all exchanges handle all commodities. Among the world's major commodity exchanges are the following.

In the United States:
New York Board of Trade/Intercontinental Exchange (ICE; agricultural products and biofuels
URL: https://www.theice.com/homepage.jhtml

New York Mercantile Exchange (agricultural products, energy, industrial and precious metals)
URL: http://www.nymex.com

Chicago Mercantile Exchange (CME, often called the "Merc")
URL: http://www.cme.com/

Kansas City Board of Trade (agricultural products)
URL: http://www.kcbt.com/

Outside the United States:
Brazilian Mercantile and Futures Exchange (Brazil; agricultural products, biofuels, precious metals)
URL (English): http://www.bmf.com.br/portal/portal_english.asp

Dalian Commodity Exchange (China; agricultural products, plastics)
URL (English): http://www.dce.com.cn/portal/en/index.jsp

London Metal Exchange (Great Britain; nonferrous metals, plastics)
URL: http://www.lme.co.uk/

NYSE Euronext (Europe; agricultural products)
URL: http://www.euronext.com/landing/indexMarket-18812-EN.html

Tokyo Commodity Exchange (Japan; agricultural products, energy, industrial and precious metals)
URL (English): http://www.tocom.or.jp/

Of course, the commodity exchanges listed above are not the only commodity exchanges in the world, just some of the largest. If your company is already involved with commodities, then you are probably familiar with one or more of the commodity exchanges. Moving into an international market, however, may require that you start looking at commodity markets outside the U.S. You will want to do your homework on the commodity markets of interest to your business. The point is that this information is often readily available via the internet, and you should be proactive in gaining the knowledge you'll need to stay current with the markets serving your international enterprises.

INFORMATION SOURCES USED TO WRITE THIS BOOK

The sources used while writing this book (listed below) can provide additional information for you as you learn more about international business operations.

Print Sources:

Czinkota, Michael R., and Masaaki Kotabe, eds. *Trends in International Business: Critical Perspectives.* New York: John Wiley & Sons, Incorporated, 1998.

Dunning, John H. *Multinational* Enterprises *and the Global Economy.* Upper Saddle River, NJ: Financial Times/Prentice Hall, 1992.

Graham, Edward M., and Paul Krugman. *Foreign Direct Investment in the United States.* New York: Peterson Institute for International Economics, 1995.

Hill, Charles W. L. *International Business: Competing in the Global Marketplace,* 5th ed. Boston: McGraw-Hill/Irwin, 2005.

James, Peter, with Nick Thorpe. *Ancient Inventions.* New York: Random House Publishing Group, 1995.

Jeannet, Jean-Perre, and Hubert D. Hennessey. *International Marketing Management.* Boston: Houghton Mifflin Company, 1988.

Meloan, Taylor W., and John L. Graham. *International and Global Marketing: Concepts and Cases.* Grand Rapids, MI: Irwin Professional, 1997.

Nelson, Carl A. *Import/Export: How to Get Started in International Trade.* New York: McGraw-Hill Education, 2000.

Nicholas, William G., James M. McHugh, and Susan M. McHugh. *Understanding Business,* 8th edition. Boston: McGraw-Hill Irwin, 2008.

Reuters. *An Introduction to Foreign Exchange and Money Markets.* New York: John Wiley & Sons Canada, Limited, 1999.

Taoka, George M. *International Business.* New York: Addison-Wesley Longman, Limited, 1991.

Online Sources:

The online sources provided below are sorted by the topic for which they were used.

Bank for International Settlements

This institution has its own Web site that describes its operation and role. URL: http://www.bis.org/

Bretton Woods Conference and System

There are many sources on the Web for information about the 1944 Bretton Woods Conference and System. Here are two:

http://web.worldbank.org/WBSITE/EXTERNAL/EXTABOUTUS/ EXTARCHIVES/0,,contentMDK:64054691~menuPK:64319211~ pagePK:36726~piPK:36092~theSitePK:29506,00.html

http://economics.about.com/od/foreigntrade/a/bretton_woods.htm

Currency Exchange Market

In addition to general sources, there are more detailed sources of information on the currency exchange market. Here are three:

The U.S. Treasury
http://www.treas.gov/education/faq/markets/foreignex.shtml

Federal Reserve Bank of New York
http://www.newyorkfed.org/education/fx/foreign.html

World Bank
http://www.worldbank.org/fandd/english/1296/articles/051296.htm

Forward, Future, and Options Contracts

From Duke University
http://www.duke.edu/~charvey/Classes/ba350_1997/futures/lecture.htm

From the Federal Reserve
http://www.federalreserve.gov/boarddocs/supmanual/bhc/200701/ 2000p7.pdf

Gold Standard

Many online references include information on the gold standard. Here are two:
http://www.uiowa.edu/ifdebook/faq/faq_docs/gold_standard.shtml
http://www.auburn.edu/~garriro/g4gold.htm

International Monetary Fund

In this book, information on the International Monetary Fund (IMF) and SDRs came in large part from the IMF Web site.
http://www.imf.org/

In addition to general information about the IMF, you can also find a great deal of other useful data on this site. Some of the IMF data requires payment; most does not.

Silk Road

If you have an interest in the history of international trade, one good source of information on the Silk Road is the international organization devoted to this ancient route.

http://www.silkroadproject.org/

Other Ancient Trading Routes

There are many online sources about ancient trading routes. Here's one resource:

http://www.metmuseum.org/toah/hd/trade/hd_trade.htm

Minnesota State University also has an interesting site on ancient trading routes:

http://www.mnsu.edu/emuseum/history/trade/variousroutes2.htm

Vehicle Currency

In addition to the general information found in international business texts, the following two sources can add to your depth of understanding.

http://www.econ.umn.edu/macro/2005/shi.pdf

http://www.newyorkfed.org/research/staff_reports/sr200.pdf

World Bank and World Bank Group

The World Bank maintains a Web site that describes their programs and work. It includes information on their programs and opportunities for business. Much of the information provided in this book came from the World Bank site. In addition, part of their site includes information on business opportunities related to World Bank projects.

http://www.worldbank.org/

General Information

Although the use of Wikipedia can occasionally be misleading (their information sources can be unreliable), if you are just beginning your investigation into a topic, this online source can help you get started.

http://en.wikipedia.org/wiki/

Appendix B:
Trading Partners and What's Traded

Several sources track United States trading patterns, but the most exhaustive and authoritative data is compiled by the U.S. Census Bureau. The following information is up-to-date as of the publication of this book, but as we've discussed many times, the international trade environment is one of rapid change. If you want up-to-the-month figures, you can find them at www.census.gov.

Total Trade of Goods, July 2007–July 2008: Top 15 Trading Partners (In $Billions)

Rank	Country	Exports (Year-to-Date)	Imports (Year-to-Date)	Total Trade (Year-to-Date)	Percent of Total Trade
—	Total, All Countries	776.8	1,258.1	2,034.9	100.0%
—	Total, Top 15 Countries	533.5	907.3	1,440.8	70.8%
1	Canada	158.7	205.8	364.5	17.9%
2	China	43.1	185.5	228.6	11.2%
3	Mexico	87.8	128.9	216.7	10.7%
4	Japan	39.7	85.7	125.3	6.2%
5	Federal Republic of Germany	32.7	60	92.7	4.6%
6	United Kingdom	34	34.8	68.7	3.4%
7	Korea, South	21.6	28.9	50.4	2.5%
8	France	17.4	26.1	43.5	2.1%
9	Saudi Arabia	6.2	34.1	40.4	2.0%
10	Venezuela	6.6	32.2	38.7	1.9%

Total Trade of Goods, July 2007–July 2008: Top 15 Trading Partners (In $Billions) *(Continued)*

Rank	Country	Exports (Year-to-Date)	Imports (Year-to-Date)	Total Trade (Year-to-Date)	Percent of Total Trade
11	Taiwan	16.8	21.3	38.1	1.9%
12	Netherlands	23.9	12.6	36.4	1.8%
13	Brazil	17.8	17.9	35.7	1.8%
14	Italy	9.6	22.3	31.9	1.6%
15	Belgium	17.7	11.3	29	1.4%

Top 15 Trading Partners, July 2007–July 2008

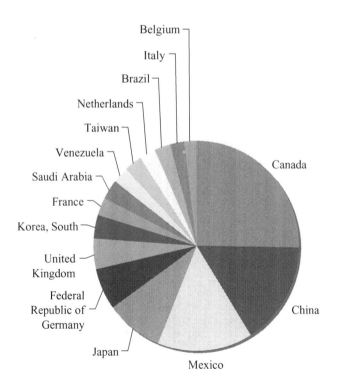

Note that there is a trade deficit (imports to the United States exceed U.S. exports) with 13 of the 15 top trade partners in this period. Also note that Mexico and Canada, our neighbors and NAFTA partners, accounted for more than a quarter of U.S. total trade in this time period.

Keep in mind, as you hear about the rise of China, that—although its current growth rate is nothing to scoff at and suggests that it may become our number-one trading partner at some point in the future—it has yet to pass up Canada for total trade with the United States.

You may also note that the above figures do not include India. India currently ranks as our 16th-largest trade partner, so the top-15 figures do not include it, but most predictions suggest that India will be moving up substantially on the list of largest trading partners in the next decade, and may push into the top 15 trading partners within a year or two. The United States' current 15th-largest trading partner is Belgium, and a country with a population of over one billion probably won't take long to surpass the Belgians, given its current rate of economic growth.

The United States International Trade Commission is an independent federal agency that tracks international trade, specifically with an eye to protecting American businesses. They do this by keeping abreast of issues involving intellectual property (international copyright law, patents, etc.) and antidumping trade agreements. The following table about overall U.S. international trade is compiled from Department of Commerce statistics by the International Trade Commission.

You can see a significant increase in exporting across all of the industries measured in this table. Perhaps most significant, although it is a smaller amount traded, is the 97.5% year-to-date increase in the exportation of energy-related products. A high level of trade in a particular item does not necessarily indicate where that item is being exported to, and you should keep this in mind. It will be important, in identifying national markets for your product, to know not only how it's selling abroad, but where it's already being sold.

Negative values in the "Percent Change Year-to-Date" column imply that there are some products that Americans either demand less of or are acquiring from internal sources. Overall, we imported 12.6% more, but note that there are many product categories in which imports are trending downward.

U.S. Exports of Domestic Merchandise

Item	2006	2007	2007 YTD	2008 YTD	Absolute Change YTD 2007–2008	Percent Change YTD 2007–2008
			Million Dollars			
Agricultural products	76,924	96,041	42,502	61,424	18,923	44.5%
Forest products	30,156	33,088	15,982	17,840	1,858	11.6%
Chemicals and related products	149,848	169,409	83,428	95,876	12,448	14.9%
Energy-related products	38,999	46,674	20,333	40,156	19,822	97.5%
Textiles and apparel	18,088	17,535	8,834	9,026	192	2.2%
Footwear	573	578	273	316	43	15.6%
Minerals and metals	82,944	100,260	48,519	62,848	14,329	29.5%
Machinery	92,886	101,289	50,292	55,320	5,028	10.0%
Transportation equipment	218,326	249,421	119,909	132,757	12,848	10.7%
Electronic products	169,381	172,502	84,829	88,603	3,774	4.4%
Miscellaneous	22,438	25,954	12,815	14,065	1,250	9.8%
Special provisions	28,925	33,607	16,307	17,887	1,580	9.7%
Total:	929,486	1,046,358	504,023	596,118	92,095	18.3%

U.S. Imports of Merchandise for Consumption

Item	2006	2007	2007 YTD	2008 YTD	Absolute Change YTD 2007–2008	Percent Change YTD 2007–2008
			Million Dollars			
Agricultural products	81,456	88,136	43,561	47,929	4,367	10.0%
Forest products	50,416	46,561	22,931	21,317	-1,615	-7.0%
Chemicals and related products	179,410	194,331	96,108	110,527	14,419	15.0%
Energy-related products	319,168	344,829	154,494	236,877	82,383	53.3%
Textiles and apparel	104,563	107,678	50,541	49,092	-1,449	-2.9%
Footwear	19,038	19,270	9,648	9,425	-223	-2.3%
Minerals and metals	169,510	174,207	86,458	92,530	6,071	7.0%
Machinery	131,091	139,131	68,136	71,792	3,656	5.4%
Transportation equipment	303,979	309,924	153,674	155,056	1,383	0.9%
Electronic products	332,485	353,009	165,581	173,650	8,069	4.9%
Miscellaneous	94,099	103,905	47,150	46,360	-789	-1.7%
Special provisions	59,837	61,882	30,515	31,503	987	3.2%
Total:	**1,845,053**	**1,942,863**	**928,798**	**1,046,058**	**117,260**	**12.6%**

U.S. Merchandise Trade Balance

Item	2006	2007	2007 YTD	2008 YTD	Absolute Change YTD 2007–2008	Percent Change YTD 2007–2008
			Million Dollars			
Agricultural products	-4,532	7,906	-1,060	13,496	14,555	Not Meaningful
Forest products	-20,260	-13,473	-6,950	-3,476	3,473	50.0%
Chemicals and related products	-29,562	-24,923	-12,681	-14,652	-1,971	-15.5%
Energy-related products	-280,170	-298,155	-134,161	-196,721	-62,560	-46.6%
Textiles and apparel	-86,476	-90,143	-41,707	-40,066	1,641	3.9%
Footwear	-18,465	-18,692	-9,375	-9,110	265	2.8%
Minerals and metals	-86,567	-73,947	-37,939	-29,681	8,257	21.8%
Machinery	-38,205	-37,842	-17,844	-16,472	1,372	7.7%
Transportation equipment	-85,654	-60,503	-33,764	-22,299	11,465	34.0%
Electronic products	-163,105	-180,507	-80,752	-85,047	-4,295	-5.3%
Miscellaneous	-71,661	-77,951	-34,334	-32,296	2,039	5.9%
Special provisions	-30,912	-28,275	-14,208	-13,615	593	4.2%
Total:	**-915,567**	**-896,505**	**-424,775**	**-449,940**	**-25,165**	**-5.9%**

The final table is a summary of the previous two, although we felt it necessary to include the overall trade balance in these product categories. As a reminder, negative numbers imply a trade deficit, meaning that Americans are importing more of that product category than they are exporting. But a negative percent change means that the deficit or surplus shrunk, year over year.

There's simply too much data, and too much variation from country to country, for this book to include more than a brief snapshot of what goods are traded. We give an example here of goods traded with Canada and China, from TradeStats Express, a feature on www.export.gov. You can find national trading data there, with a profile of U.S. trade with any individual country, by going to the Web address http://tse.export.gov and selecting "National Trade Data" to see what goods are being traded already with the country you are researching.

This is not a complete list, only the products exported from the U.S. to Canada exceeding $1 billion in value. But you can see that a diverse

Exports to Canada for 2007	($Thousands)
87—VEHICLES, EXCEPT RAILWAY OR TRAMWAY, AND PARTS, ETC.	49,778,223
84—NUCLEAR REACTORS, BOILERS, MACHINERY, ETC.; PARTS	42,201,069
85—ELECTRIC MACHINERY, ETC.; SOUND EQUIP; TV EQUIP; PTS	23,959,159
39—PLASTICS AND ARTICLES THEREOF	10,778,275
27—MINERAL FUEL, OIL, ETC.; BITUMIN SUBST; MINERAL WAX	10,382,926
98—SPECIAL CLASSIFICATION PROVISIONS, NESOI	7,690,966
90—OPTIC, PHOTO, ETC.; MEDIC OR SURGICAL INSTRMENTS, ETC.	7,609,763
73—ARTICLES OF IRON OR STEEL	5,697,938
72—IRON AND STEEL	5,663,000
48—PAPER & PAPERBOARD & ARTICLES (INC PAPR PULP ARTL)	5,223,999
94—FURNITURE; BEDDING ETC.; LAMPS NESOI, ETC.; PREFAB BD.	4,455,788
88—AIRCRAFT, SPACECRAFT, AND PARTS THEREOF	4,209,822
29—ORGANIC CHEMICALS	3,826,557
40—RUBBER AND ARTICLES THEREOF	3,669,701

Exports to Canada for 2007 *(Continued)* ($Thousands)

76—ALUMINUM AND ARTICLES THEREOF	3,283,558
30—PHARMACEUTICAL PRODUCTS	3,187,279
71—NAT, ETC., PEARLS; PREC. ETC., STONES, PR. MET., ETC.; COIN	3,055,389
38—MISCELLANEOUS CHEMICAL PRODUCTS	2,967,956
49—PRINTED BOOKS, NEWSPAPERS, ETC.; MANUSCRIPTS, ETC.	2,780,559
95—TOYS, GAMES, & SPORT EQUIPMENT; PARTS & ACCESSORIES	2,523,212
08—EDIBLE FRUIT & NUTS; CITRUS FRUIT OR MELON PEEL	2,405,325
44—WOOD AND ARTICLES OF WOOD; WOOD CHARCOAL	2,378,300
33—ESSENTIAL OILS, ETC.; PERFUMERY, COSMETIC, ETC., PREPS	1,968,257
07—EDIBLE VEGETABLES & CERTAIN ROOTS & TUBERS	1,913,385
26—ORES, SLAG, AND ASH	1,810,700
70—GLASS AND GLASSWARE	1,591,311
34—SOAP, ETC.; WAXES, POLISH, ETC.; CANDLES; DENTAL PREPS	1,584,095
32—TANNING & DYE EXT., ETC; DYE, PAINT, PUTTY, ETC.; INKS	1,583,181
83—MISCELLANEOUS ARTICLES OF BASE METAL	1,582,315
28—INORG. CHEM.; PREC. & RARE-EARTH MET. & RADIOACT. COMPD.	1,548,390
19—PREP. CEREAL, FLOUR, STARCH, OR MILK; BAKERS WARES	1,447,074
74—COPPER AND ARTICLES THEREOF	1,433,422
82—TOOLS, CUTLERY, ETC., OF BASE METAL, & PARTS THEREOF	1,344,577
21—MISCELLANEOUS EDIBLE PREPARATIONS	1,242,269
02—MEAT AND EDIBLE MEAT OFFAL	1,166,577
20—PREP. VEGETABLES, FRUIT, NUTS, OR OTHER PLANT PARTS	1,144,271
22—BEVERAGES, SPIRITS, AND VINEGAR	1,115,500
23—FOOD INDUSTRY RESIDUES & WASTE; PREP. ANIMAL FEED	1,065,261

offering is traded with our neighbor to the north. The list includes both finished and unfinished products, which denotes a broad economic partnership across a wide range of industries.

As the Top 15 Trading Partners table showed, we export more than three times as much to Canada as we do to China, which we can also see in this table of goods exported. But what is also significant, because the two tables of goods exported are both for goods that are $1 billion or higher, is that the list for China is much shorter—meaning that there is less diversification in the types of industry that are exported to China. This is partially an indication of the resources that China does not need to import in the first place, but it is also an indication of opportunities for other industries to play a heavier hand in exporting goods to China.

On a broad level of world trade analysis, in terms of trends in U.S. trade, the United States exported 12.1% more in 2007 than it did in 2006. However, this information applies to trade of goods only, and although we hear about the trade deficit all the time, we actually have a significant

Exports to China for 2007	($Thousands)
85—ELECTRIC MACHINERY, ETC.; SOUND EQUIP; TV EQUIP; PTS	10,663,795
84—NUCLEAR REACTORS, BOILERS, MACHINERY ETC.; PARTS	8,859,365
88—AIRCRAFT, SPACECRAFT, AND PARTS THEREOF	7,198,047
12—OIL SEEDS, ETC.; MISC GRAIN, SEED, FRUIT, PLANT, ETC.	4,179,264
39—PLASTICS AND ARTICLES THEREOF	3,600,324
90—OPTIC, PHOTO, ETC.; MEDIC OR SURGICAL INSTRMENTS, ETC.	3,314,269
72—IRON AND STEEL	2,225,241
74—COPPER AND ARTICLES THEREOF	2,162,643
29—ORGANIC CHEMICALS	2,100,768
47—WOOD PULP, ETC.; RECOVD (WASTE & SCRAP) PPR & PPRBD	2,053,130
87—VEHICLES, EXCEPT RAILWAY OR TRAMWAY, AND PARTS, ETC.	1,969,510
76—ALUMINUM AND ARTICLES THEREOF	1,813,451
52—COTTON, INCLUDING YARN AND WOVEN FABRIC THEREOF	1,482,768

Trade of Services vs. Total Trade and Import-Export of Services, July 2007-July 2008 (In $Millions)

Period	Balance Total (Goods and Services)	Balance Services	Exports Services	Imports Services
2007				
July	−57,317	10,477	42,480	32,003
August	−55,333	11,339	43,589	32,250
September	−55,464	11,274	43,310	32,036
October	−56,333	11,380	43,737	32,357
November	−59,871	11,826	44,246	32,420
December	−57,579	11,930	44,302	32,372
2008				
January	−58,711	11,436	44,703	33,267
February	−61,435	11,048	44,453	33,405
March	−56,964	11,439	44,677	33,238
April	−61,508	11,442	45,035	33,593
May	−60,208	11,903	45,937	34,034
June	−58,835	12,432	46,533	34,101
July	−62,198	12,676	47,372	34,696

trade surplus in services—to the tune of approximately $11.5 billion a month from July of 2007 to July of 2008. We do not trade as heavily in services as we do in goods, but that picture is changing with the increased use of global employment and improved information and communication technology.

As the table shows, the total trade balance may be negative, but the balance of trade in services alone is a trade surplus. In 2006 (the most current data available as of the publication of this book) the World Trade organization ranked the United States as the number-one importer and exporter of commercial services.

Are you interested in a commodity or product we haven't covered here? Then try one of the sites we've mentioned above. Given the space limitations in a book like this one, we could not even begin to cover everything, and there is much more data available out there for just about any product or type of product.

Glossary

Arbitrage: the short-term purchase and resale at a known profit of an asset. In the international currency market, the asset purchased and sold is money. The key characteristic of an arbitrage exchange is that the asset is resold at a known (risk-free) profit.

Ask Price and Bid Price: the bid price is the price a willing buyer offers for a product. The ask price is the minimum price a seller wishes to accept for the product. The difference between the ask price and the bid is called the spread.

Balance of Payment (BOP): the value of goods, services, payments (including tourism, foreign aid, military expenditures, and foreign investment) coming into a country, compared to those same things going out. The BOP is similar to a nation's balance of trade, but includes more items than a balance of trade report.

Balance of Trade (BOT): the value of *exported* goods and services compared with the value of *imported* goods and services within a specified nation. A BOT may be positive or negative. A positive BOT indicates that the nation has exported more goods and services than it imported; a negative BOT indicates that the nation imported more goods and services than it exported. When imports exceed exports, more of a nation's money goes abroad than comes in. If this situation continues for an extended period of time, it can lead to economic and currency problems.

Balance Sheet Approach to International Compensation: a method of determining the compensation paid to an expatriate employee. This approach aims to achieve equality between the purchasing power an employee receives in his or her home country and the purchasing power and standard of living in the host country. Figuring this compensation takes into consideration the host country's cost of goods and services, housing costs, and taxes.

Bank of International Settlements (BIS): an entity that functions as a bank for central banks. It has a limited role in enforcing monetary policies, but it does monitor and research the effects and trends of the international financial environment.

Base Salary: the basic compensation paid to an employee. This amount is also used as a benchmark to determine the size of other compensation components.

Bid Price and Ask Price: see Ask Price and Bid Price.

Bill of Exchange: a request for payment, also known as a draft.

Bill of Lading (B/L): a document issued by a shipping carrier that serves as a contract, receipt, and identification of ownership. It is inspected by customs officials in both the nation of origin and the nation of the recipient.

Bretton Woods System: the agreement made between representatives of 44 Allied nations in 1944 that set up a fixed-rate currency exchange system and founded the World Bank and the International Monetary Fund (IMF). While the fixed-rate exchange system lasted only until 1972, the World Bank and the IMF still play important roles in the international exchange of currencies and the world economic environment.

Central Bank: a country's national bank that maintains controls over the country's national economy. Typical economic controls include establishing the required reserve ratio and setting the interest rate. These banks also hold national reserves.

Comparative Advantage Theory: is the theory that nations tend to produce the goods that they can produce most efficiently.

Convertibility: the ability to change one currency into another. Convertibility is controlled by the issuing nation.

Freely Convertible Currency: no restrictions are placed on conversion to any other currency.

Externally Convertible Currency: only individuals who are *not* residents or nationals of a nation may convert unlimited amounts of the currency to any other currency.

Nonconvertible Currency: neither residents nor nonresidents may convert currency into a foreign currency. Nations adopting this policy usually intend to protect their currency and their ability to meet payment obligations on foreign debt or imported goods.

Cost of Living Allowance: is the amount paid, in international business, to an employee to offset any differences between the cost of living in the home country and the cost of living in a host country that would cause a shift (usually downward) in the standard of living for the employee.

Countertrade: the acceptance of something other than money in payment for goods or services. This means of exchange is often used when trading with nations that have a nonconvertible currency. Countertrades may also be used when both parties have goods or services to offer the other that are considered a fair exchange under the contract. Between 10 and 20 percent of modern international trades involve at least some countertrade.

Cross-Cultural Literacy: the ability to understand and learn about another culture in a functional relationship. An employee can be said to have cross-cultural literacy if he or she can be sent, for example, to Asia and over the course of the assignment come to an understanding and acceptance of the many differences within the host country's culture.

Currency Boards: a group designed to ensure that a nation's currency will be converted into another currency upon request. Currency boards also play a role in the rates of exchange.

Currency Exchange Rate: the amount of currency that can be received in exchange for a set amount of another currency. There are four types of currency exchange rates.

Fixed-Rate Exchange: currencies are valued against one another at agreed-upon rates that are stable over extended periods. The rates may be governed by international treaty or, if only a few nations are involved, by agreements among a small number of nations. The key attribute of a fixed-rate exchange system is that the rates of exchange are those that governments agree upon and undertake to maintain.

Pegged Exchange Rate: a smaller or developing nation's currency is set at a specific rate against a larger or more economically stable nation's currency. The value of the currency pegged to another will fluctuate based on the fluctuation of the stronger currency.

Floating Exchange Rates: exchange rates are determined on the international currency market in much the same way that corporate stock values are determined on stock or commodity markets. Floating exchange rates are decided by the forces that drive the market. Many developed nations, including the United States, use a floating exchange rate for their currencies.

Spot Exchange Rate: the exchange rate at any one point (spot) in time. These rates have stipulations that the delivery of the transaction occur within two business days. The spot exchange rate can fluctuate dramatically over time and trends can be difficult to predict. A spot exchange rate is not the best measurement of a currency's valuation.

Currency Market: the international market where you can exchange one currency for another or buy currency from any nation.

Currency Market Investing: investing in money from multiple nations. This may be done by investing in currency market funds or by directly making your own purchases of a foreign currency or currencies.

Customhouse Broker: an independent company that provides import shipment services for client firms.

Draft: an order drawn to request payment, also known as a bill of exchange.

Economies of Scale: involves reducing the per-unit cost of providing a good or service. In most cases, producing large numbers of a product means that the per-unit cost goes down because more efficient production methods can be used.

Education Allowance: an amount paid to an expatriate employees to allow them to send their children to schools comparable to those in their home country.

Ethnocentric Company: a company with a headquarters orientation and structure that calls for major decisions to be made at corporate headquarters by key management personnel. Expatriate managers are used as extensions or surrogates of the headquarter's management. One of the objectives of an ethnocentric company is to transplant the headquarters business culture to the foreign location.

Expatriate: an individual from one nation who lives and—often—works in another nation.

Export-Import Bank (Ex-Im Bank): a U. S. agency that provides financial assistance to exporters.

Exporting: the sale of goods or services in one nation for use in another. In the case of goods, this involves transportation of the goods from the nation of origin to the end-user nation.

Export Management Company: an independent company that provides export services to other companies. These companies have expertise in shipping and in the export and import regulations and paperwork required for international trade.

Expropriation Law: determines how much (whether as a figure or a percentage) of a foreign subsidiary's profits can be "sent" home, whether as payment or dividend. This limits the amount of money that can be sent overseas from a subsidiary to its company headquarters.

Externally Convertible Currency: only individuals who are not residents or nationals of a nation may convert unlimited amounts of one currency to another currency.

Fair Trade: the position that a market-based approach is the way to establish equanimity in the economies of developing nations, stabilize conflicts, and end cycles of poverty. It is often considered to be the antithesis of free trade.

Fixed-Rate Exchange: currencies are valued against one another at agreed-upon rates that are stable over extended periods. The rates may be governed by international treaty or, if only a few nations are involved, by agreements between a small number of nations. The key attribute of a fixed-rate exchange system is that the rates of exchange are those that governments agree upon and undertake to maintain.

Flat Organizational Structure: when a business is organized with many layers of management, the cost of maintaining that hierarchy can be a major business cost. With flat organizational structure, savings can be achieved in administrative costs while the organization is better able to respond to change and foster innovation.

Foreign Exchange Market: the international market for the exchange of currencies. There is no one physical location for this market. Currency exchanges are handled by network offices located around the world and connected via international computer links. Currencies can be exchanged around the clock. The principal center for foreign exchange transactions is London. Other major centers include New York and Tokyo, and additional offices can be found in places such as San Francisco and Sidney, Australia.

Floating Exchange Rates: rates are determined on the international currency market in much the same way that corporate stock values are determined on stock or commodity markets. Floating exchange rates are decided by the forces that drive the market. Many developed nations, including the United States, use a floating exchange rate for their currencies.

Foreign Direct Investment (FDI): investment outside an investing entity's country of origin or residence. The capital invested may be used to build, own, or maintain a long-term production facility, raw material production site, or a power plant manufacturing business that directly contributes to the creation of goods in another country. To qualify as foreign direct investment, the investment must include not just ownership of the asset, but also control 10 percent or more of the ordinary shares or voting power of an incorporated firm, or the equivalent in an unincorporated firm. FDI involves both ownership and the power to control—at least, partially—the foreign business.

> **Horizontal FDI:** capitalizing using foreign direct investment in such a manner that the same product is produced and/or marketed in multiple countries.

Vertical FDI: capitalizing using foreign direct investment so that different sections of production and/or marketing occur in different countries. The goal of the strategy is to keep the costs for each phase of production as low as possible.

Foreign Portfolio Investment: foreign portfolio investment is similar to foreign direct investment, but involves gaining ownership of less than 10 percent of the ordinary shares or voting power of an incorporated firm, or the equivalent in an unincorporated firm. The foreign portfolio investment does not provide investors with the power to make decisions in the firm in which they have invested.

Forward Exchange: an agreement between two parties to exchange and execute a contract at a specified date in the future. The forward exchange rate is the rate agreed to in the forward exchange. The forward prices may be the same as spot prices, but that is not usually the case. In most cases, the forward price may be higher (at a premium) or lower (at a discount) than the spot price.

Franchising: turning over to an individual owner the right to operate a business according to set standards, using promotional materials stipulated by the franchise developer. Often, the franchise developer will require that individual owners buy supplies from the franchise developer. Many fast food operations are franchises operated by individual owners.

Freely Convertible Currency: no restrictions are placed on conversion of this currency into other currencies.

Free Trade: the position that products should be available internationally without the interference of government regulations and tariffs. This model for trade believes that government interventions only serve to increase costs to both consumers and producers.

Free Trade Area: a group of nations that exchange goods and services without economic barriers or government interventions. For example, the North American Free Trade Agreement (NAFTA) places the United States, Canada, and Mexico in a single free-trade area.

Futures Contracts: agreements to buy a specified quantity of something at a future date at an agreed-upon price. Futures contracts are used not only in commodity markets, but also in the currency exchange market. International businesses use futures contracts for currency to reduce the risks inherent in the currency market.

Generally Accepted Accounting Principles (GAAP): a set of accounting standards used in the United States that are set by the U.S. Financial Accounting Standards Board (FASB) in combination with the Securities and Exchange Commission (SEC). These accounting standards are not the same as the International Financial Reporting Standards (IFRS) used in many other nations.

Geocentric Company: a company that is organized as if it were nationless. Corporate resources can be moved without regard to national borders. Cultural or national differences, such as local laws or customs, can be learned or managed.

Global Investment Strategy: international companies with facilities in multiple nations, with perhaps one or two critical functions (such as research and design) in its headquarters or "home" location.

Globalization: the unification of markets and production of goods and services around the world. Unification is accomplished through the reduction or elimination of trade barriers (including tariffs and import quotas). Recent advances in information, transportation, and communication technologies have made international trade easier, even for small companies.

Global Mindset: a company-wide mentality that understands that doing business on a global scale requires an intricate understanding and acceptance of the world's political and economic structures, laws, and cultures.

Gold Standard: pegging of a nation's currency to gold. By 1880, many nations had adopted the gold standard, including the United States, Japan, Great Britain, and Germany. During the economic stresses between World War I and World War II, the standard was discontinued. It was partially revived after World War II when the United States pegged its dollar to gold ($35.00 U.S. dollars to an ounce of gold). Use of the gold standard was abandoned in the early 1970s.

Green-Field Investment: direct investment in a foreign nation that involves new facilities and the creation of entirely new manufacturing and power operations.

Hardship Premium: an amount paid to an employee to counteract the hardships of moving, changing cultures, living far from family, and the length of the assignment. The degree to which these hardships exist is used to determine the size of the premium.

Hedging: a purchase made to reduce the risk inherent in a business agreement or other activity. In international finance, this often means purchasing assets (such as stocks, bonds, government securities) in the currency about which the investor is concerned. The profit made on the asset purchased can balance or reduce possible losses on the original agreement or activity. Hedging in any currency is much the same as hedging in the commodity market.

Horizontal FDI: capitalizing using foreign direct investment in such a manner that the same product is produced and/or marketed in multiple countries.

Housing Allowance: if the company does not provide housing in the host country for an expatriate employee, they will often provide an allowance to help the employee maintain his or her standard of living while on assignment. The home company may also provide services to help employees sell or rent their residence in the home country.

Home Leave Allowance: an amount provided to an expatriate employees so they can more easily travel and visit their home during a year.

Hyperinflation: extreme and very rapid inflation of a nation's currency. Hyperinflation can destroy the value of a currency with a relatively short period of time.

International Human Resource Manager (IHRM): the individual who provides company-wide leadership in the hiring, assignment, and compensation for employees in the host countries where the company operates.

Importing: the purchase of goods or services in one nation for use in another. In the case of goods, this involves the transportation of the goods from the nation of origin to the end-user nation.

Indexed Contract: a multicurrency contract in which the amount the buyer will pay the seller upon delivery is indexed or figured based on the exchange rate at the time of delivery.

Inflation: occurs when the value of a currency declines both in buying power and the power to exchange it for other currencies. Inflation involves both an excess supply of currency from the issuing nation and a loss of confidence in that currency.

International Finance Center: a unit within a business whose purpose is to focus on international finance management, including corporate tax strategy, translating financial statements prepared to a foreign set of standards, and management of currency risk and opportunity.

International Financial Reporting Standards (IFRS): a set of accounting standards set by the International Accounting Standards Board (IASB) and used in many nations outside the United States. This set of standards is not identical to the U.S. Generally Accepted Accounting Principles (GAAP).

International Monetary Fund (IMF): along with the World Bank, the IMF acts as a safety net for national currencies. The IMF provides assistance (usually loans) to economically struggling nations to help bolster their economies.

Joint Venture: going into business with a partner business. In international business, this may be the only way a U.S. company can gain access to a foreign market. For example, to do business in Malaysia, you need to partner with (pay money to) Bhumiputras.

Law of One Price: the theory that in an ideal world market, each good sold should have only one price, no matter where it is sold.

Letter of Credit (LC): a document issued by a bank that guarantees payment when specific conditions have been met.

Licensing: selling to another business the right to manufacture a product you developed.

Means of Production (MoP): a term that describes the necessity of having the tools and materials needed to create products (goods and services).

Money: a currency or symbol of value that facilitates the exchange of goods and services. Currency is issued by most nations. In business, profit or loss is measured in money.

Multidomestic Strategy: a strategy of foreign investment that involves investing in autonomous units in multiple countries. The investment in each nation is geared toward sales in that nation, not exporting to other nations or supplying the investing company. This is a decentralized investment strategy.

Multinational Business: a company with holdings in multiple nations.

National Business: any business that has offices and employees in only one country.

Net Asset Value: the underlying value of an asset. When the market price of the asset is higher than the net asset value, it is said to be trading at a premium. When the market price of the asset is lower than the net asset value, it is said to be trading at a discount.

Nonconvertible Currency: no one, not residents or nonresidents, may convert a nation's currency into a foreign currency. Nations adopting this policy are usually seeking to protect their currency and their ability to meet payment obligations on foreign debt or needed imported goods.

Organizational Culture: the system of beliefs and values that prevail within a given organization.

Outsourcing: using another company, often one in another nation, to handle some business function. Outsourcing may involve parts production, call-center activities, payroll processing, or any of hundreds of business functions. The advantage of outsourcing is that you can pay another company to do what they do best, while concentrating your business's efforts on those tasks that your employees do best.

Pegged Exchange Rate: one nation's currency, usually a smaller or developing nation's money, is set at a specific rate against another nation's currency, usually a larger or more economically stable nation. The value of the currency pegged to another will fluctuate based on the fluctuation of the stronger currency.

Polycentric Company: companies with a strong orientation to the host country or countries involved in the business. Managers in each nation are from the host nation, along with most of the staff. There is more autonomy for the foreign subsidiaries.

Production Cost: the total cost of producing a good or service, including raw materials, labor, transportation costs, and import duties.

Purchasing Power Parity (PPP): a theory developed by Gustav Cassel in 1920. Under PPP, the exchange rates for currencies are based on the compared purchasing power in each nation, based on a standard basket of identical goods. The base idea is the law of one price, the theory that in an ideal world market, each good sold should have only one price no matter where it is sold. PPP takes into account such factors as cost of living and inflation rates. There are differences—often quite large ones—between PPP rates and exchange rates. The most widely used PPP exchange rate is the Geary-Khamis dollar, sometimes called the "international dollar."

Relocation Allowance: an amount paid to an employee to offset the cost of moving to and from the host country. The allowance often includes shipping and storage costs, as well as the purchase of new home goods such as furniture and appliances.

Special Drawing Rights (SDRs): an international reserve asset created by the International Monetary Funds to supplement the official reserves of member nations. The value of an SDR is based on a basket of key international currencies reviewed every ten years.

Spot Exchange Rate: this is the exchange rate at any one point (spot) in time. These rates have stipulations that the delivery of the transaction takes place within two business days. The spot exchange rate can fluctuate dramatically over time and trends can be difficult to predict. A spot exchange rate is not the best measurement of a currency's valuation.

Trading at a Premium/Discount: any asset can be traded at either a premium or a discount. The net asset value is the underlying value of the asset. When the market price of the asset is higher than the net asset value, it is said to be trading at a premium. When the market price of the asset is lower than the net asset value, it is said to be trading at a discount.

Transaction Costs: the costs of doing business within the cost of doing business. In international businesses, the transaction costs associated with converting your home currency to the host country currency is a transaction cost. Other common transaction costs include transfer fees for moving money to a bank abroad and fees to exchange dealers.

Transfer Prices: what one unit of a company charges another unit of the same company for designated goods or services.

Transnational Business: a type of international business that operates in multiple nations but as a single entity. A transnational business will have a world headquarters in one country and subsidiary offices in one or more other nations.

Turnkey Projects: building a manufacturing facility or other means of production for a client. This arrangement is called "turnkey," because when the project is completed, you hand the client the key to his or her new facility and walk away.

Vehicle Currency: a currency used to facilitate the exchange of other currencies. Today, both the U.S. dollar and the Japanese yen are frequently used as vehicle currencies. Vehicle currencies are important in both the currency exchange market and in several commodity markets for products such as grain and oil.

Vertical FDI: capitalizing using foreign direct investment, so that different sections of production and/or marketing occur in different countries. The goal of this strategy is to keep the costs for each phase of production as low as possible.

World Bank: founded as a part of the Bretton Woods agreements in 1944, the World Bank makes low interest loans to developing nations, primarily for development projects that can help improve the lives of ordinary citizens and enhance economic conditions and maintain currency values.

Index

3M, 92, 123–124

A

Accounts payable, 207–208
Accounts receivable
  definition of, 207
  philosophy of, 207–208
Accounting standards, 204–207
  acquisition governed by, 205
  analysis governed by, 204
  contrasted, 205
  convergence of, 206, 207
  Financial Accounting Standards Board
    (FASB) sets, 204
  goodwill treated differently by, 205
  international, 118, 204
  International Accounting Standards Board
    (IASB) sets, 204
  merger complicated by, 118
  Securities and Exchange Commission (SEC)
    sets, 204
  subjectivity of, 206
  types of, 118, 204
  understanding important, 204–206
  U.S., 118, 204
  valuation of company governed by, 204,
    206
Acquisition
  accounting standards' role in, 205
  advantages of, 41, 116
  analysis before, 5
  analysis of, example of, 121–122
  company culture a complication of, 115
  definition of, 41, 58, 129
  disadvantages of, 117
  duplication common in, 88

Generally Agreed Accounting Practices
  (GAAP) method of recording, 205
global strategy uses, 116
as hedging, 116
international business built on, 116
International Financial Reporting Standards
  (IFRS) method of recording, 205
multidomestic strategy uses, 116
multinational business built on, 5
outsourcing versus, 89
pitfalls of, 41, 115
rivalry a threat to, 116
rivalry decreased by, 122
sunk-cost fallacy during, 115–116
value of a foreign company overestimated
  during, 41, 114
as vertical foreign direct investment, 115
Adaptation
  to foreign consumers, 84
  to a foreign culture, 9
  to international business, 84
  to a local environment, 87–88
  of products a sign of rivalry, 57
  risk to international business brought about
    by lack of, 83
  turnkey projects a cause of, 109–110
  understanding a cause of, 141
  universally applicable, 85
Advanced Fibre Communication (AFC), 9–10
Advising banks
  definition of, 135, 136
  role of, example of, 134–135
AFC (Advanced Fibre Communication), 9–10
Agriculture
  developing countries opposed to developed
    countries regarding, 48

Agriculture (*continued*)

International Bank for Reconstruction and Development (IBRD) supports, 69

International Center for Settlement of Investment Disputes (ICSID) supports, 69

International Development Association (IDA) supports, 69

International Finance Corporation (IFC) supports, 69

North American Agreement on Environmental Cooperation (NAAEC) focuses on liberalizing, 55

North American Free Trade Agreement (NAFTA) focuses on, 55

Multilateral Investment Guarantee Agency (MIGA) supports, 69

World Bank Group supports, 69

World Bank supports, 69

Air freight, 146

Airmail

use of, 145–146

valuation may require customs declaration, 146

Alcoa, 99

Analysis

accounting standards' role in, 204

acquisition preceded by, 5

example of, 162–164

exportation preceded by, 134

of finances, 198–217

of labor regulations, 181

of legal environment, 7–8

manufacturing preceded by, 173

marketing plan requires, 144

of market using Five Forces model, 119–123

new-market entry preceded by, 7, 56, 99, 141

purchasing preceded by, 158, 173

role of, examples of, 121–122, 134–135

of taxation, 201

Annual average currency exchange rates, 207

Arbitrage, 73

Ask price, 74

Audits

transfer pricing discovered by, 203

understanding foreign important, 201–202

B

Balance of payments (BOP)

definition of, 38

economic health of a nation indicated by, 39

Balance of trade (BOT)

definition of, 38

economic health of a nation indicated by, 37–38, 39

exportation affects, 38

importation affects, 38

Balance sheet approach, 184

Bank for International Settlements (BIS), 71

Banking, 61–62

Bargaining power

analysis of, example of, 121–122

differentiation of products to increase, 120–121

knowledge transfer capitalizing on, 120

of purchasers according to the Five Forces model, 119–120

of purchasers makes exportation advantageous when high, 122–123

of sellers according to the Five Forces model, 119–120

Barriers to cross-cultural communication

education level, 22

e-mail, 17–18

idiom, 17

Barriers to new-market entry

advantages of, 120

analysis of, example of, 121–122

bureaucracy, 19, 20

corruption, 20

definition of, 120

Five Forces model of, 120

green-fields advantageous when low, 122

laws when restrictive, 49

rivalry varies inversely with, 101

Barter

as countertrade, 142

definition of, 60, 142

Bayer, 125

Bid price, 74

Bills of exchange, 137

Bills of lading (B/L)

definition of, 135, 137, 147

role of, 137, 147

role of, example of, 134–135

types, 137

BIS (Bank for International Settlements), 71

B/L. *See* Bills of lading

Body language, 17

Boeing, 67–68

BOP. *See* Balance of payments (BOP)

BOT. *See* Balance of trade (BOT)

Bretton Woods system, 63–64
Bribery, 128
Bureaucracy, 19, 20
Buyback. *See* Compensation
Buying. *See* Purchasing

C
CAFTA (Dominican Republic Central America Free Trade Agreement), 54–56
Capital
  diversification to lower average cost of, 214
  foreign portfolio investment (FPI) supplies market for, 42
  for exportation provided by government agencies, 138–139
  for exportation, sources of, 138–139
  market for, 8
  markets of host nations sources for raising, 216
  paperwork required for receipt of, 135–137
Capital accounts, 39
Capital flight, 67
Case studies
  3M, 92, 123–124
  Advanced Fibre Communication (AFC), 9–10
  Alcoa, 99
  Bayer, 125
  Boeing, 67–68
  Caterpillar, 68, 97–98
  Cemex, 46
  centralization, 95
  China, 43–44
  countertrade, 67–68
  Daimler-Benz, 206
  economies of scale, 97–98
  favorable business environment creation, 45
  favorable business environment exploitation, 46
  Fertile Crescent, 156
  Ford, 100
  Fujisawa, 125
  GE, 127
  Generally Agreed Accounting Practices (GAAP), 206
  global strategy, 99
  green-fields, 123–124
  IBM, 124–125
  inflexibility, 127
  International Financial Reporting Standards (IFRS), 206
  international strategy, 100
  Ireland, 45
  Japan, 113
  joint ventures, 113
  licensing, 125
  local responsiveness, 90, 100
  locational advantage, 155, 156
  long-term relationship, 99
  Merck, 125
  Middle East, 156
  MTV, 100
  multidomestic strategy, 100
  Orbitz, 167
  price comparison Web sites, 167
  profit potential, 9–10
  Sematech, 127
  small-scale investment, 123–124
  strategic alliances, 124–125, 127
  3M, 92, 123–124
  Toyota, 90
  transnational strategy, 100
  Travelocity, 167
  Unilever, 95
  U.S. automotive industry, 155
  win-win situation, 167
  Xerox, 100
Caterpillar, 68, 97–98
Cemex, 46
Central banks, 70–71
Centralization
  case study, 95
  definition of, 168
  diagrammed, 169
  ethnocentrism marked by, 177–178
Centralized depositories
  certificates of deposit as, 215
  currency repatriation restrictions a barrier to, 215
  definition of, 214
  money markets as, 215
  purposes of, 214
  types of, 214–215
Central reserve assets, 71
Certificates of deposit, 215
Chambers of commerce, 149
Change
  legal environment a driver of, 7
  in legal environment creates new markets, 21
  opportunity created by, 218
  unpredictability of, 217, 219

China, 43–44
Collection, 207–209
  international disputes over, adjudication
    of, 209
  philosophy of, 209
Collectivism. *See* Individualism/Collectivism
Comity
  definition of, 20
  international agreements of, 20
  international transactions, importance in,
    209
Communication. *See* Cross-cultural
    communication
Company culture
  acquisition complicated by, 115
  controlling, 104–105
  effects of, 105
  marketing plan affected by, 144
  transplanting through expatriation, 176
Comparative advantage
  definition of, 164
  opportunity cost related to, 165
Compensation, 182–184
Competition. *See* Rivalry
Competitive advantage
  through contracting internationally, 4
  through expansion, 87
  through exploiting currency exchange rates,
    78
  through exploiting gaps between cultures,
    16
  through exploiting gaps in technology
    between cultures, 18
  through investment, 8
Complications of international business
  cultural difference, 9, 23–24
  currency exchange, 8, 62, 75
Conflict
  class-based a contributor to disputes in
    labor relations, 23
  religious a contributor to intracompany
    tension, 21–22
Consultants
  financial, 216
  legal, 19, 200, 201
Contracting, 4
Contracts
  futures (*see* Futures contracts)
  indexed, 78
  negotiation of, 13

Convertibility of currency
  external, 66–67
  free, 66
  non (*see* Nonconvertibility of currency)
Cooperation
  femininity marked by, 15
  within a transnational business, 6, 13
Co-opetition, 127
Coordination
  global strategy requires, 103
  multidomestic strategy requires less of, 103
  strategic alliances hampered by
    requirements for, 126
Corruption
  barrier to foreign-market entry, 20
  of foreign legal systems, 20
  restricted by U.S. law, 127–128
Cost pressure
  business strategies charted against, 91, 101
  definition of, 90
  global strategy expects, 93
  international business's relation to, example
    of, 102
  international strategy expects minimal, 91
Cost savings
  through economies of scale, 84, 97–98
  through ethnocentrism, 178
  through foreign economic environments,
    85, 86
  through foreign labor when inexpensive,
    5, 83
  through foreign natural resources, 83, 85
  through foreign profit potential, 85
  through foreign talent, 85–86
  through foreign technology, 85
  through government incentives, 20, 42, 48,
    49, 84
  through networking, 141
  through polycentrism, 178
  through reducing costs of production,
    83–84
  through relocation, 83–84
  through transportation via airliners and
    freight liners, 18
  varies inversely with employee education, 22
Counsel. *See* Consultants
Counterpurchase, 142–143
Counterpurchase credits, 143
Countertrade
  barter (*see* Barter)

case study, 67–68
compensation (see Compensation)
counterpurchase, 142–143
  nonconvertibility of currency circumvented
    by, 67–68
  offset trading, 143
  switch trading, 143
  types of, 142–143
Credit, 207–209
Cross-cultural bias
  anti-American, 25
  through stereotyping, 25–27
Cross-cultural communication
  via body language, 17
  via e-mail, 17–18
  idiom, 17
  via interpreter, 17
  merger requires, 119
  misunderstandings during, 28–29
  preparation for, 27
Cross-cultural literacy
  cultural toughness, 186
  definition of, 184
  employees valuable who have, 24–25, 185
  expatriate failure avoided by, 179
  others-orientedness, 185
  perceptual dimension, 185
  selection of employees possessing, 185–186
  self-orientedness, 185
Cultural dimensions
  Individualism/Collectivism (see
    Individualism/Collectivism)
  Long-term/Short-term orientation (see
    Long-term/Short-term orientation)
  Masculinity/Femininity (see Masculinity/
    Femininity)
  Power distance (see Power distance)
  Uncertainty avoidance (see Uncertainty
    Avoidance)
Culture, 11–31
  adaptation to foreign, 9
  aspects of, 16–23
  company (see Company culture)
  competitive advantage through taking
    advantage of gaps between, 16
  complications of international business
    arise from differences between, 9, 23–24
  definition of, 11
  dimensions of, 12–16
  economic structure as an aspect of, 20–21

education as an aspect of (see Education)
  gaps between, 16, 31
  green-fields, capitalizing on similarities
    among when establishing, 117
  individualism/collectivism as a dimension
    of (see Individualism/Collectivism)
  knowledge transfer among multidomestic
    subsidiaries hindered by gaps between, 95
  language as an aspect of (see Language)
  legal environment as an aspect of (see Legal
    environment)
  long-term/short-term orientation as a
    dimension of (see Long-term/Short-term
    orientation)
  masculinity/femininity as a dimension of
    (see Masculinity/Femininity)
  power distance as a dimension of (see Power
    distance)
  religion as an aspect of, 21–22
  researching foreign, 27
  shock (see Culture shock)
  social structure as an aspect of (see Social
    structure)
  technology as an aspect of (see Technology)
  training (see Language and culture training)
  uncertainty avoidance as a dimension of
    (see Uncertainty avoidance)
  understanding foreign, 9
  unfamiliarity with a risk in international
    business, 83
Culture shock
  definition of, 16–17
  described, 190
  examples of, 189
  language and culture training minimizes,
    190–191
  others-orientedness alleviates, 185
  reverse, 193
Currency
  definition of, 60
  direct purchase of, 72, 73, 76
  exchange of (see Currency exchange,
    Currency exchange rates)
  externally convertible, 66–67
  freely convertible, 66
  history of, 60
  intangible qualities of, 66
  investment in market for, 72
  nonconvertible, 67
  transfer of (see Repatriation of currency)

Currency (*continued*)
    valued using international monetary
        system, 8
    value of decreased by capital flight, 67
    value of tied to purchasing power, 65
    vehicle (*see* Vehicle currency)
Currency boards, 70
Currency exchange, 75–79
    complication of international business, 8,
        62, 75
    complication of multinational business, 75
    definition of, 75
    global center of, 76
    major centers of, 76
    nature of, 75–76
Currency exchange markets, 64–80
    international business use of, 76, 79
    role of, 75
Currency exchange rates
    complication of international business, 8,
        62, 75
    competitive advantage through taking
        advantage of, 78
    financial statements governed by, 207
    fixed rates of, 71
    floating rates of (*see* Floating currency
        exchange rates)
    foreign portfolio investment (FPI) climate
        affected by, 43
    gold standard as a system of, 63
    pegged rates of, 71
    rates of return skewed by, 217
    researching of a foreign country, 78
    spot rates of (*see* Spot currency exchange
        rates)
Currency fund, 72
Current accounts, 38–39
Customization. *See* Adaptation, Differentiation
Customs, 146
Customs broker houses
    globalization affects, 50
    importation uses, 50–51, 149–150

D
Daimler-Benz, 206
Debt, 214
Decentralization
    definition of, 168–169
    diagrammed, 170
    of labor relations, 195

polycentrism marked by, 177–178
transnational strategy requires, 97
Department of Commerce (DOC)
    foreign direct investment (FDI) controlled
        by standards of, 37
    services provided by, 43, 58
Depreciation
    debt repayment related to, 214
    Generally Agreed Accounting Practices
        (GAAP) method of recording, 205
    International Financial Reporting Standards
        (IFRS) method of recording, 205
    schedule, choosing when calculating the
        value of a foreign company, 206
Developing countries
    agricultural positions opposed to those of
        developed countries, 48
    environmental positions opposed to those
        of developed countries, 48
    free trade positions opposed to those of
        developed countries, 53
    tariff positions opposed to those of
        developed countries, 48
    remedy positions opposed to those of
        developed countries, 48
    services positions opposed to those of
        developed countries, 48
    World Trade Organization (WTO) aids, 52
Development
    funded by currency restricted from
        repatriation, 215, 219
    strategic alliances to promote, 124–125
Differentiation, 120–121
Distribution system, 83
Diversification, 214
DOC. *See* Department of Commerce (DOC)
Documentation, 133–152
    customs clearance requires, 146
    export/import financing receipt requires,
        135–137
    freight forwarding agencies complete, 146
Doha Development Round
    concerns of members, 53
    purpose of, 48
Domestic business. *See* National business
Dominican Republic Central America Free
        Trade Agreement (CAFTA), 54–56
Drafts, 137
DR-CAFTA (Dominican Republican Central
        America Free Trade Agreement), 54–56

Drivers of change, 7
Drivers of international business, 8
Duke University study, 47–48
Duplication, 88
Duties. *See* Tariffs

E
Economic power, 23
Economic structure
  an aspect of culture, 20–21
  government governs, 20–21
  legal environment governs, 20
Economic warfare, 68
Economies of scale
  case study, 97–98
  cost savings through, 84, 97–98
Economy, 8
Education
  barrier to cross-cultural communication, 22
  cultural attitude toward tied to power
    distance and social structure, 22
  of employees inversely tied to cost savings of
    foreign labor, 22
  of expatriate children, 188
  International Bank for Reconstruction and
    Development (IBRD) promotes, 69
  International Center for Settlement of
    Investment Disputes (ICSID) promotes, 69
  International Development Association
    (IDA) promotes, 69
  International Finance Corporation (IFC)
    promotes, 69
  language of choice governed by, 22
  Multilateral Investment Guarantee Agency
    (MIGA) promotes, 69
  necessary for certain kinds of employment, 22
  social structure stratified by, 22
  World Bank Group promotes, 69
  World Bank promotes, 69
E-mail, 17–18
EMC. *See* Export management company
Employee retention
  after expatriation and repatriation, 179,
    192–193
  human resources' effect on, 193
  importance of, 193, 195
  uncertainty avoidance related to, 14
Employees
  compensation calculated using balance
    sheet approach, 184

cross-cultural literacy desirable in, 24–25
education of inversely tied to cost savings, 22
hiring additional to conduct research,
    141–142
retention of (*see* Employee retention)
selection of possessing cross-cultural
    literacy, 185–186
Employment, 22
Entrepreneurism
  foreign largely responsible for creating U.S.
    intellectual property, 46–47
  individualism related to, 13
  innovation related to, 47
  multidomestic strategy fosters, 95
Environment
  developing countries opposed to developed
    countries regarding, 48
  ethical considerations of exploiting, 159
  International Bank for Reconstruction and
    Development (IBRD) protects, 69
  International Center for Settlement of
    Investment Disputes (ICSID) protects, 69
  International Development Association
    (IDA) protects, 69
  international dispute over, 54, 55
  International Finance Corporation (IFC)
    protects, 69
  Multilateral Investment Guarantee Agency
    (MIGA) protects, 69
  North American Agreement on
    Environmental Cooperation (NAAEC)
    focuses on protecting, 55
  World Bank Group protects, 69
  World Bank protects, 69
Equity
  Generally Agreed Accounting Practices
    (GAAP) reporting method, 205
  International Financial Reporting
    Standards (IFRS) reporting method, 205
  use of abroad, 216
Escrow accounts, 78
Ethical considerations
  in environmental exploitation, 159
  in flexible manufacturing, 172
  in foreign labor use, 159
  in outsourcing, 159, 172
  in purchasing, 159
Ethnocentrism
  advantages of, 178
  cost savings through, 178

Ethnocentrism (*continued*)
  definition of, 177–178, 195
  disadvantages of, 178–179
  international business initially built on, 178
  language and cultural training manifests
    neglect as, 189
  polycentrism versus, 179
European Union (EU)
  labor regulations imposed by, 181
  role of, 164
Exchange. *See* Currency exchange, Currency
  exchange rates
Ex-Im Bank. *See* Export Import Bank (Ex-Im
  Bank)
Expatriated children
  concerns regarding, 187, 188
  language and culture training for, 188
Expatriated spouse
  challenges facing, 187
  expatriate success and failure affected by
    adjustment level of, 187
  human resources aid to, 187–188
  language and culture training for, 188
Expatriate failure
  causes of, 178–179, 192
  cross-cultural literacy avoids, 179
  definition of, 178, 179
  polycentrism avoids, 179
  human resources can prevent, 179
  spousal maladjustment can cause, 186–187
Expatriation
  definition of, 175
  employee retention after, 179
  expensive, 176, 180
  family, effects on (*see* Expatriated spouse,
    Expatriated children)
  human resources' role in, 177
  importance of language and culture
    training after, 192
  purposes of, 176
  research before, 176
  transplanting company culture through, 176
  transportation costs hamper, 180
  visa requirements hamper, 180
Export Assistance Centers, 148
Exportation
  advantageous when bargaining power of
    purchasers high, 122–123
  advantages of, 108
  aid in, 108, 148

analysis of market before, 134
capital sources for, 138–139
counterpurchasing creates flexibility in, 143
customs broker houses facilitate, 50
government agencies providing assistance
  in, 148
government agencies providing capital for,
  138–139
government incentives for, 200
insurance offered for, 138
Interest-Charge Domestic International
  Sales Corporation (ICDISC) a taxation
  loophole for small businesses dealing in,
  200–201
international business builds on, 109
international strategy builds on, 91
market entry through, 108–109
offset trading creates flexibility in, 143
paperwork required for receipt of capital for,
  135–137
to a pilot market to limit risk, 140–141
procedures of, 145–148
profit potential lost through, 109
strategies for, 140–144
transportation governs, 145
World Trade Organization (WTO)
  regulates, 51
Export Import Bank (Ex-Im Bank)
  history of, 138
  services provided by, 138–139
Export license, 147
Export management company (EMC)
  advantages of, 140
  legal information from, 142
  locating, 140
  role of, 91, 140
Expropriation. *See* Repatriation of currency
External convertibility of currency, 66–67

F
Face
  long-term orientation increases importance
    of, 15
  saving and losing, 29–30
Fair trade, 53
FASB (Financial Accounting Standards Board),
  204
FCIA (Foreign Credit Insurance Association),
  139
FCPA (Foreign Corrupt Practices Act), 127–128

FCSA (Foreign Commercial Service Agency), 43, 58
FDI. *See* Foreign direct investment (FDI)
Femininity. *See* Masculinity/Femininity
Fertile Crescent, 155
Financial Accounting Standards Board (FASB), 204
Financial institutions, 69–71
    Bank for International Settlements (BIS), 71
    Central banks, 70–71
    Currency boards, 70
    International Bank for Reconstruction and Development (IBRD) (*see* International Bank for Reconstruction and Development (IBRD))
    International Center for Settlement of Investment Disputes (ICSID), 69
    International Development Association (IDA), 69
    International Finance Corporation (IFC), 69
    International Monetary Fund (IMF) (*see* International Monetary Fund (IMF))
    Multilateral Investment Guarantee Agency (MIGA), 69
    World Bank, 69
    World Bank Group, 69
Financial statements
    currency exchange rates govern, 207
    Generally Agreed Accounting Practices (GAAP) method of recording, 205
    importance of, 207
    International Financial Reporting Standards (IFRS) method of recording, 205
    of subsidiaries in local currency, 206
Financial structure
    definition of, 213
    examples of, 213
    purpose of, 213, 219
First impressions
    importance of, 25
    positive, 25, 27
Five Forces model
    analysis of market using, 119–123
    bargaining power of purchasers according to, 119–120
    bargaining power of sellers according to, 119–120
    barriers to new-market entry according to, 120
    rivalry according to, 121
    threat of substitutes according to, 120–121

Fixed currency exchange rates, 71
Flexible manufacturing
    advantages of, 171
    definition of, 170
    disadvantages of, 171–172
    ethical considerations in, 172
    example of, 170
    lean manufacturing built on, 171
Floating currency exchange rates
    definition of, 65, 72
    history of, 63–64
    inflation governs, 65–66, 79
Ford, 100
Foreign Commercial Service Agency (FCSA), 43, 58
Foreign Corrupt Practices Act (FCPA), 127–128
Foreign Credit Insurance Association (FCIA), 139
Foreign direct investment (FDI), 35–58
    competitive advantage through, 8
    in countries having high rates of return, 8
    currency repatriation restrictions discourage, 66, 67, 79
    currency repatriation restrictions encourage, 199
    definition of, 9, 36, 37, 58
    foreign portfolio investment (FPI) versus, 43
    governmental attitudes' variance toward, 20–21
    government incentives for, 7, 20, 42
    history of, 35
    horizontal (*see* Horizontal foreign direct investment)
    low taxation rate as an incentive for, 201
    standards controlling, 37
    taxation rate affected by, 37
    tied to relative rate of economic growth, 44–45
    in the United States, 45, 46
    U.S., 44–45
    vertical (*see* Vertical foreign direct investment)
Foreign exchange markets. *See* Currency exchange markets
Foreign exchange. *See* Currency exchange
Foreign investment market, 42–56
Foreign labor
    cost savings of varies with employee education, 22
    cost savings through using, 5, 83
    culturally complex, 5
    ethical considerations of, 159

Foreign perceptions of the United States
counteracting, 25
through experience of U.S. culture, 22–23
stereotypical, 25–26
as taught by foreign education systems, 22
understanding, 25
Foreign portfolio investment (FPI)
aids to, 43
definition of, 43
exchange rate affects climate for, 43
foreign direct investment (FDI) versus, 43
interest rate affects climate for, 43
market for capital supplied by, 42
taxation rate affects climate for, 43
Foreign subsidiaries
financial statements made in local currency, 206
innovation difficult to spread among in a
multidomestic business, 95
ownership by a multinational business, 5
ownership by a transnational business, 6
rivalry between in a multidomestic
business, 95
For-profit business, 59
Forward exchange, 74
FPI. See Foreign portfolio investment
Franchising
definition of, 111, 112
risk of diminishing brand value through,
111–112
Free convertibility of currency, 66
Free trade
blamed for condition of U.S. economy, 53,
55–56
definition of, 53
developing countries opposed to developed
countries regarding, 48
Freight forwarding agencies, 146
Fronting loans
definition of, 211
diagrammed, 211
example of, 211–212
Fujisawa, 125
Futures contracts
definition of, 77
issued to guarantee payment, 43
limitation of risk by using, 77

G
GAAP. See Generally Accepted Accounting
Principles (GAAP)

GATT (General Agreement on Tariffs and
Trade), 52
GE, 127
Geary-Khamis dollar, 74–75
General Agreement on Tariffs and Trade
(GATT), 52
Generally Accepted Accounting Principles (GAAP)
acquisition according to, 205
case study, 206
depreciation according to, 205
equity according to, 205
financial statements according to, 205
International Financial Reporting
Standards (IFRS) versus, 205
role of, 118, 204
Geocentrism
advantages of, 180
definition of, 178, 180, 195
disadvantages of, 180–181
managers' response to, 180
Global business. See Transnational business
Global economy, 8
Globalization
customs broker houses affected by, 50
definition of, 4
legal environment affects level of, 7
production shifted by, 7
Global mindset
definition of, 176
example of, 176–177
Global strategy
acquisition as a part of, 116
case study, 99
commodities, suited to sale of, 99
coordination important to, 103
cost pressure expected by, 93
definition of, 57, 93, 106
horizontal foreign direct investment an aid
to, 56–57
joint ventures as a part of, 114
local responsiveness expected minimal by, 93
product adaptation expected minimal by, 93
rivalry between commodity dealers best
addressed by, 99
taxation negotiation difficult in, 199
Total Quality Management (TQM) aids, 93
transnational strategy built on, 97
weakness of, 93–94
Global supply chain. See Production
Gold standard, 63

Goodwill
  accounting standards' differing treatment
    of, 205
  definition of, 118
Government
  agencies providing capital for exportation,
    138–139
  corruption in, 20
  economic structure governed by, 20–21
  incentives for exportation, 200
  incentives for foreign direct investment
    (FDI), 7, 20, 42
  incentives for manufacturing, 160
  International Bank for Reconstruction and
    Development (IBRD) supports stability
    in, 69
  International Center for Settlement of
    Investment Disputes (ICSID) supports
    stability in, 69
  International Development Association
    (IDA) supports stability in, 69
  International Finance Corporation (IFC)
    supports stability in, 69
  monopolies, 20–21
  Multilateral Investment Guarantee Agency
    (MIGA) supports stability in, 69
  researching foreign, 27
  variance in attitudes toward foreign direct
    investment (FDI), 20–21
  World Bank Group supports stability in, 69
  World Bank supports stability in, 69
Green-fields
  advantageous when barriers to new-market
    entry low, 122
  capitalizing on similarities among cultures
    when establishing, 117
  case study, 123–124
  definition of, 41, 58, 116, 129
  difficulties of creating, 41
  disadvantages of, 117
  duplication common in, 88
  human resources' role in, 117
  international business built on, 116
  limitation of risk in, 116
  transnational strategy benefited by, 117
Growth
  of markets, 6–7
  of markets affected by customs broker
    houses, 50
  relative rate of economic, 44–45

H
Harmonized System, 150
Harmonized Tariff Schedule of the United
    States (HTUSA)
  definition of, 150, 151
  example of, 151
Headquarters
  of an ethnocentric business, 177–178
  of a geocentric business, 178, 180
  of a multinational business, 5
  of a national business, 4
  of a polycentric business, 178, 180
Health
  International Bank for Reconstruction and
    Development (IBRD) promotes, 69
  International Center for Settlement of
    Investment Disputes (ICSID) promotes,
    69
  International Development Association
    (IDA) promotes, 69
  International Finance Corporation (IFC)
    promotes, 69
  Multilateral Investment Guarantee Agency
    (MIGA) promotes, 69
  World Bank Group promotes, 69
  World Bank promotes, 69
Hedging
  through acquisition, 116
  in international markets by institutions, 46
  through purchasing foreign securities to
    limit risk, 77–78
High-demand products, 47
Hofstede, Geert, 12
Holdings
  of a multinational business, 5
  of a national business, 4
  restrictions of, 49
  of a transnational business, 6
Hollowing out, 126
Horizontal foreign direct investment
  definition of, 39–40, 58
  multidomestic strategy aided by, 56
  purposes of, 40
  by transportation minimization creates cost
    savings, 40
HTUSA. See Harmonized Tariff Schedule of
    the United States (HTUSA)
Human resources, 175–196
  compensation goals of, 182–183
  employee retention affected by, 193

Human resources (*continued*)
  ethnocentrism as a strategy in (*see*
    Ethnocentrism)
  expatriated spouses aided by, 187–188
  expatriate failure prevented by, 179
  expatriation aided by, 177
  foreign managers aid, 182
  geocentrism as a strategy in (*see*
    Geocentrism)
  green-fields aided by, 117
  labor regulations a concern of, 195
  polycentrism as a strategy in (*see*
    Polycentrism)
  strategies in, 177–181
Human rights, 54
Hyperinflation
  definition of, 65
  instances of, 65–66

I

IASB (International Accounting Standards
  Board), 204
IBM, 124–125
IBRD. *See* International Bank for
  Reconstruction and Development (IBRD)
ICCH (International Commodities Clearing
  House), 43
ICDISC. *See* Interest-Charge Domestic
  International Sales Corporation
  (ICDISC)
ICSID (International Center for Settlement of
  Investment Disputes), 69
IDA (International Development Association),
  69
Idiom, 17
IFC (International Finance Corporation), 69
IFRS. *See* International Financial Reporting
  Standards (IFRS)
IHRM. *See* Human resources
IMF. *See* International Monetary Fund (IMF)
Importation
  chambers of commerce aid, 149
  customs broker houses' role in, 50–51,
    149–150
  duties imposed for, vii
  facilitated by customs broker houses, 50
  international disputes caused by, 48
  Internet sources aid, 149
  labor relations disputes threaten, 195
  market entry through, 108–109

from multiple suppliers to limit risk, 195
  paperwork required for receipt of capital for,
    135–137
  researching before, 149
  sources for, 148–149
  trade promotion organizations aid, 149
  trade shows aid, 149
  World Trade Organization (WTO)
    regulates, 51
Impressions. *See* First impressions
Incentives to foreign-market entry
  deregulation, 49
  government agency–provided, 42
  grants, 49
  insurance, 48–49
  loans, 49
  subsidies, 48, 49
  tax breaks, 20, 48, 49, 198, 200
  tariffs, decreased, 7, 20
  work permits, 20
Indexed contracts, 78
Individualism/Collectivism
  attitude toward company policy affected
    by, 13
  charted, 16
  contract negotiation affected by, 13
  definition of, 12, 31
  entrepreneurism related to, 13
  power distance related to, 13
Inflation
  definition of, 65
  floating currency exchange rates governed
    by, 65–66, 79
  instances of, 65–66
  nonconvertibility of currency a result of, 67
Inflexibility
  case study, 127
  strategic alliances hampered by, 126–127
Infrastructure
  International Bank for Reconstruction and
    Development (IBRD) supports, 69
  International Center for Settlement of
    Investment Disputes (ICSID) supports, 69
  International Development Association
    (IDA) supports, 69
  International Finance Corporation (IFC)
    supports, 69
  Multilateral Investment Guarantee Agency
    (MIGA) supports, 69
  World Bank Group supports, 69

World Bank supports, 69
Innovation
    entrepreneurism related to, 47
    multidomestic strategy fosters, 95
    small businesses depend on, 47
    of subsidiaries of multidomestic business difficult to spread, 95
Insurance
    certificate of, 147
    collection aided by, 208, 219
    exportation, offered for, 138
    investment, offered for certain kinds of outward, 48–49
    sources of for credit extension, 208
Integration, 103
Intellectual property, 47–48
Interest-Charge Domestic International Sales Corporation (ICDISC)
    legal counsel necessary to use, 201
    taxation loophole for small businesses dealing in exportation, 200–201
Interest rates
    foreign portfolio investment (FPI) climate affected by, 43
    low promoted as attractive for investment, 46
International Accounting Standards Board (IASB), 204
International agreements
    of comity, 20
    of trade (see International trade agreements)
International Bank for Reconstruction and Development (IBRD)
    agricultural support, 69
    education promotion, 69
    environmental protection, 69
    government stability support, 69
    health promotion, 69
    infrastructure support, 69
    origin of, 64
International business
    acquisition an immediate step into, 116
    adapting to, 84
    complications of (see Complications of international business)
    currency exchange markets' use to, 76
    definition of, 3
    exportation as a first step into, 109
    factors shaping, 6–9
    global economy a driver of, 8
    green-fields an immediate step into, 116
    human resources' role in, 177
    international strategy a first step into, 92–93
    legal environment a driver of change in, 7
    merger an immediate step into, 116
    methods of conducting (see Methods of conducting international business)
    risk to through failure to adapt products or services, 83
    risk to through lack of a distribution system, 83
    risk to through unfamiliarity with a foreign culture, 83
    types of, 3–6, 10
International Center for Settlement of Investment Disputes (ICSID), 69
International Chamber of Commerce, 148
International Commodities Clearing House (ICCH), 43
International Development Association (IDA), 69
International disputes
    adjudication of by the World Trade Organization (WTO), 52–53
    adjudication of by UK courts, 20, 209
    adjudication of collection disputes, 209
    adjudication of, negotiating, 209
    over human rights, 54
    over the environment, 54, 55
    over wages, 54
International dollar, 74–75
International finance center
    definition of, 212
    purpose of, 212, 219
    role of, 212
    small businesses require, 212–213
International Finance Corporation (IFC), 69
International finance specialist, 212
International Financial Reporting Standards (IFRS)
    acquisition according to, 205
    case study, 206
    depreciation according to, 205
    equity according to, 205
    financial statements according to, 205
    Generally Agreed Accounting Practices (GAAP) versus, 205
    role of, 118, 204
International human resources management (IHRM). See Human resources
International Monetary Fund (IMF), 64, 69–70

International monetary system
  currency valued using, 8
  history of, 60–64
International strategy
  analysis of, example of, 121–122
  case study, 100
  commodities, suited to sale of, 99
  cost pressure minimally expected by, 91
  definition of, 91, 106
  exportation a foundation for, 91
  international business built on, 92–93
  joint ventures as a part of, 114
  local responsiveness minimally expected
    by, 91
  product adaptation minimally expected by, 91
  strength of, 93
  transnational strategy built on, 97
International trade
  agreements (see International trade
    agreements)
  environment a point of dispute in, 54, 55
  examples of, 134–135, 156–157
  exporters' role in, 134
  history of, vii, 35
  human rights a point of dispute in, 54
  importers' role in, 134
  nonconvertibility of currency restricts, 67
  parties involved in, 134
  risks of, 138
  routes, vii
  wages a point of dispute in, 54
International trade agreements
  Dominican Republic Central America Free
    Trade Agreement (CAFTA), 54–56
  enforcement levels of, increasing, 7
  international disputes caused when broken, 52
  between members of the World Trade
    Organization (WTO), 51
  North American Free Trade Agreement (see
    North American Free Trade Agreement
    (NAFTA))
  scope of, increasing, 7
International trade organizations, 49–56
  customs broker houses (see customs broker
    houses)
  international business governed by
    standards of, 56
  World Trade Organization (see World Trade
    Organization (WTO))
Internet, 149

Interpreters
  foreign nationals having experience of the
    United States ideal as, 23
  language and culture training leading to
    cultural understanding unable to be
    replaced by, 27, 189
  risks of using, 189
  use of, 17
Intracompany tension
  class-based conflict a contributor to, 23
  religious conflict a contributor to, 21–22
Investment
  accepting from countries having low rates
    of return, 8
  in currency funds, 72
  in the currency market, 72
  foreign direct (see Foreign direct investment
    (FDI))
  interest rate promoted as attractive for when
    low, 46
  inward, 49
  outward, 48–49
  reasons for abroad, 46–48
  small-scale, case study of, 123–124
  small-scale to limit risk, 46–47
Inward investment, 49
Ireland, 45

J
Japan, 113
Joint ventures
  advantages of, 112
  case study, 113
  definition of, 4, 129
  disadvantages of, 113–114
  global strategy includes, 114
  international strategy includes, 114
  knowledge transfer a risk of, 113–114
  limitation of risk, 4
  method of conducting international
    business, 4, 10
  multidomestic strategy includes, 114
  national business use of, 4
Jurisdiction, 209

K
Knowledge transfer
  bargaining power capitalized on by, 120
  gaps between cultures hinder among
    multidomestic subsidiaries, 95

as horizontal integration, 103
risk of joint ventures, 113–114
transnational strategy requires, 97
transnational strategy requires cross-
culturally, 97, 98

L
Labor regulations, 54, 181, 195
Labor relations, 23, 194–195
Labor
foreign (*see* Foreign labor)
regulations (*see* Labor regulations)
relations (*see* Labor relations)
Lag strategy, 209
Language, 17–18, 22
training (*see* Language and culture training)
Language and culture training
cultural awareness training, 191
culture shock minimized by, 190–191
expatriation, importance of after, 192
instruction, practical, 191–192
language training, 191
neglecting, fallacy of, 188–189
resources aiding, 30–31
visits, host-country, 191
Laws
civil, 19
common, 19
constituent of legal environment, 7–8
foreign, 7–8, 19–20
importation and exportation complicated
by, 50
researching foreign, 27
restricting repatriation of currency, 67, 199
restricting transfer pricing, 202, 203
restrictive a barrier to foreign-market entry,
49
small businesses supported by, 47, 54
transportation complicated by, 50
LC. *See* Letter of credit
LCP (Local currency pricing), 76
Lead strategy, 209
Lean manufacturing, 171
Legal environment
analysis of, 7–8
global, 19–20
globalization affected by, 7
laws constituting (*see* Laws)
power distance affects, 19
understanding through consultants, 19

Legal systems, 20
Letters of credit (LC)
definition of, 136
role of, 136–137
role of, example of, 134–135
Licensing
case study, 125
definition of, 111, 112, 129
risk of creating rivalry through, 112
Limitation of risk
through diversification, 214
through escrow accounts, 78
through futures contract issue, 77
in green-fields, 116–117
through hedging by purchasing foreign
securities, 77–78
through importation from multiple
suppliers, 195
through intracompany loans, 212
through joint ventures, 4
laws barring foreign-market entry create as
a side effect, 49
through multidomestic strategy, 96
through networking with government
officials, 215
through a pilot market, 141
through small-scale investment, 46–47,
140–141
through turnkey projects, 109, 110
Loans
fronting, 211
intracompany, 211–212
limitation of risk through intracompany, 212
Lobbying, 215
Local currency pricing (LCP), 76
Local responsiveness
business strategies charted against, 91, 101
case studies of, 90, 100
definition of, 90
global strategy expects minimal, 93
international business relation to, example
of, 102
international strategy expects minimal, 91
Localization. *See* Local responsiveness
Logistics, 36. *See also* Production
Long-term/Short-term orientation
case study, 99
charted, 16
definition of, 12, 31
face related to, 15

Long-term/Short-term orientation (*continued*)
  international transactions governed by,
    99, 210
  technology related to, 18
Loss, 59

M
Making. *See* Manufacturing
Management fee, 203
Managers
  of an ethnocentric business, 177–179
  of a geocentric business, 178, 180
  geocentrism's effects on, 180
  human resources aided by foreign, 182
  of a polycentric business, 178, 179
Manufacturing
  advantages of, 159–161, 173
  disadvantages of, 161–162, 173
  government incentives for, 160
  logistical barriers to, 161
  patriotic incentives for, 160
  political incentives for, 160
  Six Sigma's role in, 161
  understanding production through, 160–161
Market entry
  bureaucracy hinders, 19, 20
  corruption hinders, 20
  modes of, 107–129
  scale of, 123–124
  timing of, 124
Marketing
  balance of trade (BOT) and balance of
    payments (BOP) affect, 39
  masculinity affects, 14
  mix, 144
  plan (*see* Marketing plan)
  stereotypes hinder, 26–27
Marketing mix, 144
Marketing plan
  description of, 143–144
  role of, 134, 144
Markets
  analysis of, 7
  analysis of using Five Forces model, 119–123
  bureaucracy a barrier to entry into foreign,
    19, 20
  for capital, 8
  capital-raising in host-country, 216
  for capital supplied by foreign portfolio
    investment (FPI), 43

corruption a barrier to entry in foreign, 20
currency exchange, 75
entry into (*see* Market entry)
for foreign investments, 42–56
growth of, 6–7
growth of affected by customs broker
  houses, 50
investment in for currency, 72
new (*see* New markets)
volatility of (*see* Market volatility)
Market volatility
  caused by many factors, 154–155
  caused by political environment, 160,
    163–164
  small-scale investment a method of
    counteracting, 46–47
Masculinity/Femininity
  assertiveness related to, 14
  charted, 16
  definition of, 12, 31
  marketing affected by, 14
  sexes, attitudes of related to, 14
Means of production (MoP), 36
Merck, 125
Merger
  advantages of, 118
  complications of, 118, 119
  cross-cultural communication essential
    during, 119
  definition of, 41, 58, 129
  disadvantages of, 118–119
  international business built on, 116
  rivalry decreased by, 118, 122
  transnational strategy built on, 119
Methods of conducting international business
  acquisition (*see* Acquisition)
  foreign direct investment (*see* Foreign direct
    investment (FDI))
  green-fields (*see* Green-fields)
  joint ventures (*see* Joint ventures)
  merger (*see* Merger)
  outsourcing (*see* Outsourcing)
  purchasing (*see* Purchasing)
  selling (*see* Selling)
Micro-multinational
  definition of, 86–87
  technology a strength of, 169
Middle East, 156
MIGA (Multilateral Investment Guarantee
  Agency), 69

Money. *See* Currency
Money markets, 215
Monopolies, 20–21
MoP (Means of production), 36
MTV, 100
Multidomestic strategy
  acquisition as a part of, 116
  case study, 100
  coordination not essential to, 103
  definition of, 57, 94, 106
  entrepreneurism fostered by, 95
  horizontal foreign direct investment an aid
    to, 56
  innovation fostered by, 95
  joint ventures as a part of, 114
  limiting risk through, 96
  local responsiveness expected by, 95
  performance ambiguity low in, 104
  product adaptation expected by, 95
  rivalry between technology dealers best
    addressed by, 99
  services a strength of, 95
  technology, suited to selling, 99
  time to market increased by, 95
  transnational strategy built on, 97
  weakness of, 95, 96
Multilateral Investment Guarantee Agency
  (MIGA), 69
Multilateral netting, 210
Multinational business
  acquisition to become, 5
  consultant use by, 216
  currency exchange a complication of, 75
  definition of, 5, 10
  foreign direct investment (FDI) affects, 37
  headquarters of, 5
  holdings of, 5
  outsourcing versus, 5
  regional manufacturing use by, 85
  subsidiaries of, 5, 95
  transnational business versus, 6

N
NAAEC. *See* North American Agreement
  on Environmental Cooperation
  (NAAEC)
NAALC (North American Agreement on
  Labor Cooperation), 54
NAFTA. *See* North American Free Trade
  Agreement (NAFTA)

National business, 4–5, 10, 75
National Customs Brokers & Forwarders of
  America, 148
Negotiation. 13, 76–77, 134–135, 199
Netting, 210
Networking
  cost savings through, 141
  with government officials to limit risk, 215
  importance of, 141
  understanding through, 141
New markets
  analysis of, 7
  causes of creation of, 21
  entry into as a pilot market a means of
    understanding, 140–141
  identification of through understanding of
    foreign markets, 154
  profit potential offered by, 18
Nonconvertibility of currency
  countertrade to circumvent, 67–68
  definition of, 67
  indexed contracts opposed because of, 78
  inflation causes, 67
  international trade restricted by, 67
Nonprofit business, 59
North American Agreement on Environmental
  Cooperation (NAAEC)
  agricultural liberalization, 55
  environmental preservation, 55
North American Agreement on Labor
  Cooperation (NAALC), 54
North American Free Trade Agreement
  (NAFTA), 54, 55, 164

O
Ocean freight, 146
OECD. *See* Organisation for Economic
  Co-operation and Development
  (OECD)
Offset trading, 143
Offshoring. *See* Outsourcing
OPEC (Organization of the Petroleum
  Exporting Countries), 164
Opening bank, 136
Opportunity, 218
Opportunity cost
  definition of, 165
  examples of, 165, 166
  types of, 165–166
Orbitz, 167

Organisation for Economic Co-operation and Development (OECD)
members, 199
role of, 198–199
Organizational structure, 85
Organization of the Petroleum Exporting Countries (OPEC), 164
Outsourcing, 4–5, 6, 10, 48–49, 56, 89
Outward investment, 48–49
Ownership
of foreign subsidiaries, 5, 6
of a national business, 4
restrictions on, 49

P
Paperwork. *See* Documentation
Patriotism, 160
PCP (Producer's currency), 76
Pegged currency exchange rates, 71
Performance ambiguity, 104
Pilot market
limitation of risk through entry into, 140–141
understanding a new market using, 141
Policy, 13
Polycentrism, 178, 179–180, 195
Power distance
charted, 16
definition of, 12, 31
education affected by, 22
legal environment affected by, 19
power distribution related to, 13
PPP. *See* Purchasing Power Parity (PPP)
Price comparison Web sites, 167
Pricing, 76
Producer's currency (PCP), 76
Product classification, 151–152
Production, 153–173
decreasing costs of, 83–84
globalization affects, 8
labor relations disputes increase costs of, 23
location of affects taxation negotiation, 199
relocation to take advantage of lower costs of, 85
simplified through manufacturing, 159–160
tied to location, 153–156
understanding important to, 153–154
understanding through manufacturing, 160–161

Products
adaptation of a sign of rivalry, 57
adaptation of not a major feature of global strategy, 93
adaptation of not a major feature of international strategy, 91
classification of, 151–152
differentiation of to increase bargaining power, 120–121
high-demand, 47
importance of, 153
international strategy expects minimal adaptation of, 91
relocation to market to foreign consumers, 85
risk to international business through failure to adapt, 83
Professional certifications, 20
Profit
definition of, 59
potential offered by new markets, 18
Profit potential
case study, 9–10
exportation limits, 109
new markets offer, 18
relocation to take advantage of, 85
rivalry decreases, 121
turnkey projects limit, 109
Purchasing
advantages of, 159, 173
analysis before, 158
disadvantages of, 157–158, 173
ethical considerations in, 159
foreign labor a consideration of, 157
method of conducting international business, 4, 10
national business use of, 4
reasons for, 157
through strategic alliances, 161–162
tariffs a consideration of, 157
transportation a consideration of, 157
Purchasing power
new markets created by increases in, 21
parity of (*see* Purchasing power parity (PPP))
value of currency tied to, 65
Purchasing Power Parity (PPP)
currency exchange rate versus, 74–75
deficiencies of, 75
definition of, 74, 79

Q

Quality assurance, 103
Quotas, 150

R

Rate of return
  accepting investment from countries having
    low, 8
  investment in countries having high, 8
  skewed by international considerations, 217
Reciprocity, 15
Relationships
  case study of long-term, 99
  importance of long-term, 99, 210
Relative rate of economic growth, 44–45
Religion, 21–22
Relocation, 83–84, 85, 86, 173, 184
Repatriation of currency
  barriers to, 67, 198
  definition of, 197
  development funded by currency restricted
    from, 215
  example of, 67–68
  laws restricting, 57, 142, 198, 199
  lobbying funded by currency restricted
    from, 215
  philosophy of, 216–217, 219
  research funded by currency restricted
    from, 215
  restriction, a barrier to centralized
    depositories, 215
  restriction, causes of, 57, 142, 198, 199
  restriction, purposes of, 67, 199
  transfer pricing to circumvent restriction
    of, 203
Repatriation of employees
  advantages of, 179, 192–193
  employee retention after, 192–193
Required reserve ratio, 70
Research
  of capital-raising in host-country markets,
    216
  of currency exchange rate, 78–79
  of economic environment, 37–39, 58
  before expatriation, 149
  of a foreign company's credit, 208
  of foreign cultures, 27
  of foreign governments, 27
  of foreign laws, 27
  funded by currency restricted from

  repatriation, 215, 219
  hiring new employees to conduct, 141–142
  before importation, 149
  incomplete unavoidable, 217
  of labor regulations, 182
  marketing plan based on, 144
  of options necessary to choose business
    strategy, 57
  strategic alliances to promote, 124–125
  before transacting, 208
Restrictions
  on convertibility of currency, 66–67
  on ownership and holdings, 49
Reverse culture shock. *See* Culture shock
Risk
  barrier to international expansion, 98
  of failing to adapt products or services, 83
  of franchising, 111–112
  of international trade, 138
  of interpreter use, 198
  of knowledge transfer through joint
    ventures, 113–114
  of lacking a distribution system, 83
  of licensing creating rivalry, 112
  limiting (see Limitation of risk)
  of rivalry, 121
  uncertainty avoidance related to, 14
  of unfamiliarity with a foreign culture, 83
Rivalry
  acquisition decreases, 122
  acquisition threatened by, 116
  adaptation of products a sign of, 57
  between commodity dealers best addressed
    by the global strategy, 99
  Five Forces model of, 121
  with former collaborators, 89, 106, 110, 112,
    113–114
  licensing risks creating, 112
  masculinity marked by, 14–15
  merger decreases, 118, 122
  between multidomestic subsidiaries, 95
  new-market entry caused by, 120
  profit potential decreased by, 121
  risks of, 121
  strategic alliances hampered by, 127
  success a cause of, 88
  between technology dealers best addressed
    by the multidomestic strategy, 99
  varies inversely with barriers to foreign-
    market entry, 101

S

SBA. *See* Small Business Administration (SBA)

SBIDA (Small Business Development Act), 47

SBIR (Small Business Innovation Research Program), 47

Scale of market entry, 123–124

SDR (Special drawing right), 70

SEC (Securities and Exchange Commission), 204

Securities, 77–78

Securities and Exchange Commission (SEC), 204

Selling

method of international business, 4, 10

national business use of, 4

Sematech, 127

Services

developing countries opposed to developed countries regarding, 48

multidomestic strategy well-positioned to offer, 95

provided by Department of Commerce (DOC), 43, 58

provided by Export Assistance Centers, 148

provided by Export Import Bank (Ex-Im Bank), 138–139

provided by Foreign Commercial Service Agency (FCSA), 43, 58

provided by Foreign Credit Insurance Association (FCIA), 139

provided by Freight forwarding agencies, 146

provided by International Chamber of Commerce, 148

provided by International Commodities Clearing House (ICCH), 43

provided by National Customs Brokers & Forwarders of America, 148

provided by Small Business Administration (SBA), 139, 148

provided by Trade Information Center, 148

risk to international business from failure to adapt, 83

Shipping. *See* Transportation

Sight draft, 137

Six Sigma, 161

Small Business Administration (SBA)

history of, 139

services provided by, 139, 148

Small Business Development Act (SBIDA), 47

Small businesses

high-demand products often the foundation of, 47

innovation a strength of, 47

Interest-Charge Domestic International Sales Corporation (ICDISC) a taxation loophole for when dealing in exportation, 200–201

international finance centers' role in, 212–213

international finance specialists' role in, 212

laws to support, 47, 54

resources aiding, 47

strategic alliances advantageous to, 126

Small Business Innovation Research (SBIR) Program, 47

Social structure

economic power rooted in, 23

education governed by, 22

education's stratification of, 23

tribal identity governs, 23

Special drawing right (SDR), 70

Spot currency exchange rates

definition of, 72

role of, 206–207

Standardization. *See* Cost pressure

Stereotypes, 25–27

Strategic alliances, 124–125, 126–127, 161–162

Strategy

changing, example of, 101–102

choosing, 83–106

choosing, questions when, 99

global strategy (*see* Global strategy)

international strategy (*see* International strategy)

multidomestic strategy (*see* Multidomestic strategy)

transnational strategy (*see* Transnational strategy)

Structure, organizational, 85

Subsidiaries. *See* Foreign subsidiaries

Substitutes

analysis of, example of, 121–122

threat of according to the Five Forces model, 120–121

Sunk-cost fallacy, 115–116

Supply chain. *See* Production

Surface shipping, 146

Switch trading, 143

T

Tariffs, 7, 48, 50, 151–152, 157–158, 202–203

Taxation, 198–202
  analysis of, 201
  double, 198–199
  Interest-Charge Domestic International
    Sales Corporation (ICDISC) a loophole
    for for small businesses dealing in
    exportation, 200–201
  negotiation difficulties in global strategy,
    199
  negotiation difficulties in transnational
    strategy, 199
  negotiation of, 199
  negotiation of affected by production
    location, 199
  transfer pricing to circumvent, 202, 203
  understanding liability, 219

Taxation rates
  foreign direct investment (FDI) affects, 37
  foreign portfolio investment (FPI) climate
    affected by, 43
  low as an incentive for foreign direct
    investment (FDI), 201
  manipulation of, 202–204

Technology
  competitive advantage through taking
    advantage of gaps in between cultures, 18
  long-term/short-term orientation related
    to, 18
  micro-multinationals often deal in, 169
  strategic alliances often support, 125
  transnational strategy suited to sale of, 99

Tension. *See* Intracompany tension

Threat of substitutes. *See* Substitutes, threat of

3M, 92, 123–124

Time draft
  definition of, 137
  role of, example of, 134–135

Time to market
  acquisition decreases, 114
  multidomestic strategy increases, 95

Timing of market entry, 124

Total Quality Management (TQM), 93

Toyota, 90

TQM (Total Quality Management), 93

Trade. *See* International trade

Trade at a discount, 74

Trade at a premium, 74

Trade deficit, 38

Trade Information Center, 148

Trade promotion organizations, 149

Trade relations, 151

Trade shows, 149

Training, 178

Transaction costs, 209–211
  definition of, 203, 209–210
  minimizing, 210, 219

Transfer of currency. *See* Repatriation of
  currency

Transfer of knowledge. *See* Knowledge transfer

Transfer of resources, 38

Transfer pricing, 202–204
  advantages of, 202–203
  audits to discover, 203
  currency repatriation restrictions
    circumvented by, 203
  definition of, 202
  laws regarding, 202, 203
  scope of, 203–204
  tariffs circumvented by, 202–203
  taxation circumvented by, 202, 203

Translators. *See* Interpreters

Transnational business
  cooperation within, 6
  definition of, 6, 10
  holdings of, 6
  multinational business versus, 6
  performance ambiguity high in, 104

Transnational strategy
  case study, 100
  cross-cultural knowledge transfer required
    by, 97, 98
  decentralization required by, 97
  definition of, 96–97, 106
  global strategy a foundation for, 97
  green-fields, advantages of in, 117
  international strategy a foundation for, 97
  merger a foundation for, 119
  multidomestic strategy a foundation for, 97
  taxation negotiation difficult in, 199
  technology, suited to sale of, 99

Transportation
  cost savings of using airliners and freight
    liners to provide, 18
  cost savings through horizontal foreign
    direct investment, 40
  cost savings through networking, 141

Transportation (*continued*)
  costs hamper expatriation, 180
  exportation affected by, 145
  international business increasingly has as
    paradigm, 36
  laws complicate, 158
  methods of, 145–146
  purchasing affected by, 157–158
  reliability of, 158
  relocation to reduce the costs of, 83–84
  workforce required to handle, 158
Travelocity, 167
Treaties. *See* International agreements
Turnkey projects, 109–110, 111, 129

U
UK. *See* United Kingdom (UK)
UN. *See* United Nations (UN)
Uncertainty avoidance
  charted, 16
  definition of, 12, 31
  employee retention related to, 14
  risk related to, 14
Unilever, 95
United Kingdom (UK)
  courts of commonly used to settle
    international disputes, 20
  foreign portfolio investment (FPI) aided
    by, 43
United Nations (UN), 37, 181
U.S. automotive industry, 155
U.S. perceptions of foreign countries, 22, 26–27

V
Value
  accounting standards' role in calculating of
    company, 204, 206
  of airmail may require customs declaration,
    146
  of currency, 8
  of currency decreased by capital flight, 67
  of currency tied to purchasing power, 65

of a foreign company, choosing depreciation
    schedule when calculating, 206
  overestimation of during acquisition, 41, 114
  risk of diminishing of brand through
    franchising, 111–112
Vehicle currency
  definition of, 73
  Japanese yen as current, 73, 79
  U.S. dollar as current, 73, 79
Vehicle currency pricing (VCP), 76
Vertical foreign direct investment
  through acquisition, 115
  definition of, 40, 58
  global strategy aided by, 56
  purposes of, 40
Volatility. *See* Market volatility
VSP. Vehicle currency pricing (VCP)

W
Wages, 54
Win-win situation
  case study, 167
  definition of, 167
  example of, 168
World Bank, 69
World Bank Group, 69
World economy, 8
World Trade Organization (WTO)
  activities of, 52
  criticisms of, 53
  developing countries aided by, 52
  disputes between members of, 52
  governance of, 51
  international disputes adjudicated by,
    52–53
  membership of, 51
  standards of controlling importation and
    exportation, 51
WTO. *See* World Trade Organization (WTO)

X
Xerox, 100

About the Author

With business administration training in both India and the United States, Dr. Rajesh Iyer is a graduate-level business education professor and writer with unusual insight into international business. His outlook is firmly rooted in the real-world concerns of business leaders. A faculty member of the Foster College of Business Administration at Bradley University, Dr. Iyer teaches graduate-level courses in marketing management, international business, and global issues in international business. Respected as both a teacher and a widely published researcher and writer for professional journals, Dr. Iyer has special interests in marketing research, business ethics, and related topics in international business. He brings a practical, global view to this introduction to international business.

Made in the USA
Monee, IL
28 January 2023

26620395R00160